The Promise of Power

Under what conditions are some developing countries able to create stable democracies while others have slid into instability and authoritarianism? To address this classic question at the centre of policy and academic debates, *The Promise of Power* investigates a striking puzzle: why, upon the 1947 Partition of British India, was India able to establish a stable democracy while Pakistan created an unstable autocracy?

Drawing on interviews, colonial correspondence, and early government records to document the genesis of two of the twentieth century's most celebrated independence movements, Maya Tudor refutes the prevailing notion that a country's democratization prospects can be directly attributed to its levels of economic development or inequality. Instead, she demonstrates that the differential strengths of India's and Pakistan's independence movements directly accounts for their divergent democratization trajectories. She also establishes that these movements were initially constructed to pursue historically conditioned class interests. By illuminating the source of this enduring contrast, *The Promise of Power* offers a broad theory of democracy's origins that will interest scholars and students of comparative politics, democratization, state-building, and South Asian political history.

Maya Tudor is a Fellow in Politics at St John's College, Oxford University. Her dissertation, upon which this book is based, won the American Political Science Association's Gabriel Almond Award for the Best Dissertation in Comparative Politics.

The Promise of Power

The Origins of Democracy in India and Autocracy in Pakistan

MAYA TUDOR

University of Oxford

CAMBRIDGE
UNIVERSITY PRESS

CAMBRIDGE
UNIVERSITY PRESS

University Printing House, Cambridge CB2 8BS, United Kingdom

Cambridge University Press is part of the University of Cambridge.

It furthers the University's mission by disseminating knowledge in the pursuit of education, learning and research at the highest international levels of excellence.

www.cambridge.org
Information on this title: www.cambridge.org/9781316635247

© Maya Tudor 2013

First published 2013
First paperback edition 2016

A catalogue record for this publication is available from the British Library

Library of Congress Cataloguing in Publication data
Tudor, Maya Jessica, 1975–
The promise of power : the origins of democracy in India and autocracy in Pakistan / Maya Tudor.
pages cm
Includes bibliographical references and index.
ISBN 978-1-107-03296-5 (hardback)
1. India – Politics and government – 1947– 2. Pakistan – Politics and government. 3. Democracy. 4. Authoritarianism. I. Title.
JQ231.T83 2013
320.954–dc23
2012043729

ISBN 978-1-107-03296-5 Hardback
ISBN 978-1-316-63524-7 Paperback

For
Loren

Contents

Contents

Table, figures and maps

Acknowledgments

How did two of the world's most populous countries emerge from a shared colonial legacy with radically divergent and historically enduring political regimes? Investigating that question has been my professional preoccupation for the last decade. That I have finally crafted an answer in the form of this book is a testament to the extraordinary support of a great many individuals and institutions. As such, I would be remiss not to acknowledge some of the hands that have steadied my progress and encouraged my spirits along the gratifying path to the book's completion.

The earliest seed of this project formed over a decade ago when I spent six months working in Dhaka for a microfinance organization. At the time, I was struck by the considerable political differences between Bangladesh and India, despite their common colonial legacy. The idea of systematically exploring the origins of these differences germinated during my enrollment in Atul Kohli's graduate course the Comparative Political Economy of Development, at Princeton. This engaging and provocative course, which asked ambitious questions about the origins of worldwide patterns of economic development, charted the kind of bold intellectual terrain that inspired my enrollment in a political science doctoral program and that directly led to the writing of this book.

The argument advanced within these pages was most critically formed during 13 months I spent immersed in archival research and interviewing in Pakistan, India and England. To the many dozens of academics, civil servants, journalists, military officers, and other experts who so generously gave of their time and expertise, I am deeply grateful. The hospitable warmth of dozens of Pakistanis brightened my visits to Lahore and

Islamabad, but I would particularly like to thank Ejaz Haider, Hasan Askari-Rizvi, and Mohammed Waseem for informative conversations, the staff at the National Documentation Centre in Islamabad for graciously assisting me in my scouring of early government records, Sara Sebhai for her marvelous hosting in Islamabad, and Omer and Sheryar Salamaat for introducing me to competitive kite flying on Lahore's rooftops. My greatest debt of gratitude in Pakistan goes to Mehvesh and Naeem Ahmed and their family. Their gracious kindness and protectiveness literally created a home away from home. In India, I would like to thank Mridula and Aditya Mukherjee as well as Bipin Chandra for guiding my archival research, Pratap Bhanu Mehta at the Centre for Policy Research for providing me with office space, the staff at the Nehru Memorial Museum and Library for tolerating my seemingly endless requests for archived papers, and Prerna Singh for much-needed laughter and even timely medical assistance.

Upon my return from field research, I found myself ensconced in the unequalled scholarly community at Princeton, both in the Woodrow Wilson School and in the Politics department. I owe a profound debt of gratitude to my dissertation committee for its unstinting support of the earliest form of this book. Atul Kohli's steadfast encouragement and incisive questioning always sharpened my thinking and roused my spirits, especially after the birth of my daughter when writing at all seemed a distant priority. Deborah Yashar's support came in manifold forms, perhaps most clearly in the countless pearls of wisdom she shared from the crafting of her own comparative historical investigation into democratization in *Demanding Democracy* and in the tough, ever-brilliant role model she so ably continues to be. Stephen Cohen encouraged this project from an early stage, critically appraising my interpretation of historical events in ways that have immeasurably improved the final result, and Carles Boix enthusiastically read and commented upon each chapter.

A heartfelt thank you is also extended to the fantastic writing group that first formed at Princeton: Sarah Chartock, Ludmila Krytynskaia, Rachel Beatty Riedl, and Prerna Singh. First as fellow graduate students, and now as friends and colleagues, these women have painstakingly read through repeated iterations of this book, balancing thoughtful critiques with unbridled laughter. For insightful comments at various stages of writing at Princeton, I would also like to thank Gary Bass, Jason Brownlee, Arudra Burra, Wolfgang Danspeckgruber, Tyler Dickovick, Joanne Gowa, Stan Katz, Evan Lieberman, Zia Mian, Ilan Nam, Anne Sartori, and Kathryn Stoner-Weiss.

This book has also been molded and improved by a broader scholarly community. Eva Bellin, Nancy Bermeo, Malfrid Braut-Heggehammer, Rachel Gisselquist, Patrick Heller, Steve Levitsky, Steve Miller, Vipin Narang, Robert Rotberg, Alexandra Scacco, Lee Seymour, Dan Slater, Hillel Soifer, Paul Staniland, Ashutosh Varshney, Steve Walt, Jeremy Weinstein, Steve Wilkinson, Adam Zeigfeld, and Daniel Ziblatt are all to be thanked for giving generously of their time at various stages of the writing and the presenting of this manuscript. A special note of thanks is extended to my friend Pavan Ahluwalia, who read through every single page of the book as I endeavored to cut its unwieldy size, often commenting in detail on footnotes that I doubt few scholarly experts will even read.

No less importantly, I am indebted to a wide array of institutions for their support. At Princeton, this included the Woodrow Wilson School, the Princeton Institute for International and Regional Studies, and the Fellowship of Woodrow Wilson Scholars. During field research, this included the Center for Democracy, Development and Rule of Law at Stanford University, the David L. Boren Fellowship, the Lahore University of Management Sciences, and the Centre for Policy Research. And as I wrote up the research, this included the vibrant scholarly community at the Belfer Center in the Kennedy School of Government at Harvard University, the Centre for the Study of Inequality and Democracy at Oxford University, and St John's College, Oxford University.

Marigold Acland, Sarika Narula, Lucy Rhymer, and Elizabeth Spicer at Cambridge University Press and Rob Wilkinson at Out of House Publishing were all unfailingly competent and encouraging as they ushered this manuscript to its final completion. I also wish to thank the two anonymous reviewers of this manuscript for their valuable comments and suggestions.

My soulful tribe of friends, all in their own ways, supported the writing of this book by repeatedly reminding me that there was life beyond it. Thank you to Ollie Babson, Casey Budeslich, MacGregor Duncan, Caroline Flintoft, Katherine Greig, Anu Gupta, Jessica Hartman Jacobs, Peter Jewett, Jessa Lewis, Steve Murphy, Ritesh Shah, Susie Smith, Marie Soller, and Rachel Tobey.

I owe the love of different cultures and of animated political debate that ignited my interest in the topic of this book to my far-flung but close-knit family: Jan Tudor, Naomi Tudor, Kim Tudor, Ana Gonzales-Trigas, Patrick Mullen, Harpal Singh, Tom Tudor, Eunim Tudor, Hanna Tudor, Rajeshwar Dayal, Indira Dayal, Aarti Dayal, Harsh Vardhan, Barbara

Griffith, and a missed Harry Griffith. My dear sister, fellow graduate student, friend, confidante, and colleague Rani Mullen deserves a special note of gratitude for always believing in me and for remembering and cheering me on at every important milestone of my life. The support of my mother, Marlies Kurtz-Singh, has made it possible for me to write this book in ways both ordinary and extraordinary. Her unwavering optimism, her high-minded idealism, and her thoughtful dedication to her children and grandchildren continues to inspire me.

Coming to life as they did during the years that this book was in the making, my beloved daughter Amelia and son Theo have, through their beautiful laughter and love, supported the writing of this book by reminding me every morning and evening of what really matters.

Finally, mere words hardly suffice to express my gratitude to my partner, Loren Griffith. He has accompanied me intellectually in the writing of this book by asking thought-provoking questions on late nights, by providing insight on every iteration of this manuscript, and by drawing detailed flow charts of my argument. He has accompanied me physically in the writing of this book, grinning through our Old Delhi rickshaw rides and falling in love with the incomparable beauty of the Indian subcontinent. And he has accompanied me emotionally in the writing of this book with his ever-ready laugh, with his steadfast and unrivalled parenting, and with his unconditional love. I dedicate this book to him.

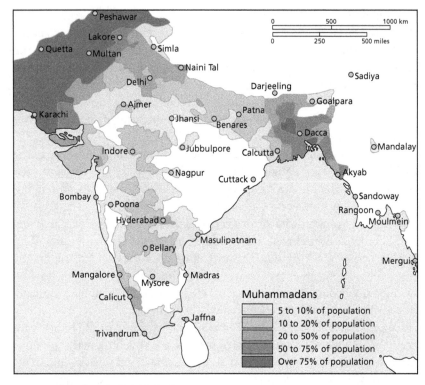

MAP I. Muslims in British India.

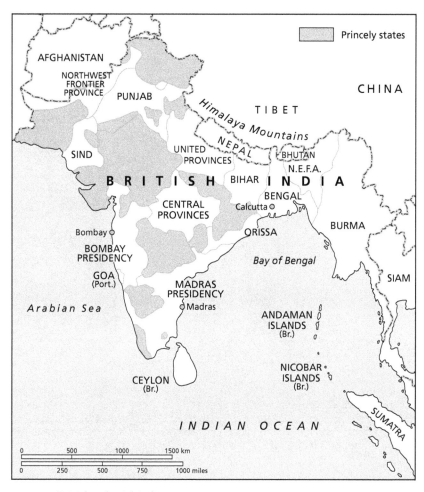

MAP 2. British colonial India, 1935.

Disputed border

Jammu and Kashmir

PAKISTAN

Punjab

Delhi

Rajasthan

Karachi

Gujarat

BANGLADESH
(East Pakistan
until 1971)

Dacca

West
Bengal
Calcutta

INDIA

| 0 | 500 | 1000 km |
| 0 | 250 | 500 miles |

MAP 3. India and Pakistan.

How India institutionalized democracy and Pakistan promoted autocracy

At the stroke of midnight on August 14 and August 15, 1947, the former independence leaders Mohammed Ali Jinnah and Jawaharlal Nehru respectively presided over the creation of Pakistan and India, two new countries carved out from British India that should have been equally unlikely to become stable democracies. Both countries emerged from nearly a century of shared colonial rule with broadly similar state institutions, both were governed as infant democracies until their sovereign constituent assemblies wrote new constitutions, and both countries were beset by massive refugee crises, though Pakistan's was larger relative to its population. Both ethnically diverse countries were destabilized by external and sub-national challenges to their territorial integrities and both countries were governed by single dominant parties, supported by multi-class coalitions, which had some experience governing at provincial levels prior to independence.

Yet, despite such striking similarities, these two countries embarked upon markedly different democratic trajectories immediately upon their twin independences. Pakistan's constitution-making process was from the start mired in conflict and national elections were perpetually delayed while eight national administrations cycled through power with increasing rapidity. Pakistan's tentative democratic experiment foundered on the shoals of two extra-legal 'bureaucratic coups' in 1953 and 1954 and formally ended with a military coup in 1958. In contrast, India rapidly ratified the world's longest constitution in early 1950, held free and fair national elections on the basis of universal adult suffrage in 1952, and installed an elected chief executive who subordinated the military and civilian bureaucracy. These democratic differences, as indicated in

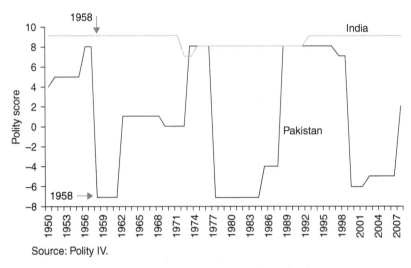

Source: Polity IV.

FIGURE 1.1. Divergent regime trajectories in India and Pakistan.

Figure 1.1, can be understood as varying along the dimensions of regime *type* (how democratic each country was, conceptualized as the average of each country's Polity IV score during the post-independence decade) and regime *stability* (how stable its regime was, conceptualized as the variation around the average of each country's Polity IV score during the post-independence decade), though these are not entirely analytically separable. Noticeably, India's democratic stability and Pakistan's autocratic instability emerged immediately after independence and were clearly established by 1958. What explains this puzzling divergence in India's and Pakistan's democratic trajectories?

In answering that question, this book seeks to help shed new light on the causes of democratization in post-colonial countries. How and why have some newly independent states been able to establish durable democracies whereas others frequently oscillate between fragile democracies and unstable autocracies? Understanding the conditions under which post-colonial states were able to create both democratic regimes and stable regimes is of critical importance to political scientists and policy-makers alike.

Like India and Pakistan, many post-colonial countries shared similar features in that they gained independence in the two decades after the end of World War II and in that they did so with relatively under-developed economies and the vestiges of a colonial state. Yet the literature explaining democratization, with few exceptions, has not generalized comparative lessons from the democratization experiences of South Asia. Learning from the democratization experiences of countries in the world's most populous region has the potential to contribute to and possibly modify our explanations of post-colonial democratization experiences elsewhere.

Investigating the variance in political development in India and Pakistan is also important because they are two large, politically significant countries whose regime outcomes have seldom been compared systematically.[1] Dismissing the Indian case of democratization as an empirical outlier, as many studies of democratization do, is simply inadequate when that case constitutes over one-sixth of the world's population. An inability to explain or predict India's democracy signifies a central problem with our theoretical understanding of democratization and regime stability in a low-income setting.

Yet if the study of comparative democratization seeks to distill a set of logically consistent causes that explicate a broad range of democratization experiences, any explanation of India's democratic stability ought also to be able to elucidate the failure of the same in Pakistan. While many studies have investigated the success of India's democracy in isolation, very few have simultaneously judged their causal explanations against the experience of Pakistan.[2] A close historical comparison with a country whose regime trajectory was very different while its major structural features were largely similar enables a compelling causal analysis.

The remainder of this introductory chapter is structured as follows. In the first section, I detail my argument. The second section explains in greater depth how this argument contributes to the existing scholarly literature on democratization. A third section examines the alternative historical and theoretical explanations for regime outcomes in India and Pakistan. And a fourth section briefly describes the further organization of the book.

I. THE ARGUMENT

The core argument advanced in this book is that, first, the kinds of social classes leading each country's independence movement and, second, the

---

[1] The only in-depth comparison of India and Pakistan's democratic divergence based on a thorough review of both primary and secondary sources is Jalal (1995). Other comparative works, discussed in the alternative explanations, include Chadda (2000), Talbot (2000), Stern (2001), and Oldenberg (2010).

[2] The most prominent case-specific analyses of regime outcomes are, for India, Rudolph and Rudolph (1967), Kothari (1970), and Kohli (2001) and for Pakistan, Sayeed (1968), Jalal (1990), McGrath (1996), Talbot (1988), and Cohen (2004).

strength of the dominant political party at independence were the most important causes of India's and Pakistan's divergent democratic trajectories. Specifically, the first of the book's two organizing claims is that the class interests dominating each country's independence movement critically impacted its post-independence regime *type*. All social groups in British India desired material gains and greater social prestige. But which political goals were perceived to promote upward mobility was relative to not just the wealth and social status of other class groupings but existing patterns of colonial patronage, the social identities available for mobilization, and the range of alliance partners. In particular, the fact that a colonially entrenched landed aristocracy formed and dominated the independence movement for Pakistan made it highly unlikely that a country governed by such a movement would become democratic. This is because the landed aristocracy was a politically over-represented and disproportionately powerful social group that stood to lose substantially by adopting a genuinely representative system of government in which it could not guarantee its continued political dominance. A landed aristocracy with a disproportionate share of material resources and political power was quite likely to oppose a regime which would institutionalize opportunities for the redeployment of material resources and political capital to other social groups.

The fact that an urban, educated middle class formed and dominated the Indian independence movement made it possible, though by no means inevitable, that a post-independence India would be democratic. Middle classes strategically forge whatever alliances they can to best promote upward mobility. In the historically specific context of a well-developed state apparatus, an under-developed economy, and a colonial regime that entrenched large landowners and was unwilling to devolve power, the urban, educated middle class of colonial India stood to gain (employment and political power) by advocating for a more representative political regime. While this class initially sought only limited enfranchisement, the strategic pursuit of its interests led to the propagation and institutionalization of universal adult franchise and other democratic institutions in the pre-independence decades. Class interests, historically understood, thus had a powerful impact on the *type* of regime each movement was likely to establish upon independence.

The second organizing claim of this book is that, in the decades before independence, these different social classes created political parties which varied in their strengths and that this strength was the most important explanation for each country's regime *stability* upon independence. I define party strength along the three constituent sub-variables of programmatic ideology (programmatic versus vague), coherent distributive alliances (coherent if the distributive interests were relatively aligned), and robust intra-party organization (well-developed versus undeveloped).

On the first dimension of programmatic ideology, I show below how the strategic pursuit of narrow class interests led to the formulation of nationalist ideologies that, over time, began to differ in their programmatic content. The *presence* of programmatic content within its nationalist ideology substantially affected each country's likelihood of regime *stability* after independence because such content facilitated the party's ability to broker compromises among its diverse membership. This organizational resource, where it existed, could be utilized to resolve new conflicts in the post-independence era. Pakistani nationalism was not programmatic, defined almost wholly by its opposition to Congress rule, and was characterized by neither clear principles nor practices associated with those principles. This weak form of nationalism meant that Pakistan's political party was unable to invoke a programmatic basis for reconciling regime-building political conflicts. Indian nationalism was defined not only in opposition to colonial rule but also by an adherence to a set of economic and social principles and costly actions associated with those principles. The presence of a programmatic nationalism which became valued in and of itself in India meant that, upon independence, India's governing political party was more able to reconcile post-independence state-building conflicts by invoking the substantive goals of nationalism as a basis for political compromise.

At the same time, the *content* of the nationalism that each party espoused in the lead-up to independence substantially affected post-independence regime *type* because such programmatic content, where it existed, provided the organizing ideas for governing in the inevitably chaotic aftermath of independence. If nationalism was centered upon egalitarian norms before independence, as it was in India, then democratic forms of government were more likely to be adopted after independence, both because these norms had become the institutional basis for party organization and because the norms had become symbolically important to party members. Upon Indian independence, there was little benefit and substantial cost to rejecting egalitarian norms. In contrast, Pakistani nationalism was not egalitarian, but this mattered little because that nationalism remained weakly institutionalized. All in all, the presence of a programmatic nationalism made the political party stronger and substantially more able to provide for post-independence regime *stability* while the substantive content of that nationalism impacted the *type* of stable regime that was created.

On the second dimension of coherent distributive alliances, I show below how the strategic pursuit of narrow class interests in each country led to the creation of alliances that differed in terms of their distributive coherence and that greater distributive coherence critically supported post-independence regime *stability*. To marshal mass support for colonial independence, Pakistan's nascent nationalist movement created alliances with a landed aristocracy and a peasant movement, two social groups that subsequently formed the core support bases of Pakistan's independence movement. Because the distributive interests of its two core alliance partners were in almost diametric opposition to each other, this alliance rapidly dissolved when post-independence regime-building required power-sharing compromises. By contrast, India's independence movement was, at the time of independence, substantively based on an alliance between the urban and rural middle classes. These social classes shared an interest in marginal redistribution away from the colonial regime and the large landed aristocracy but also in preventing any downwards redistribution toward subordinate socio-economic groups. The representation of relatively coherent distributive interests within India's dominant political party meant the party was better able to broker state-building compromises after independence, thus providing for regime *stability*.

Finally, on the dimension of intra-party organization, I demonstrate that the pursuit of narrow class interests in each country led to the creation of intra-party organizations which varied in their robustness and that this variation critically affected the likelihood of post-independence regime *stability*. At independence, Pakistan's dominant political party was minimally developed and heavily dependent upon its charismatic leadership while India's independence movement resembled a relatively disciplined and centralized party organization. Upon independence, the presence of a more developed intra-party organization meant that India's dominant political party was able to more quickly and decisively broker regime-building compromises after independence, thus providing for regime *stability*.

In sum, this study argues that the strategic pursuit of class interests in a historically specific context led to the alternate promotion of or resistance to representative democracy and the consequent construction of stronger or weaker political parties. Upon independence, the nature of dominant class interests and the content of its nationalist ideology primarily

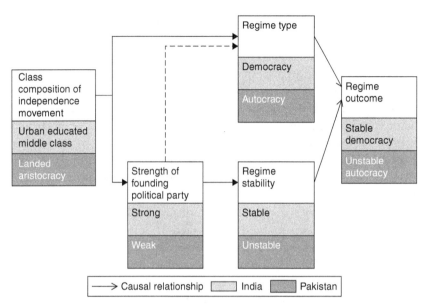

FIGURE I.2. The argument of the book.

explains each country's choice of regime type (democracy or autocracy) while the strength of its dominant political party largely explains regime stability. As Figure 1.2 indicates, the divergent democratic trajectories of India and Pakistan thus pivoted upon the nature of their dominant class interests and the strength of their political parties.

Defining democracy

As serious normative and definitional problems arise when democracy is defined either in terms of its sources or its effects, this study adopts a procedural definition in which democracy is defined as "that institutional arrangement for arriving at political decisions in which individuals acquire the power to decide by means of a competitive struggle for the people's vote."[3] This Schumpeterian definition views a regime as democratic to the extent it enables candidates to freely compete for votes in an election as well as the presence of civil and political liberties that make such competition meaningful. To the extent that military coups, rigged elections, jailing of political opponents, and the censorship of media characterize a regime, it is less democratic. By this definition, for almost

[3] Schumpeter (1942: 269).

all of the years since their twin independences, India has been a democracy and Pakistan has not.

A democracy is also procedurally defined by decision-making according to the majoritarian principle of "one individual, one vote," given the important qualification that such decision-making respects a basic set of rights. Said differently, so long as majoritarian rule does not substantively impinge on the enumerated or implied rights of protected groups or individuals, the process of decision-making by a popular majority, with one vote accorded to each person, procedurally defines democratic decision-making because it is taken to best operationalize political equality.[4] Democratic theorists tend to view constitutional or legal protections for discrete cultural practices of minority groups (particularly so in ethnically divided societies) or individual rights (such as freedom of press and association) as entirely consistent with majoritarian rule. Permanently allocating specific groups extra-proportional representation, such that the procedural basis of "one person, one vote" is violated, is generally thought of as procedurally inconsistent with democracy.[5]

Practically speaking, while a movement advocating for the protection of minority rights in specific, restricted domains (e.g. language, the protection of certain cultural and religious practices, or minority veto rights on specifically enumerated issues) can be entirely consistent with the establishment of a democratic regime, permanent decision-making procedures that are *not* based on "one individual, one vote" violate a defining characteristic of democracy. This distinction is germane to the argument developed below because Pakistan's independence movement ultimately sought not to carve out specific domains for the protection of Muslim rights (e.g. the right of regional languages to be recognized, discrete religious practices, or even proportional representation, all of which would have been entirely consistent with the establishment of a democracy) but instead sought to permanently institutionalize a governing system whereby a Muslim vote would procedurally count as *more than* one non-Muslim vote. By the standard democratic definition of majoritarian rule then, Pakistan's independence movement could not be termed a proto-democratic movement.

[4] Sartori (1987: Chapter 6).
[5] For example, Rawls (1971: 356) writes that "Some form of majority rule is justified as the best available way of insuring just and effective legislation. It is compatible with equal liberty and possesses a certain naturalness; for if minority rule is allowed, there is no obvious criterion to select which one is to decide and equality is violated."

In addition to seeking to understand why India and Pakistan quickly established different regime *types*, this book also seeks to understand why post-independence India and Pakistan established regimes which varied tremendously with respect to their *stability*, given that regime stability is defined by the adherence to a set of regular, constitutionally defined procedures for organizing, checking, and transferring power. To the extent that the executive power of a country is irregularly seized or such a seizure attempted, its regime is less stable. As evidenced by Figure 1.1, a difference in regime stability was already marked in 1950, when the Polity IV dataset began. The comparative historical analysis shows that these differences in regime stability were in fact already noticeable upon independence in 1947. The question taken up below is: what explains the initial emergence of such differences?

Defining social classes

Social classes are not necessarily conscious or organized actors with cogent or distinctive worldviews. Particularly because the popular conceptualizations of class are overlaid with multiple ideological and political connotations, it is necessary to carefully define the meaning of social classes in the context of this book. This study employs a Weberian definition of class which defines classes not as objective communities but as "merely represent(ing) possible, and frequent, bases for communal action." Individuals who own comparable objects of exchange and who, as a result of similar positions in the marketplace, "share in common a specific causal component of their life-chances" are objectively defined as members of the same class. However, an objective definition of class categories is analytically distinct from both the consciousness of a shared class position and from organized action on the basis of class interests.[6]

This Weberian class definition is not strictly structural-functional, assuming as it does that class situations are determined by economic markets *as well as* by markers of status and that these markers are to some extent socially constructed. This is a particularly important distinction in the context of developing countries, where, typically, markets are poorly developed and social relations are regulated by traditional hierarchies. Theoretically, I take seriously Weber's ideal-type distinction between "class" and "status" (whereby class position is determined by production and acquisition of goods in the marketplace and status grouping is

---

[6] Weber (1991 [1947]: 181).

determined by the principles of group consumption and by special "styles of life"). The argument developed below thus makes reference to both shared life-chances as well as shared markers of status in ascribing class positions. While theoretically distinct, however, empirical observations of class and status groupings frequently overlap.

The study also adopts a Weberian understanding of class because it does not presume a relationship between a given class situation and either the consciousness of that situation or subsequent political organization on the basis of class interests. In the cases discussed below, action on the basis of shared class and status positions depended on first perceiving a causal basis for class positions. The argument developed below does not presume a relationship between a given class situation or status grouping and the subsequent formation of a political organization to pursue class interests. Instead, it investigates the extent to which objective class groups did in fact translate into the perception of a shared class position and into the consequent formation of social or political organizations.

Adapting from Maddison (1971), the indigenous social structure of British India during the late nineteenth and early twentieth centuries can be broken down into four ideal-type class groupings at the most extreme level of generalization. For conceptual clarity, the *upper class* refers in rural areas to the pre-capitalist landed aristocracy that owned large tracts of land (over 50 acres) but did not engage in its direct cultivation and who typically possessed a titled or hereditary right to such land. This class predominantly existed in swaths of northern India. In urban areas, upper classes refers to a small but growing and increasingly powerful social group in colonial India which owned large-scale capital or large-scale trading enterprises. I refer to this group as large capitalists. *Lower classes* refers, in rural areas, to those individuals earning a subsistence or just above subsistence income from pre-capitalist agricultural activity and, in urban areas, to those individuals earning a subsistence or just above subsistence income from selling labor to industrial or commercial enterprises.

Middle classes refers to professional individuals in urban and upwardly mobile areas who are neither landed aristocracy, the large capitalists, or members of the lower classes. In urban areas, this typically consisted of the principal professions such as lawyers, doctors, and professors, the salaried executives and technical staff of trading and manufacturing firms, civil servants, well-to-do shopkeepers, small-scale shopkeepers, traders, and moneylenders. In rural areas, this typically consisted of the dominant peasantry, who are both the holders of the middle grades of proprietary tenures of land (typically less than 50 acres) and "farmers of revenue, living on unearned income or partially personal management, exclusive of the largest and some of the smallest holders of estates."[7]

Of course, caste and not class was the overwhelmingly salient social category in colonial India. Nevertheless, since both independence movements eschewed caste categories and sought to mobilize on the basis of other identities, this starkly generalized typology of class structure in colonial British India helps to broadly situate the social origins of the independence movements of India and Pakistan independently of caste. This can be done because, on the whole, caste categories heavily overlapped with class categories.

This study suggests that classes, as opposed to status groups, are more likely to influence political outcomes when a society is undergoing major economic changes, as was typical of colonial societies. Class tends to become a more important determinant of political action in a society undergoing big economic changes because changes in the economic structure of society – typically toward greater industrialization, urbanization, and international integration – are often accompanied by changes in social structure and in political institutions that had heretofore reflected the status quo. The emergence of an industrial sector in an agrarian economy typically creates economically powerful individuals without commensurate political power or social recognition. How this new economic group understands its interests to be best advanced and how these interests are politically accommodated is an important influence, if not the critical influence, on subsequent regime outcomes.

By definition, a democracy is a political system in which the popular majority procedurally decides political outcomes. This system offers opportunities for political entrepreneurs to organize among popular groups and to affect the distribution of resources and power. It is this potential for redistributive policies that can render the adoption of a democratic regime threatening to groups advantaged by the status quo distribution of power. But the actual likelihood of a democratic regime being accepted and enduring hinges on the *perception* of various groups or classes that democratic governance serves their interests, to the extent that such groups are indeed conscious of shared interests.

---

[7] Misra (1961: Introduction and Chapter 1).

Using this conceptualization of class as a frame of reference, the comparative historical analysis of regime outcomes developed below assesses the extent to which various classes in colonial British India perceived themselves advantaged by the pre-colonial and colonial distribution of power. It then investigates whether and how the economic changes wrought by colonialism impacted powerful social classes, how those impacts were subjectively understood, the kinds of coalitions those social classes formed as a result, and the degree to which those coalitions were institutionalized within political parties. In short, this study problematizes the causal link between social class (as an approximation of socioeconomic structure) and regime type, through the mediation of political parties.

Defining strong political parties

Because I argue that political party strength exerts a central influence on regime outcomes, it is important to both conceptualize and operationalize party strength in a non-tautological manner. As Figure 1.3 indicates, I define party strength along the three dimensions: the distributive coherence of its core alliance, the extent of programmatic nationalist commitment, and the development of intra-party organization. Throughout the empirical narrative, I substantiate the claim that the dominant political parties in India and Pakistan varied along each of these three dimensions.

Among these three dimensions, the development of programmatic nationalism among party supporters is perhaps the most prone to tautological claims and the most difficult to empirically demonstrate. Nonetheless, the importance of supporters' ideational commitment has been well established in political party literature. Theorists such as Selznick (1957) and Huntington (1968) have both posited that political parties become stronger and more adaptable to change when party supporters transition from pursuing specific short-term goals through the party to viewing party perpetuation as a goal itself. Selznick argues that parties which are only "rational instrument[s] engineered to do a job" are not likely to survive beyond the achievement of that specific job. By contrast, party institutionalization occurs when supporters seek to maintain the organization independently of narrow and often short-term goals. When this happens, the party transforms from "an expendable tool into a valued source of personal satisfaction."[8] Similarly, Huntington

---

[8] Selznick (1957: 5–21).

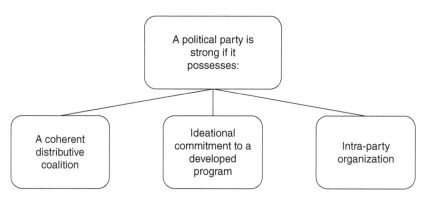

FIGURE 1.3. Defining political party strength.

suggests that parties become stronger and more adaptable when the party "develops a life of its own quite apart from the specific functions it may perform at any given time."[9] The ideational dimension of party strength is particularly important to measure in political parties created during colonial regimes because such parties were often created for the specific purpose of advancing independence from colonial rule. Independence parties valued wholly as a means of achieving the goal of colonial independence were often less equipped to make a transition to the changed circumstances of a post-independence period.

To avoid advancing tautological claims, this book shows that ideational commitment among party supporters existed before colonial independence so as to demonstrate that its members valued the party organization prior to the key episode of organizational change – in this case, national independence.[10] To substantiate the claim that party supporters possessed varying degrees of ideational (as opposed to only instrumental) commitment to India's and Pakistan's independence parties, I show below how supporters of India's Congress Party made some costly decisions that did not directly promote their short-term political interests whereas such decisions were not made by supporters of Pakistan's Muslim League. Upon independence, consensus around and commitment to the programmatic goals of its nationalism greatly impacted regime stability while the content of that commitment critically shaped regime type.

The second definitional dimension of party strength is a party's degree of internal organization, particularly the extent to which a party

---

[9] Huntington (1968: 15–17).
[10] Levitsky (1998: 85).

is governed by regularized rules and procedures. Institutional theorists have long argued that institutions, including political parties, structure behavior through consistent rules and informal codes and defined party strength by the degree to which "regularized patterns of interaction are known, practiced, and regularly accepted."[11] Party organization is the single dimension along which political parties are regularly compared – Diamond and Gunther's sweeping analysis of party types, for example, conceptualizes variation among 15 ideal-type parties along the basis of organization, which lies on a spectrum between wholly elite-based or "thin" organization and wholly mass-based or "thick" organization.[12] The depth of intra-party organization is commonly used to characterize party strength because the more that political behavior is organized and altered through the party bureaucracy, the more the party itself (as opposed to extra-party processes or organizations) represents access to political power.

To be sure, highly bureaucratized parties are in some ways less able to innovate, evidencing that there is no uniform relationship between party organization and party strength.[13] Nonetheless, in the case of post-colonial developing countries, political parties were typically prone to too little rather than too much party organization. In the subset of political parties which emerged in low-income, post-colonial settings then, intra-party organization is taken to indicate party strength rather than weakness. To show that intra-party organization varied in the cases of India and Pakistan, I highlight the varying degree to which regularized rules and procedures governed the decision-making processes within each party before independence. Upon independence, I argue that the existence of regularized rules facilitated the creation of regime stability.

The third definitional dimension of party strength, the distributive coherence of its core coalition, draws upon but also extends the existing scholarly literature on political parties. Mainwaring and Scully define strong parties as those with "stable roots in society" which have "encapsulated" major social organizations.[14] Similarly, Shefter suggests that party leaders who construct an "extensive popular following" create more enduring political parties.[15] But while these works emphasize the

---

[11] O'Donnell (1994: 57) and North (1990).
[12] Diamond and Gunther (2001: 13).
[13] Kitschelt (1994: 213).
[14] Mainwaring and Scully (1995: 9–12).
[15] Shefter (1994: 32).

stability of party linkages to society, they do not make typically clear that the stability of such interests is often premised on a distributive logic.

I argue that when parties are built on linkages between social groups who share relatively more in the way of distributive interests, this coalition is more likely to prove stable and enduring. By this definition, a core coalition of party support drawn from segments of the middle class which share an interest in redistribution away from upper classes but also in preventing downwards redistribution away from itself towards subordinate social groups is substantially more stable than a core coalition of party support drawn from a wealthy landed aristocracy interested in virtually no downwards redistribution and a landless laboring class interested in radical redistribution. In the following chapters, I show that the party leaders in India and Pakistan, though they both organized multiclass coalitions, nonetheless forged coalitions which varied greatly with respect to this distributive coherence. The coherence of its core support coalition, in turn, critically affected each political party's ability to broker regime stability upon independence.

II. THEORETICAL CONTRIBUTION

In early modern times too, a decisive precondition for modern democracy has been the emergence of a rough balance between the crown and the nobility.

(Moore 1966: 417)

A strong political party system has the capability, first, to expand participation through the system and thus to preempt or to divert anomic or revolutionary political activity, and, second, to moderate and channel the participation of newly mobilized groups in such a manner as not to disrupt the system ... The development of such party institutions is the prerequisite for political stability.

(Huntington 1968: 412)

The social origins of political parties

The above quotations frame two seemingly alternative approaches to the classic but still contested question of what explains regime outcomes. In their separate endeavors to explicate why regimes varied in type and in stability across countries, Huntington and Moore provided distinct theoretical answers. Moore explained regime outcomes with reference to the relative distribution of power between social classes, inspiring a rich sociological research tradition. Huntington argued that regime stability was explained by the presence of strong political institutions, similarly generating an expansive scholarly literature emphasizing political parties as purveyors of regime stability. A major contribution of the present inquiry is to argue that these analytically separate literatures – one on the sociological origins of democracy and democratic stability and the other on the institutional mechanisms undergirding regime stability – can fruitfully be considered in tandem.

On the one hand, this book contributes to a well-developed research tradition emphasizing the relative distribution of power among social classes in explaining regime outcomes. Beginning with Barrington Moore's landmark *The Social Origins of Dictatorship and Democracy*, this vibrant research tradition has explored the ways in which the distribution of power between social groups matters for regime outcomes. Moore essentialized two causal relationships in his explanation of regime outcomes – stressing the importance of both a substantial commercializing middle class and a weakening landed aristocracy to the emergence of democratic regimes.

Like numerous comparative historical works, this book cautiously but conditionally validates Moore's central hypotheses. An important group of scholars has demonstrated that Moore's own historical interpretation of several pivotal cases was problematic,[16] while a complementary group of scholars has extended Moore's class-coalitional arguments to explaining regime outcomes, notably in Latin America.[17] This extensive body of literature has on the whole confirmed Moore's explanatory emphasis on the central role of a commercializing middle class in promoting democracy, explicating that capitalist development matters because it is associated with a change in the traditional balance of class power of a society – often a weakening of the traditional landed aristocracy as well as a strengthening of other subordinate classes. How those changes in economic power are politically accommodated deeply impacts the likelihood of a democratic regime being established.

Yet scholars working the Moore tradition have shown that, across regions and times, emergent middle classes have hardly consistently championed democratic regimes. Rather, middle classes have typically only sought their own political inclusion. Mobilization and organization among subordinate social classes has been just as important in facilitating

---

[16] Skocpol (1979), Luebbert (1991), and Rueschemeyer *et al.* (1992).
[17] Yashar (1997), Paige (1997), Collier (1999), and Mahoney (2001).

democratization.[18] Given the right set of historical circumstances, how-ever, the middle class has cautiously cultivated the support of subor-dinate classes in order to compel its own political inclusion, thereby creating an alliance that promoted broad-based democratization. The present inquiry validates those findings, demonstrating how a politically powerful but factionalized landed aristocracy blocked democratization and induced regime instability in Pakistan while an emergent middle class seeking only its own enfranchisement mobilized support among subordinate social classes as a way of compelling reform in India.

To the sociological literature emphasizing the relative distribution of power among class actors, then, this comparative historical analysis makes two contributions. First, it shows that arguments emphasizing the linchpin role of social classes can generate compelling explanations of regime outcomes in post-colonial, developing country cases. With some exceptions, this literature has not examined cases of democratization in the post-colonial world outside of Latin America and Europe, and indeed, no single work has to my knowledge sought to wield the insights from this sociological research tradition to explain democratization in South Asia.

A second and perhaps more important contribution to this research tradition is to emphasize that a key mechanism through which class inter-ests matter for regime outcomes is through class incentives to establish party institutions. While some scholars centralizing the interests of dom-inant social classes have shown that political parties matter for regime outcomes, this research tradition has not devoted as much attention to the institutionalization of class coalitions as it has to conditions facilitat-ing the emergence of those coalitions.[19]

In the cases of India and Pakistan, I show below that regime stability was most proximately explained not by class interests nor by the military or bureaucracy in each country, but rather by the strength of its political party. When the party was strong before the transition to independence, it was able to effectively govern and establish supremacy over bureau-cratic and military institutions after independence. Where the dominant political party was weak before the transition to independence, however, the inability of the party to provide an institutional locus for reconciling

---

[18] Rueschemeyer *et al.* (1992), Bermeo (1997), Paige (1997), and Collier (1999).
[19] Rueschemeyer *et al.* (1992: 287). Luebbert (1991) and Collier (1999) do theoretically centralize political parties however.

and limiting conflict quickly led powerful elites representing distinct class groups to defect from the party and politicize the army, eventually inviting the relatively stronger colonial institutions of state to intervene and govern. This book thus concurs with Huntington's assessment that "military coups do not destroy parties; they simply ratify the deterioration which has already occurred."[20]

This book advances the Barrington Moore research tradition on the origins of democracy because it highlights how sociological explanations for regime outcomes have neglected to examine how institutional arrangements – be they constitutions or political party norms – undergird the democratic pacts between class groups. In particular, the argument developed below emphasizes that political parties are created by elites representing particular class groups at particular historical moments but that, once established, political parties themselves causally impact the political strategies of class groups in and of themselves.

At the same time as it underscores the need for sociological analyses of regime outcomes to consider the independent role of political parties in explaining regime trajectories, the book also contributes to a burgeoning literature on the role of political parties. In particular, while a variety of institutionalist scholars have shown that political parties are critical mechanisms of regime stability, this work has tended to focus on the way that political parties maintain or alter an institutional equilibrium rather than on the sociological foundations of this institutional equilibrium.[21] By not asking the analytically prior question of under what structural conditions do effective party institutions arise, this literature generally neglects to fully consider the causal force of antecedent conditions.

Focusing as it does on the creation of political parties before moments of colonial independence, this study contributes to the institutionalist research tradition by showing how political parties in two post-colonial states emerged before key moments of transition in order to advance the historically defined interests of powerful social classes. Once these political parties were established, however, they worked independently of class interests by changing individual preferences, lengthening time horizons, and by providing a locus of coordination for access to political power.

---

[20] Huntington (1968: 409).
[21] Haggard and Kaufman (1995), Geddes (1999), Magaloni (2006), and Brownlee (2007). Two important exceptions are Mahoney (2001) and Slater (2010).

The history in politics

A second key contribution of this book is to emphasize that the link between economic development and democracy is endogenous to the institutionalization of political alliances that are forged in a historically specific context. Consequently, regime outcomes cannot be read off of crude development or inequality levels. Decades ago, modernization theorists such as Lipset (1959) hypothesized that there was a positive, causal, and probabilistic relationship between a country's level of economic development and its propensity to democratize. Generally, economic development was hypothesized to reduce scarcity and produce a middle class that attenuated redistributive conflicts and that could more readily organize for political accommodation. This argument has been tested in myriad comparative historical investigations of democratization, many of which have found that the weakening of the landed aristocracy and the growth of capitalist development are indeed associated with democratization, though not in any facile, functionalist manner. These studies have underscored that the sequencing of coalition-making affects democratization.[22]

This sociological emphasis on sequencing and historically contingent causal pathways to regime outcomes has co-existed uneasily with statistical studies which have emphasized the economic prerequisites to democracy. For example, Przeworski and Limongi (1997) and Boix and Stokes (2003), while debating the precise nature of the causal pathway, have both emphasized that economic development is causally responsible for democratization.

Other works underscoring the structural requisites of democracy have formalized the sociological emphasis on class. Boix (2003) suggests that levels of inequality and the nature of capital mobility determines elite attitudes toward democratization. Building on this, Acemoglu and Robinson (2006) predict that democratization will occur at middling levels of inequality. Taken as a whole, however, these theories tend to argue that the distribution of resources itself, rather than the political coalitions which contingently arise from this distribution, is the most important causal driver of democratization. While the argument of this book validates the centrality of distributive interests as the causal engine driving democratization and regime stability, it sounds a cautionary note on theories that predict democratization predominantly on the basis of

---

[22] Yashar (1997) and Mahoney (2001).

inequality and development. Through a comparative historical examination of two countries with similar levels of economic development and
inequality but with different regime outcomes, this book underscores that
the preferences of individuals and group actors do not correspond to
their class positions in a one-to-one fashion. Instead, the examination
of a particular, historically specific distribution of political power deeply
affects whether, for example, a middle class is interested in promoting or
retarding the growth of representative politics.

A narrow focus on the economic interests of major social actors does
not adequately reflect the ways in which existing political institutions
themselves impact and structure political preferences. In particular,
while economic interests were central in motivating actors to choose
their alliances and mobilization strategies, the regime outcomes in India
and Pakistan cannot be understood without reference to how these strategies were operationalized in a particular colonial environment where
power was already distributed to distinct social groups. And indeed, statistical studies by some of the same authors previously emphasizing the
economic origins of democratization have shown that when accounting
for the historically specific political trajectories of each country, there
are *no* economic requisites for democracy.[23] That quantitative analysis
of regime outcomes thus suggests, as does this comparative historical
analysis, that historically conditioned perceptions of material interest
and the institutions which framed these perceptions, just as much as the
objective measurements of income and inequality, critically affect regime
trajectories.

Expanding regional narratives of democratization

The third major contribution this book makes is to bring two regime
outcomes in a crucial region of the world to bear on mainstream democratization literature. To date, democratization literature has mostly generated its theory from European or Latin American histories. Rather than
being marginalized as an exceptional case, the origins of the world's largest and most enduring post-colonial democracy must be elucidated by
such models if this literature is to be considered compelling. To the extent
that theories of democratization and democratic endurance can be used
to explain the South Asian cases, they are simply more valid theories.

[23] Acemoglu *et al.* (2008).

Despite a plethora of studies by political scientists explaining regime outcomes in a single South Asian country, most regional accounts of democratization have not considered the regime outcomes of India and Pakistan in tandem and, as such, are less able to make compelling causal claims. Literature suggesting that Indian or Pakistani regime outcomes were largely driven by the differential legacies of British colonialism must contend with the fact that the colonial legacies in India and Pakistan were, with the exception of the disproportionate inheritance of military personnel in Pakistan, largely similar, particularly relative to the substantial variation in the cross-national institutional inheritances of post-colonial states elsewhere.[24]

Investigations of Indian democratization that focus on the transformative nature of Indian nationalism in creating an imagined community are convincing but incomplete because they are silent on the role of discrete social groups in initially defining nationalism.[25] Explanations of Indian democratization focusing on the importance of the Congress Party to India's regime stability, while they foreshadow elements of the argument developed below, do so without reference to the antecedent class interests that this book suggests is critical to understanding why Congress was initially created.[26] Finally, a series of notable works on Indian democracy describe important aspects of the Indian party system which were ultimately conducive to the maintenance of Indian democracy.[27] However, the question posed in this study is an altogether different one of why India *initially* emerged from independence with a party that was able to envelop factionalism or contain ethnic differences while another country facing similar challenges did not.

Scholarly analyses of Pakistan's regime instability have tended to focus on the analytical consequences rather than causes of autocracy and regime instability. Some scholars have argued that Pakistan turned to authoritarianism because of the extraordinary challenges of constructing a state upon independence and the military's consequent ability to exploit this position while others explained the same through the extraordinary power of the civilian bureaucracy to subvert democracy.[28] Yet these

[24] Jalal (1995).
[25] Chandra (1966) and Varshney (1998). Also Anderson (1983).
[26] Kothari (1970) on India and Oldenberg (2010) on India and Pakistan.
[27] Kohli (1990), Kohli (2001), Varshney (2003), Chandra (2004), and Wilkinson (2006).
[28] Sayeed (1968), Jalal (1990), and McGrath (1996).

arguments raise the unanswered question of why these legacies were so different in India.

Indeed, only Jalal (1995) has squarely compared regime outcomes in India to its historically similar neighbor Pakistan through an in-depth primary source analysis. The argument developed below refers to the same primary source data, but disputes the assessment therein that formal categories of democracy in India and authoritarianism in Pakistan are of little substantive relevance, in addition to making a different theoretical argument. The argument developed herein takes seriously the "different colonial inheritances of a central state apparatus, the relatively milder impact of the economic and strategic consequences of partition on India than on Pakistan and the nature of their international links" but suggests that these were not among the most important factors leading to the divergent democratic outcomes.[29] While these differences helped strengthen authoritarian instability, the nature and party-based organization of class interests were the most important causes of authoritarian instability in Pakistan.

III. EXISTING EXPLANATIONS AND THEIR LIMITATIONS

In making a sociological and institutional argument about the origins of divergent regime trajectories in South Asia, this book considers theoretical explanations for democratization and regime stability that have been utilized in cross-country comparisons of divergent regime outcomes or have been centralized in specific explanations of regime outcomes in India and Pakistan. Each of these alternative explanations is evaluated in turn.

High command or sole spokesman? The real but limited role of leadership

This book expands upon agency-based explanations that emphasize how the leader of each independence movement, such as Mahatma Gandhi, Jawaharlal Nehru or Mohammed Ali Jinnah, primarily accounts for divergent democratization trajectories in question.[30] Indeed, the role of leadership was frequently cited during interviews as the key differentiating factor in India's and Pakistan's independence movements. And to be

[29] Jalal (1995: 38).
[30] Jalal (1985) and Rudolph and Rudolph (2008: 62).

sure, leaders' chosen ideologies and strategies certainly contributed to the divergent regime trajectories in question.

But simply put, Pakistan's independence movement was and India's independence movement was not particularly vulnerable to the elimination of a top party leader – a difference that is largely attributable to party strength. India's Congress Party was able to function and even mobilize support when its top leaders were jailed in the pre-independence decades, sometimes for years at a time. The Indian National Congress was a mass movement led by not one but many leaders that became known as its "high command." India's democracy may have looked different if Jawaharlal Nehru had not survived India's independence, but there is little doubt that it would still have functioned as a democracy under the leadership of any one of a handful of top Congress leaders. By contrast, Pakistan's independence movement was largely contingent upon the whims of its "sole spokesman," Mohammed Ali Jinnah.[31] By tenuously tethering together regional movements beneath the umbrella of a national-religious ideology, Jinnah achieved the independent state of Pakistan. But Jinnah did not groom effective party leaders who would survive him, reluctant as he was to cede power. Thus the difference between the two movements was not the presence of charismatic leadership. Instead, the difference was that upon independence, India's independence party movement maintained a reservoir of able leaders whose careers had been defined by that party and who would have governed India as a democracy.

Another way of explaining divergent democratization trajectories through a focus on leadership is by emphasizing the causal role of political elites as a whole in brokering democratic settlements. Democratization literature abounds with explanations focused on groups of powerful individuals, defining elites as those who are in a position to strongly and regularly influence the exercise of political power.[32] While the argument developed herein does employ the concept of elites, it also suggests that elites are better understood as a mediating theoretical concept between social groups (sometimes classes) and political institutions. Centralizing elite autonomy in explaining regime outcomes tends not to acknowledge that individuals are elites precisely because they formally or informally represent certain social or political groups within societies. Elite-based

---

[31] Jalal (1985).
[32] Dahl (1971), O'Donnell and Schmitter (1986), Bermeo (1997), and Higley and Burton (2006).

explanations of democratization are not typically able to explain why elites have the preferences that they do. Focusing on the strategic interaction between elites, then, such studies tend to neglect moving further back along the causal chain to understand whence elite preferences originated.

The present inquiry suggests that the class situation of elites, in the context of a historically defined distribution of power, importantly defines elite preferences. In the cases examined below, elite actions were regularly and continually constrained by the support such elites were able to marshal among their core constituencies. The leaders of India's and Pakistan's independence movements made their alliances not in a political vacuum, but by seeking to frame their goals so as to be seen both as advancing their supporters' interests and as being compatible with the interests of other social classes. Party leaders were continually constrained by their bases of support, even as these support bases were growing and changing.

All this is not to argue that elite interests did not substantially affect regime outcomes. The argument developed herein concurs with the view that "each type of elite has had a 'foundational origin' in the sense that it formed in the process of founding an independent national state."[33] Indeed, this book argues that at particular points in history, elite interests and the power-sharing norms that evolved to mediate those interests deeply impacted regime outcomes. At the same time, however, this book emphasizes that elite autonomy is heavily constrained by the social groups that these elites represent, particularly once a given perception of interests is institutionalized.

The (lack of) economic requisites for democracy

This book underscores the limited explanatory value of emphasizing the economic requisites for democratization. The most celebrated explanation of democratization suggests that higher levels of economic development facilitate the establishment of enduring democracies. The classic argument that a society moving from traditional to modern demographics – characterized by increasing economic and spatial mobility, growing literacy, and increasing urbanization – is likely to adopt democratic forms of governance remains compelling. Myriad scholars have hypothesized

[33] Higley and Burton (2006: 24).

that higher levels of economic development are causally related to democratization and democratic endurance largely because the establishment
of a middle class attenuates socio-economic conflict and generates pressure for responsive and open forms of governance.[34]

Another economic explanation for the lack of democratization is
an abundant endowment of particular natural resources, the so-called
resource curse. Cross-national studies have demonstrated a statistically
significant, negative relationship between abundant natural resources
and economic growth, an argument which has been extended to democratic endurance. Scholars have hypothesized that abundant and easily
monopolized natural resources are likely to engender rent-seeking activities in the domestic political arena, leading vested interests to capture the
state and generating a resource curse which is particularly pronounced in
oil-rich economies.[35]

Finally, both higher levels of inequality and higher levels of capital
mobility are also hypothesized to diminish the likelihood of democratization.[36] The theoretical link between these variables and regime outcomes is mediated through an analytic framework which assumes that
a democratic regime, where all individuals possess the right to vote and
where relatively more of the franchise possesses an interest in redistribution, is more likely to redistribute assets away from the well-off than
an authoritarian regime, where regime influence is by definition limited
to a few. A democracy gives greater representation to redistributive pressures than does an authoritarian regime which is by definition captured
by elites. Its potential for redistribution means that democracy poses
a greater threat to elites in a more unequal society. Conversely, as the
distribution of income becomes more equal, the prospect of democratic
governance (and the rising likelihood of redistribution which accom-
panies democratic governance) appears less threatening to the well-off.
Capital mobility similarly mitigates the threat of democratic redistribution, because elites can simply transfer their capital abroad and evade
redistribution.

All three of these arguments would suggest that the roots of different political regimes in India and Pakistan might lie in different natural
resource endowments or in differing crude rates of economic growth,

---

[34] Lipset (1959), Przeworski and Limongi (1997), Geddes (1999), and Boix and Stokes
(2003).
[35] Sachs and Warner (1997), Karl (1997), and Ross (2001).
[36] Boix (2003).

capital mobility, or income inequality. Yet comparative data, where available, provides little traction for these possibilities because these characteristics are not thought of as markedly different upon independence.[37] Forming approximately one-quarter of the geographic territory of undivided British India, Pakistan at independence inherited 18 percent of its population, just under 10 percent of its industrial base, and approximately 7 percent of the employment facilities. Nonetheless its post-independence growth rates matched that of India. By 1960, Pakistan performed marginally better on the key indicator of per capita income, which would on balance lead us to believe that its economic conditions render it more conducive to democratic creation and consolidation.

Though reliable data on historical income inequality is lacking, the best extrapolations of land inequality suggest that India and Pakistan's distribution of income were not substantially different at independence.[38] Explanations which directly link economic variables, such as income and inequality levels, to regime outcomes without reference to the contingent nature of class interests and political coalitions thus form weak primary explanations for the divergent regime trajectories of India and Pakistan.

A limited role for differing colonial inheritances

This book considers but ultimately finds wanting several types of institutionalist arguments which causally attribute divergent democratization outcomes in India and Pakistan to the nature of inherited colonial institutions, that is, the nature or size of the bureaucracy and the military. The efficacy (and relatedly, the stability) of a regime is often hypothesized to pivot upon the professionalization of its bureaucracy. The failure to establish or maintain a professional corps of bureaucrats is typically linked to the inability of a functioning state to emerge and tentative democratic regimes to consolidate.

Because autocratic intervention by the bureaucracy and the military did formally end Pakistan's early democracy, several scholars have contended along the lines of this theory that India was relatively advantaged by gaining (a) a *greater proportion* of the colonial civil service; (b) a more *professionalized* portion of the colonial civil service; and/or (c) a *smaller proportion* of the colonial army when British India was cleaved into India and Pakistan and that this differential primarily explains the divergent

[37] Maddison (1971).
[38] Maddison (1971: Comparison of Table VI-1 and Table VII-1).

TABLE 1.1. *India and Pakistan compared*

	India	Pakistan
Population (in millions)		
1960	435	46
1970	548	61
1980	687	83
1990	850	108
2000	1,016	138
Urban population (%)		
1960	18	22
1970	20	25
1980	23	28
1990	26	31
2000	28	33
GDP per capita (constant 2000 $US)		
1960	175	186
1970	207	283
1980	222	327
1990	316	461
2000	450	531
Industry (% of GDP)		
1960	19	16
1970	21	22
1980	24	25
1990	28	25
2000	27	23
Agriculture (% of GDP)		
1960	47	46
1970	46	37
1980	39	30
1990	31	26
2000	25	27

Source: World Development Indicators, World Bank.

regime trajectories in question. Specifically focusing on the role of the bureaucracy in thwarting Pakistan's democratic stabilization, Sayeed (1968) argues that Pakistan inherited a colonial tradition of centralized, despotic rule (the "viceregal tradition"); Potter (1986) implies that India's bureaucracy was likely more professionalized because Muslim civil servants were more likely to have been appointed than selected through merit; and Jalal (1995) posits that India's relatively stronger institutional inheritance relative to Pakistan (both in terms of state infrastructure such as a

stronger military and a weaker civilian officer corps) tipped a fragile balance between elected and unelected institutions toward the latter, ending
formal democracy in Pakistan.[39]

An examination of the empirical facts provides limited support for
these theses. Twenty percent of the non-British civil servants were Muslim,
very nearly proportionate to the Muslim population of India and virtually all joined the Pakistani civil service upon independence.[40] Even if the
selection of many Muslim civil servants was initially on less meritorious
grounds than their Hindu counterparts, all civil servants and military
officers serving at the time of the observed regime divergence in India and
Pakistan (namely, the five years after independence) were similarly trained
and professionalized in the British colonial state before independence,
with strong professional ethics being inculcated that limited bureaucratic
politicization.[41] Upon independence in 1947, Pakistan and India each
came into being with an approximately population-proportionate share
of civil servants. Moreover, several dozen highly experienced British civil
servants stayed on and served in the bureaucratic machinery of Pakistan
(and *not* India) for several years into independence, thereby significantly
attenuating any professionalization deficit in Pakistan's civil service.[42] All
in all, the deficit in bureaucratic capacity upon independence was marginal and thereby unable to fully account for the democratic divergence
in question.

Finally, if the bureaucratic tradition within West Pakistan was less
democratic under British colonial rule than elsewhere in British India
(though this remains a contested claim, as large parts of what became
India were also annexed late in British colonial rule and also inherited
the viceregal tradition in which the executive and judicial functions were
not separated), one would have expected the bureaucracy to immediately
assert its authority over provincial elites as well as national politicians.
But post-independence political power was overwhelmingly concentrated in West Pakistan (and specifically in the hands of provincial elites
in Punjab and the Sindh) – and not in the civilian bureaucracy. The defining political struggles in Pakistan's early decade were *either* between the
central government and provincial elites, that is, the weak party leaders

---

[39] Jalal (1995), Jaffrelot (2002), and Oldenberg (2010).
[40] Potter (1986: 117).
[41] Potter (1986: Chapters 1 and 2).
[42] Potter (1986: 143).

who possessed very little in the way of popular support and provincial elites as well as traditional leaders who were loathe to relinquish any power to the central government *or* between provincial elites themselves. There is little evidence of a bureaucracy or military eager to intervene to arrest democratic politics until well after Pakistan's dominant political party had amply failed to provide stable governance. On the whole, then, relatively marginal differences in the size or quality of Pakistan's bureaucratic inheritance cannot primarily account for its post-independence democratic divergence from India.

A more plausible version of the institutionalist argument centralizes the size of Pakistan's military in explaining the divergent regime paths, contending that Pakistan's absorption of the lion's share of the British colonial army set it on an early autocratic path. Evidence substantiating this causal claim is not readily found however. To be sure, *since* the Pakistani military initiated its first military coup in 1958, its changed institutional norms, its power-maintenance incentives, external support for military rule and even the relatively large percentage of the population with links to military have likely all combined to perpetuate regular military interventions in Pakistan. Indeed, as Londregan and Poole (1990) have shown, initial military coups significantly increase the risk of a subsequent coup within the same country. What initially drove the first military intervention of 1958 is an altogether different question for which the evidence should be carefully examined.

To this end, scholars have effectively demonstrated that the most populous and powerful province in West Pakistan – Punjab – was on the eve of independence characterized by a deeply entrenched nexus between former military officers and smaller landlords that was created during the colonial period in order to both settle the newly irrigated canal colonies as well as to safely retire ex-military officers. An astonishing number of recruits into the British colonial army were drawn from a few districts in Punjab, all of which became part of Pakistani Punjab upon independence.[43] Nevertheless, as Israel – a stable democracy with a high proportion of military personnel per capita – demonstrates, it does not necessarily follow that a state with a large militarized population or a high proportion of military officers cannot create a stable or democratic regime.

---

[43] Ali (2003) and Yong (2005).

An in-depth review of political developments in the post-independence decade provides more convincing evidence for the thesis that it was the presence of a weak political leadership at the helm of the Pakistani state which proved unable to govern that precipitated bureaucratic and military intervention. Not only was the Pakistani Commander-in-Chief a British officer until 1951, but the leadership of the dominant political party in Pakistan was so weak that it needed to regularly call upon the military to ensure that its writ was effectively enforced. For example, top League leaders, in a struggle for power with a Punjabi landlord, declared martial law in Lahore in 1953 in order to quash riots that were threatening the stability of the administration, thereby politicizing the military. Following the imposition of martial law, a top American embassy official stated that the military was "ready" but "reluctant" to arrest democratic politics in the face of political instability.[44] Despite the fact that there was similar economic and political stress in India, with early civil agitation to promote the linguistic reorganization of the state for example, India's political leaders governed without calling in the military to quell civil unrest – attesting to the more proximate importance of the dominant political party in explaining divergent democratization paths.

When Pakistan's civilian bureaucracy dismissed the Constituent Assemblies in 1953 and 1954, it was in the context of governing administrations that had been unable to produce any real power-sharing compromises among Pakistan's constituent units for over five years and the attendant (often dubiously justified) dismissal of every provincial government in Pakistan. In India, which was also characterized by constitutional conflict between the center and the states, the instrument of political consensus was a relatively cohesive party. Finally, when Pakistan's Commander-in-Chief did announce the military coup of 1958, he claimed that he had been encouraged on numerous occasions to seize power and chose not to do so.[45] These facts are more consistent with Pakistan's dominant political party failing to provide for stable governance than with a military waiting in the wings to seize power at the earliest possible opportunity.

---

[44] Charles Withers, First Secretary to American Consulate in Lahore, recounts his conversation with General Ayub Khan on February 29, 1953: "I got the distinct impression from Ayub and from subsequent conversations with his senior officers who were in Lahore at the same time, that the Pakistan Army is definitely ready to take control should Civil Government break down, although they would be reluctant to do so." United States National Archives.

[45] Khan (1967).

Thus, though there was a difference in the institutional inheritances of the two countries, I posit that these differences were dwarfed by the differing nature of their dominant political parties. India inherited a political party capable of drawing on mostly loyal and local power bases to govern, thereby ensuring the continued subordination of civilian bureaucrats and military officers to elected leadership whereas Pakistan did not. Its independence party, much more so than the colonial bureaucracy or the military, *was* the central coordinating apparatus of the post-independence government in India. In Pakistan, the colonial bureaucracy and eventually the military assumed governing authority simply because no political organization was capable of stably representing even a limited popular mandate.

International influences

The argument developed below demonstrates that the ways in which domestic actors organized, rather than external influences (international alliances, the nature of the external security environment, geopolitical factors, or a dependent position in the global economic order), primarily explains the divergent regime outcomes in question. Democratization scholars have long suggested that international support for regimes can be an important influence on whether or not states democratize.[46]

Consistent with these arguments, this book suggests that international pressures certainly strengthened particular actors or power distributions within a domestic polity, but they cannot predominantly explain domestic developments because international linkages were still in flux when regime trajectories diverged in India and Pakistan. American support for military regimes has unequivocally entrenched anti-democratic forces in Pakistan over time. But the military alliances between Pakistan and the United States were formed between 1953 and 1955, by which time Pakistan's political party had already failed to provide for regime stability and called in the military to put down civil unrest. Moreover, the impetus for these alliances was predominantly driven by the Pakistani military, which in the absence of strong political leadership was effectively given free rein to negotiate military aid. All this is not to obfuscate the fact that US support absolutely perpetuated the authoritarian tendencies in Pakistan. Nevertheless, American support did not create these autocratic tendencies – it merely strengthened them.

[46] Huntington (1993) and Levitsky and Way (2006).

Another argument which scholars have made is that a country's external security environment conditions its regime type.[47] This literature argues that democratic regimes are the luxury of secure states such as the United States, UK, Japan, Australia, and those of Western Europe which (because of NATO) do not face serious border threats. Indeed, in the case of India and Pakistan, one scholar argues that the large gap between the share of the economy devoted to defense expenditures in Pakistan compared to India after independence causally bears on the divergent regime trajectories of the two countries.[48]

However, there is no clear theoretical or empirical reason to expect such differences to causally correlate with the creation of unstable or autocratic regimes. The literature linking high external threat to regime outcomes has found that, all other factors being equal, high external threat environments have actually tended to encourage civilian primacy in domestic politics.[49] Moreover, there are good theoretical and empirical reasons to believe that civil–military relations are deeply influenced by how broader social structures are accommodated within political institutions.[50] Thus, though Pakistan's defense spending needed to be relatively higher because it inherited a disproportionate share of the colonial army and a larger proportion of Partition refugees, there is neither a clear theoretical nor empirical link between the greater degree of resources devoted to military expenditures in Pakistan and its regime outcome.

Ethnic politics

While an argument based on ethnic differences has not been used to explain regime outcomes in India and Pakistan by any scholar, the conflict of class interests in East and West Pakistan that is central to the argument below could be argued to substantively represent ethnic differences. Any argument claiming an ethnic basis for Pakistan's autocratic instability must of course be able to account for India's considerably greater ethnic diversity. However, a more sophisticated version of this argument might point to the existence of two dominant ethnic groups, which some theorists suggest are inimical to the emergence of power-sharing norms.[51]

---

[47] Gourevitch (1978).
[48] Jalal (1995: 140–141).
[49] Huntington (1957), Posen (1984), Tilly (1992), and Desch (2001).
[50] Rosen (1996).
[51] Dahl (1971).

If ethnic, class, and geographical cleavages all overlapped, why should class rather than ethnic cleavages be privileged as the primary explanatory variable?

This study demonstrates that the two dominant issues over which state-building in Pakistan broke down were substantively class-based rather than ethnicity-based. The two key post-independence conflicts in Pakistan, over the basic form of representation to be enshrined in the constitution and over the installation of an elected chief executive, had little to no impact on Bengali identity per se. Rather, the crux of these conflicts was over the ability of a numerically dominant majority to maintain *some* but *by no means exclusive* access to state machinery.

At the time of independence, West Pakistan was itself ethnically divided into several distinct ethnic groups: Punjabis, Sindhis, Pashtuns, Balochis and the immigrant *mohajirs*, the latter themselves a heterogenous group. While Punjabis were numerically dominant in West Pakistan and heavily overrepresented in colonial institutions, the immigrant *mohajirs* dominated the Muslim League and government cabinets during the early years of independence.[52] There was thus no single ethnic community in West Pakistan whose interests were consistently prioritized over Bengalis. Moreover, in the conflict over the choice of national language, the *mohajir* tongue of Urdu, not Punjabi, was chosen as the national language.

Even in the conflict over national language, which was the most distinctly ethnic issue arising in post-independence Pakistani politics, class was closely correlated with ethnic identity. A prominent ethnic conflict scholar writes in this vein that "language is ... a potent symbolic issue because it accomplishes a double linkage. It links political claims to ownership with psychological demands for the affirmation of group worth, and it ties this aggregate matter of group status to outright careerism, thereby binding elite interests to mass concerns."[53] The East Pakistani bid for language *autonomy* was not a conflict over which ethnic group would have monopolized the state, since the proposed national language was Urdu, not Punjabi or Bengali. Bengalis were mobilizing for Bengali as one of multiple national languages and were thereby not making an exclusive ethnic claim to the state.

---

[52] Mozaffar (1981). *Mohajirs*, or refugees from the United Provinces, held 29 percent of Pakistan's Cabinet positions in 1947, including all the important ones. By 1958, this figure was just 8 percent.

[53] Horowitz (1985).

Furthermore, the conflict over language was substantively about economic opportunity since the use of Bengali as one national language would have unambiguously translated into greater Bengali access to the state machinery and greater control over national economic policies. The fact that the recognition of Bengali as a national language would have translated into greater Bengali representation in the state and heightened the possibility of redistributive policies in favor of East Pakistan made the conflict over language particularly explosive. Ethnicity may have provided an opportune frame for mobilizing group claims on the state, but the question of a national language in Pakistan also substantively represented conflict over the economic policies of the state. The economic threat posed by Bengali control over the state, and not Bengali ethnic identity per se, was the driving rationale for authoritarian intervention in Pakistan.

Islam and authoritarianism

Some scholars have found that a country with a Muslim-majority population is less likely to establish a democracy, though the reasons for this relationship have been theoretically and empirically contested. Yet none of the mechanisms which are hypothesized to account for this finding are found to exist to a greater degree in Pakistan. A few scholars have hypothesized that the concentration of easily monopolized natural resources in Muslim-majority countries (typically oil rents) facilitates the establishment of coercive state apparatuses.[54] As discussed above, neither India nor Pakistan possess such natural resources.

Another explanation for robustness of authoritarianism has focused on the differing socio-political position of women in Muslim-majority countries.[55] Yet before the passage of the Hindu Code Bills in the mid 1950s, women were just as poorly empowered in India and Pakistan. Moreover, the key indicators of female empowerment used in these studies, female infant mortality and female literacy rates, show very little difference around the time of independence.[56] Finally, Stepan and Robertson (2003)

---

[54] Ross (2001) and Bellin (2004).

[55] Fish (2002).

[56] In 1941, census data indicates that 7.3 percent of adult females in undivided British India, including figures for India and Pakistan, were literate. In 1951, 7.9 percent of Indian females in the divided successor state of India were literate. Since approximately a tenth of the population of British India seceded to Pakistan and that overall literacy rates remained virtually the same in India, the average female literacy rates of the seceding regions could not have been radically different or else literacy rates for divided India would have changed more significantly (Indiastat Database). Moreover, by 1960, the life

have found that democratic under-achievement among Muslim countries is particularly limited to the Arab world, which does not include Pakistan. The more expansive rights accorded to women in India today are a consequence rather than a cause of secular nationalist politics.

The primacy of political parties?

Perhaps most importantly, however, this study expands strictly party-based explanations for regime type. Parties are often theorized to be important to a country's democratic and regime stability prospects, leading some authors to posit that strong parties are a necessary feature of successful democratization.[57] The causal link between democratization and political instability could be applied to these cases as follows: Pakistan's authoritarian tendencies are primarily fed by the inability of political parties to resolve social disputes whereas India's democratic stability results from the effective functioning of party institutions. Several Indian scholars do in fact contend that the roots of a moderately effective civilian state in the early post-independence India lay in the ability of the Congress party to envelope political factionalism at local levels of governance within an institutionalist framework.[58] This study confirms these claims, arguing that the nature and organization of each independence movement, which became the dominant political party in the first decade of statehood, has been the most important *proximate* cause of divergent regime outcomes in India and Pakistan.

However, this book also asks the analytically prior question of why and how such a strong party was constructed in India and not Pakistan. Why was the Muslim League unable to capitalize upon its legitimacy as the party of independence to create democratic institutions in Pakistan? The answer developed below causally links the class nature of support for each independence movement to the construction of its political party. The inability of the independence movement (and eventually political party) in Pakistan to resolve class conflict created a political stalemate in which the bureaucracy and then the military overtly assumed political power. In short, party-based explanations for the observed variation in regime outcome are persuasive. But to be fully explanatory, the origins of

---

expectancy of females in Pakistan, at 46 years, was actually higher than the average life expectancy of females in India, at 41 years.

[57] Mainwaring and Scully (1995).
[58] Weiner (1967), Kothari (1970), and Kohli (2001).

such differences in party strength must be deconstructed. The nature of class alliances, though less proximate, directly drove differences in party strength.

IV. CLAIMING CAUSALITY AND THE ORGANIZATION OF THE BOOK

The central aims of this book are to explain the divergent democratization trajectories of India and Pakistan and, in doing so, to elucidate the causal factors which drive democratization in a low-income, post-colonial setting. But since scholarly work evidencing, contesting, and refining the causes of democracy forms perhaps the largest body of research on any topic in comparative politics, can any valuable theoretical insights be gained from a comparative historical analysis of just two countries? Why should those two countries be India and Pakistan? And how can causal claims be convincingly established? This book investigates the explanatory power of an institutionalization of class alliances model and the alternative explanations specified above through comparative historical case studies. In particular, the argument of the book is developed and nuanced by a systematic process analysis of the early democratization trajectories of India and Pakistan.[59]

Claiming causality

How were causal inferences about the divergent democratization trajectories of India and Pakistan drawn? From both democratization literature as well as historical accounts of regime developments before and after independence in India and Pakistan, a broad range of plausible explanations for the divergent democratization trajectories in question were identified. Some explanations, e.g., levels of economic development, levels of inequality, ethnic diversity, and British colonial rule, were readily eliminated as causes because there was little to no variation between India and Pakistan. If one factor was primarily held responsible for the regime outcome of India, then it logically stands to reason that this factor should somehow have been different in the case of Pakistan, where the regime outcome is different.

From among the remaining plausible explanations, predictions for each theory were generated and compared with the sequence of actual events

[59] Hall (2003).

that were established through a triangulation of sources. For example, as the military coup of 1958 defined Pakistan's authoritarian turn, process tracing involved establishing the sequence of events culminating in the military coup. Two strong alternative theories – that military intervention in Pakistan was driven by either its disproportionate inheritance of military personnel or by its weak political party – were then used to generate a series of predictions about what should be observed should either theory be true. If Pakistan's military coup had been primarily caused by the disproportionate inheritance of military personnel in Pakistan, one would have expected to see some mobilization among military officers for intervention in civilian politics. Yet there was little evidence of such mobilization in the immediate years after independence.

The theory that the dominance of military interests in Pakistan's government primarily drove its 1958 coup was rendered less plausible via a number of observations about Pakistan's pre-1958 political developments. Working chronologically backwards, these observations were: (1) that the coup of 1958 was initiated not by a military officer but a civilian bureaucrat who subsequently invited military intervention; (2) that the illegal dismissals of Pakistan's Constituent Assemblies in 1953 and 1954 were also initiated by civilian bureaucrats; (3) that politicians and civilian administrators called in the military to institute martial law in 1953 to quell riots that primary sources indicate were likely engineered by a provincial minister to destabilize the central government – indicating that the military was being politicized by government; (4) that a secret telegram by an American official in Pakistan in 1953 related his conversations with multiple military officers, including the general who ultimately effected the 1958 coup, and noted their reluctance to initiate a coup; (5) that primary and secondary sources agree that the failure of Pakistan's dominant political party to agree on the basic framework of a constitution between 1947 and 1953 stemmed from the inability to agree upon a power-sharing formula between the two dominant geographical areas of the country; and (6) that Pakistan was characterized by intensifying political instability immediately upon independence at a time when the Pakistan military was led by a British general and while Jinnah was still alive to govern.

All these observations indicate that, while military intervention was the direct cause of democracy's demise, Pakistan's early, pervasive, and intensifying political instability was not caused by the politicization of the military but by the inability of its dominant political party to effectively govern. The sequence of these events gives substantially greater plausibility to the theory that Pakistan's political instability caused rather than was caused by military intervention in politics. At the same time, the theory that party weakness accounted for Pakistan's early political instability was strengthened not only by an abundance of sources which directly attest to its validity in Pakistan, but also by the comparison with India's relative stability in that same period. In India, an overwhelming variety of primary and secondary sources state that this stability was brokered by India's dominant political party. In short, closely tracing out the origins of key political decisions while simultaneously seeking evidence for multiple explanatory theories, where the nature and number of observations for each theory are sufficiently numerous, evinces compelling causal claims.

Process tracing is thereby able to avoid what some quantitative researchers have called the degrees of freedom critique. Statistical researchers sometimes suggest that research based on a small number of cases lacks a sufficient number of observations to accurately estimate the effect of a particular explanatory variable (say, military interests in the case of Pakistan) on an outcome of interest (autocratic instability). Yet this criticism inaccurately employs the quantitative framework for making correlative claims to comparative historical research in which causality is differently established. Process tracing is not a method aimed exclusively at generating greater numbers of observations with which to establish statistical significance. Instead, process tracing makes causal inferences by observing sequential processes within a specific historical case, using in-depth knowledge of context and mechanisms in a way that typically provides multiple checks on the validity of causal claims. Sometimes, even a single observation made through case-study research can form a superior means of claiming causality to large numbers of data observations.[60] The explanatory power of any theory is ultimately judged by its ability to specify the exact process by which a particular cause leads to the outcome of interest. Case study research verifies this process directly.

Finally, given the credible possibility of multiple interaction effects between the dominant theoretical explanations for democratization, process tracing is a particularly appropriate means of establishing causality.[61] Statistical investigations of democratization, such as those that have focused on the explanatory role of economic development, have been

---

[60] Gerring (2007: 183), George and Bennett (2005), and Mahoney (2010).
[61] Hall (2003) and George and Bennett (2005).

able to establish that a correlation between democratization and development exists. Indeed, the best-fitting statistical model for explaining democratization focuses on the level of economic development, ascertaining that 77.5 percent of the variation in regime types can be explained by looking at per capita income alone.[62] But these statistical analyses are generally unable to speak to *why* this correlation exists. This is particularly problematic because there are strong reasons to believe that there are multiple interaction affects between many of the plausible explanations for democratization such as economic growth, the emergence of a commercial middle class, and rising inequality. Consequently, the causes of democratization can be best assessed by comparing the predictions of those theories about sequences and processes to actual observations of processes within a few cases.

Why India and Pakistan?

This book is concerned with investigating the dynamics of democratization in a low-income, post-colonial setting, but it focuses upon the countries of Pakistan and India. This choice was motivated by two analytical reasons. First, as indicated above, the relative colonial, social, political, and economic similarities between these countries means that this particular paired comparison forms a close approximation of a natural experiment, wherein making causal claims is facilitated by the lack of many confounding factors. In order to explore the argument that the nature and institutionalization of class alliances greatly influences democratization prospects, it is useful to compare countries that vary greatly along that particular dimension but which are otherwise largely similar. While both India and Pakistan created multi-class alliances before independence, the nature of those alliances and the level of party institutionalization were different. This difference, especially in light of broader similarities, enables us to more ably assess the causal effect of those factors on democratization.

Second, examining one country whose democratization trajectory is theoretically unexpected offers rich opportunities to gain new insights into the processes of democratization. Democratization literature, both in the statistical and the comparative historical analysis tradition, has established that democracy in a low-income setting is extremely unlikely.

---

[62] Przeworski *et al.* (2000: 79). See also Boix and Stokes (2003) and Epstein *et al.* (2006).

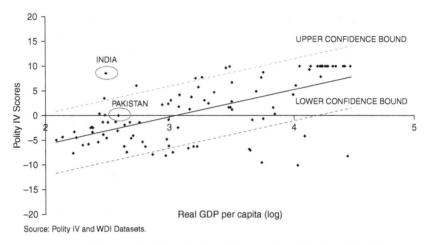

FIGURE 1.4. Cross-national correlation of economic and political development.

Figure 1.4, which depicts the correlation between the level of income per capita and democracy scores for all available countries between 1960 and 2010, demonstrates that India is an exceptional "off-the-line" case whose democracy score is highly under-predicted by its level of development, though one does find other theoretical analogues in countries such as Costa Rica. India's democratization level appears particularly exceptional when one accounts for the fact that all of the deviant countries in the lower right-hand quadrant are oil-exporting countries suffering from the so-called resource curse. Elucidating why the Indian case deviates from the statistical expectation not only helps explicate a discrete empirical puzzle but also has the potential to illustrate that a theoretical focus on economic development as explaining democracy may be deeply flawed.

The organization of the book

The remainder of the book is organized as follows. In Chapter 2, I establish the variation in the kinds of social classes dominating each independence movement, showing that the dominant political parties in India and Pakistan were created by distinct classes whose opposing attitudes toward the adoption of representative political institutions critically influenced post-independence regime trajectories. Drawing on a combination of colonial records, party papers, and personal memoirs, I show how the establishment and growth of the state in colonial British India during the late nineteenth and early twentieth centuries destabilized the rigid, religiously sanctioned social order of caste by creating an urban, educated middle class whose new status and wealth was not readily accommodated.[63] In the context of a poorly developed economy and a well-developed state apparatus, I illustrate how this emergent urban, educated middle class channeled its desire for social mobility into accessing the colonial state, in the process founding India's independence party to more effectively lobby for the establishment of representative political institutions.

I also demonstrate how the British colonial state entrenched specific social groups – in particular the landed aristocracy and Muslims – as political counterweights to the demands of the growing and increasingly organized educated middle class. I show how a subset of this group, a geographically concentrated group of Muslim landed aristocrats, established Pakistan's independence movement as a way of protecting its declining economic position and social status and that this movement therefore opposed the establishment of representative political institutions.

In Chapters 3 and 4, I substantiate how different class interests critically motivated the formation of strong and weak political parties. Both chapters take up the task of evidencing components of this claim. In Chapter 3, I substantiate the variation in ideational commitment which partly defines strong political parties. Utilizing colonial government records, party papers, newspaper reports, and personal memoirs, I document how each political party, in the decades before independence, instrumentally espoused nationalist ideologies in order to mobilize mass support for their goals. The educated, urban middle class leading in the Indian independence movement propagated and institutionalized a well-defined, programmatic nationalism that was substantively egalitarian. Though egalitarian nationalism was initially propagated as a means of more effectively mobilizing a mass base, the organization of the party along these egalitarian principles meant that upon independence, the adoption of similarly egalitarian principles as the organizing basis for national political power did not threaten the interests of the powerful social groups. The pre-independence institutionalization of an egalitarian nationalism within its dominant political party was therefore largely responsible for India's post-independence adoption of democratic rules of the game.

[63] In 1947, the geographical entity known as British India broke up into the sovereign states of India and Pakistan. In 1971, East Pakistan seceded and became Bangladesh. What was colonial British India has today become the three sovereign states of India, Pakistan, and Bangladesh.

Contrastingly, I show that Pakistan's ruling political party articulated a nationalist ideology which was not programmatic and which remained wholly instrumental throughout its independence struggle, never coming to motivate party supporters in and of itself.

In Chapter 4, I establish the variation in the distributive coherence and organization of the core coalitions. During its struggle for independence, I show that the urban middle class leading the Indian independence party allied with the rural middle class for the purposes of forcing political reform. The relative identity of economic interests between these segments of the middle class made for a stable political coalition because it created broad scope for compromise on key post-independence policy choices. The relative coherence of distributive interests of Congress' support coalition was reinforced through the creation of local, regional, and national party infrastructure, which was utilized after independence to help reconcile elite conflict.

In contrast, I show how Pakistan's independence party was supported by an incoherent distributive coalition, consisting of both a powerful landed aristocracy and a well-organized peasant movement. The disparity of economic interests between these primary bases of support created relatively little scope for compromise on key post-independence policy choices. As a result, party infrastructure was never developed at local, regional, or even national levels. Upon independence, intra-party organization could therefore do little to stabilize a fragile core coalition.

In Chapter 5, I show how after independence, the relative strength and weakness of each political party translated into democratic regime stability in India and regime instability in Pakistan. Its ideological, coalitional, and organizational strength allowed India's governing political party to broker compromises over such contentious state-building issues such as the creation of a national constitution, the creation of an elected chief executive, and the recognition of sub-national linguistic demands. In addition, the egalitarian content of Indian nationalism, which through the course of the independence struggle institutionalized plebiscitarian politics, habituated key social groups to democratic decision-making and facilitated the adoption of "democratic rules of the game." By contrast, its ideological, coalitional, and organizational weaknesses left Pakistan's governing political party unable to broker agreement between its support bases on the same contentious regime-building issues. Democracy in Pakistan thus foundered on class conflict, eventually inviting the autocratic intervention of the bureaucracy and the military.

In Chapter 6, I draw out the broader scholarly and policy implications of this argument. I describe how an argument focusing upon the institutionalization of class alliances provides a bridge between alternative theoretical approaches and thereby advances the contested literature on democratization. I propose that explaining regime outcomes across nations, cultures, and histories requires engaging with but disentangling the mutually conditioning forces of material interests, ideas, and political institutions. While ideas may initially become important because of the material or political interests they protect or advance, ideas have staying power when they become embedded in norms and organizations.

2

The social origins of pro- and anti-democratic movements (1885–1919)

This chapter links the social origins of the parallel independence movements of India and Pakistan to the distinctly pro- and anti-democratic natures of those movements. The primary argument developed herein is, *first*, that social classes with opposing interests in promoting democratic reform founded political movements toward the end of the nineteenth century in British India and, *second*, that class attitudes toward democratic reform were directly responsible for the primary goals of these independence movements, namely, to lobby for and against the adoption of representative politics. As Figure 2.1 indicates, I establish that the interest of its dominant social class was the most important driver of the political regime each movement was likely to establish.

While the empirical observations in this chapter are not entirely novel, they provide important foundations for constructing an original, comparative argument. Overall, this chapter illustrates how a class whose wealth and prestige was entrenched within the existing colonial order resisted democratic reform while an emergent, educated middle class lobbied for limited democratic reforms as a way of promoting upward mobility. In both cases, material interests were the primary motivators of political movements. These movements, in turn, were a direct consequence of a socio-economic structure that was absorbing and reacting to the imperatives of colonialism.

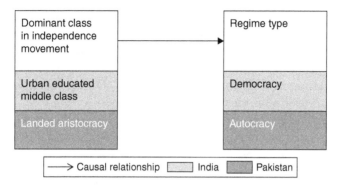

FIGURE 2.1. Argument of the chapter.

I. IMAGINED INDIANS EMBRACE DEMOCRATIC REFORM

Educated as Englishmen, imagined as Indians

During the early half of the nineteenth century, a new educated and urban middle class arose as the result of a distinct policy to create indigenous intermediaries who could assist in the maintenance of British colonial rule over a vast and highly differentiated polity. British educational policy had heretofore rejected indigenous education for many in favor of Western education for an elite few.[1] This new highly educated elite which emerged, announced a prominent member of the colonial government in 1835, should form "a class who may interpret between us and the millions whom we govern; a class of persons, Indian in blood and colour, but English in taste, opinions, in morals, and intellect."[2] The accompanying establishment of colonial institutions of higher education across British India, in combination with the erstwhile ascriptive nature of educational attainment for the Brahmin caste in Indian society, meant that a select group of high-caste individuals attained relatively high levels of education in colonial institutions, which positioned them to serve the British administration.[3]

As was not uncommon for educated, indigenous administrators in far-flung colonies, this new elite straddled two distinct social worlds, often having as much in common with their colonial administrators as they did with the traditional society from whence they came. On the one hand, these modern professionals were educated as Englishmen, typically

[1] Adams and Adams (1971).
[2] Thomas Babington Macaulay, "Minute on Indian Education," 1835, NMML.
[3] Government of India (1921: Vol. I, 296).

studying in England and residing in urban British India. Through their education, this urban, educated elite was inculcated with a liberal ideology and immersed in English social norms. By virtue of their skin color however, they were excluded by their colonial rulers from the highest echelons of power and status within government. On the other hand, such individuals had often defied religious and social orthodoxy to pursue colonial education and employment. As such, they were somewhat alienated from both traditional Indian and colonial British social structures.

Such individuals, encouraged by shared educational and social norms, formed the tentative beginnings of an imagined national community that first came together in the form of regional associations.[4] By the mid nineteenth century, the educated middle class was growing into sizeable numbers and unable to find employment for which it had been prepared in colonial institutions of higher education.[5] The high-caste status of these individuals rendered them socially unfit to assume menial jobs. Consequently, many had turned to law, teaching, journalism, and organized political activity instead, setting up regional associations which lobbied the British government to fulfill the implied promise of government jobs to English-educated Indians in the Charter Act of 1833. The future leaders of India's independence movement were still members of castes, regions, and certain religious sects, however, even if they had distanced themselves from these linkages by enrolling within the Western system of education. Though they shared a common language, the contradictions of their unique social position, and increasingly, regional associations, the emergent, educated middle class had not yet overcome traditional social divisions.

Through these newly forged regional associations, the emergent, educated elite began to lobby for greater indigenous representation within the colonial government's nominally advisory political bodies. The practice of excluding otherwise well-qualified indigenous Indians from the highest levels of power contradicted the espoused ideational foundations of British colonial rule. Versed in these ideologies and familiar with the evolution of constitutional government in other parts of the British empire, these Western-educated professionals began to lobby the colonial government to apply the same model of gradual devolution of power to colonial India.[6] In

---

[4] Anderson (1983) and Martin (1969: 237).
[5] Report of the Indian Education Commission of 1882: 269, 274.
[6] Chandra (1989: 72–73), Misra (1976: 43), and Sarkar (1983: 88).

Bengal in particular, the educated segment of the urban middle class was organizing mass meetings and petitioning England for greater indigenous representation in various parts of colonial government. They typically pursued these aims by lobbying British legislators directly or by supporting the election of British members of parliament who favored reforming British India's Legislative Councils. While such reforms would mainly benefit the 404 indigenous individuals educated in Britain in 1884 (an absolutely tiny fraction of the 200 million plus population), they were nonetheless a demand for more representative political institutions and, as such, formed the basis of a pro-democratic movement.[7]

Unsurprisingly, the colonial government resisted all efforts at democratic reform by dubbing Congress wholly unrepresentative of the manifold political interests within British India. Conceding even partial representation, colonial government officials wrote, would "place millions of men, dozens of nationalities, and hundreds of the most stupendous interests under the domination of a microscopic minority."[8] The colonial government unambiguously recognized the threat posed by these demands to the longevity of the British colonial enterprise in India. In 1884, the reigning Viceroy presciently wrote: "You may rely upon it that there are few Indian questions of greater importance in the present day than those which relate to the mode in which we are to deal with the growing body of Natives educated by ourselves in Western learning and Western ideas."[9]

By 1885, a series of pointed failures on the part of regional associations to achieve any success in promoting representative reforms led educated elites to attempt to coordinate on an all-India basis – creating what eventually became India's independence movement. By the early 1880s, numerous individuals suggested coordinating on an all-India scale. Particularly important factors in motivating the establishment of an all-India organization were the lack of success in electing reform-friendly electors, the rejection of Riponian reform attempts, and successful European opposition to the Ibert Bill in 1882–3. As a result, 72 men met in Bombay in December of 1885 to form India's eventual independence movement – the Indian National Congress.

---

[7] Statement III, Report of the Public Service Commission, 1886–7, IOL.
[8] Lord Dufferin, Letter 118, Volume 5, *Letters from Dufferin to Cross*, No. 25, Cross Papers, IOL.
[9] Ripon Viceregal Papers, I.S. 290/5, No. 18, IOL.

The germ of a "native parliament"

The founding members of the Indian National Congress (INC), which herein refers precisely to the national organization of Congress as well as to its affiliated regional and local bodies, were predominantly members of both this new educated middle class and the high-status Brahmin caste. Between 1885 and 1914, 60 of 86 leading Congressmen and 13 of 16 Congress Presidents had received advanced legal training in English educational institutions. A large majority of these were individuals whose fathers were not in the legal profession, indicating how these individuals were part of a fundamentally *new* class.[10] High-status Brahmins, for whom educational attainment had historically been an ascriptive occupation, comprised less than 6 percent of the total occupation of British India but accounted for nearly 40 percent of the 13,839 delegates who attended Congress' annual meetings between 1892 and 1909. Of the 57 most active Hindu delegates to Congress between 1885 and 1914, 38, or 67 percent, were Brahmins.[11] The simultaneous ability to represent new and old sources of social prestige made this a particularly influential social group.

During the first two decades of its existence, Congress primarily served as a forum to bring together educated professionals from across British India aiming to overcome colonial objections to devolving political power by creating what could legitimately be called a national movement. As members of the newly educated, urban professional elite, Congressmen wanted to translate their existing educational and social capital into greater political power and prosperity. They self-consciously created, in Gramscian terms, the headquarters of a movement to advance these goals in the face of colonial criticism that it was unrepresentative of the many nations of India. The primary stated goal of Congress at its opening session in 1885 was to "enable all the most earnest labourers in the cause of national progress to become personally known to each other." It was also concerned with "mould[ing] Indians into a common nation" and with forming "the germ of a Native Parliament [that] if properly conducted, will constitute in a few years an unanswerable reply to the assertion that India is still unfit for any form of representative institution."[12]

---

[10] Leading Congressmen are defined as those who spoke five or more times at Congress' annual meetings and who were appointed to at least three ad-hoc committees. McLane (1977).

[11] McLane (1977: 63, 97).

[12] Zaidi (1990: Vol. I, *The Founding Fathers*: 39).

Congress' agitation for representative politics was in substance a limited demand for democratic reform. To be sure, Congressmen freely admitted that the franchise should be limited to those with education. Moreover, the party had little institutional independence from class interests, lacking well-defined procedures, a written constitution or active standing committees. But the aim – greater indigenous representation within government – as well as the means – Congress meetings were conducted via open discussion and debate, with resolutions being passed by majority voting – were constitutive of democratic politics.

While united in its goal of seeking greater representation, Congressmen remained divided as to whether loyalist or radical strategies would best achieve that goal and, as such, remained politically impotent for the next three decades. "Moderate" Congressmen such as G.K. Gokhale, Dadabhai Naoroji, W.C. Bonnerjee, and P.N. Mehta promoted a cautious and gradualist approach that advocated limited democratic reform by direct engagement with the colonial government. Congress "Extremists" such as B.G. Tilak, B.C. Pal, and L.L. Rai advocated more aggressive methods of reform agitation and were a small but growing presence in national politics.[13] Moderates, who dominated the Congress organization and who were in control of the movement's minimal organizational infrastructure, tended to disassociate themselves from violent tactics through loud professions of loyalty and were therefore legitimized by the colonial government as the genuine voice of Congress.

The thorny question of religious reform

Advocating political reform in nineteenth-century British India necessitated engagement with the many contemporaneous religious reform movements because traditional norms of Hinduism, the religion of a large majority of British Indians, limited the possibilities for promoting national unity. This is because it did not allow for public interactions on the basis of equality. The very concept of a "public sphere" where religiously sanctioned, hierarchical caste identities did not deeply pattern social interaction simply did not exist in nineteenth-century India, thereby impeding the emergence of a nationalism based on the concept of equal citizens. Congress leaders recognized that the all-encompassing nature of the Hindu religion militated against political engagement. As a prominent

[13] Mss. Eur. E. 243 (24) p. 12. Dufferin to Cross, June 29 1888. Enclosures III and IV, IOL.

social reformer wrote in 1828, "I regret to say that the present system of religion adhered to by the Hindus is not well calculated to promote their political interest. The distinctions of castes introducing innumerable divisions and sub-divisions among them has entirely deprived them of patriotic feeling."[14] As a result, a substantial minority of early Congressmen were involved in religious reform efforts outside of Congress and a majority of Congressmen had in one form or another embraced religious reform. The advancement of religious reforms, though not entirely instrumental, nonetheless advanced the cause of political modernization because it furthered an intellectual and cultural break with the past.

Religious reforms were divisive however, not least because approximately a quarter of British India was not Hindu. Congressmen's engagement with political reform created the impression that Congress was a Hindu movement. As Indians developed an awareness of and pride in their identity, they sometimes substituted a specifically Hindu identity for an Indian identity. While Congress leaders took concrete steps to maintain a careful distinction between religious and social reform and to enshrine secular principles in Congress' founding charter, the distinction between Hindu reform and political nationalism was not easy to maintain in practice. A prominent example of the difficulty separating the Congress movement from Hindu reform movements is the Hindu cow protection movement which spread across northern British India during the closing decades of the nineteenth century. The movement to legally protect cows – sacred in the Hindu religion – from being slaughtered in observance of Islamic religious festivals arose during this period. A movement to protect cows was inevitably construed as a challenge to the Islamic practice of cow slaughter however, at times provoking riots between Hindus and Muslims. Many of the key religious figures associated with this movement were important patrons of Congress.[15] Though Congress leaders rebuffed efforts to address religious issues within the party platform, they were not able to prevent the appearance of Congress representing Hinduism.

The perceived links between its leaders and Hindu reform movements translated into limited Muslim membership within Congress. The image of Congress as a Hindu movement led some Muslim leaders to abstain from Congress participation while others launched Muslim reform movements. Between 1885 and 1905, Muslims formed between 7 and 13

[14] Hiemsath (1964) and Chandra (1989).
[15] Freitag (1980).

percent of Congress' membership, though they formed between 20 and 25 percent of the population.[16] Muslim under-representation in Congress is also partly attributable to the fact that Congress was a movement of the educated elite and that fewer Muslims were among this elite because of the historically low economic status of Islamic converts in the Indian subcontinent. Some highly educated Muslims did join Congress. Others, particularly those from the United Provinces, urged abstention from Congress politics because the advent of representative politics governance would directly diminish their wealth and influence.

The turn away from loyalism

Congressmen, encouraged by limited reforms at the turn of the nineteenth century, had held out the possibility that the colonial government would gradually cede meaningful political power at the dawn of the twentieth century. Over the course of the next decades, however, it not only became clear that colonial government was unwilling to cede political power, but that it was willing to employ brutal force to maintain its rule, thereby exposing the shallow roots of its professed liberalism. In response, Congress abandoned loyalism and devoted itself to expanding the scope of the movement in order to demonstrate that its demands for democratic reform represented the interests of a broad swath of Indian society.

Four developments were particularly important in uniting Congressmen and motivating their embrace of mass politics. First, the 1905 partition of Bengal demonstrated the unifying and effective power of mass politics. Second, the government's adoption of nearly meaningless constitutional reforms in 1909 and in 1919 finally discredited the Moderate strategy of reform. Third, the economic havoc wrought by the advent of World War I multiplied grievances with the colonial regime among broad segments of rural British India. And fourth, the limited success of reform movements under a charismatic new Congress leader exemplified how the tactic of civil disobedience could successfully advance the goal of political reform. Each development is discussed in turn.

In the early years of the twentieth century, Congressmen across British India were increasingly growing disillusioned with the lack of results from polite petitions for democratic reform. The government decision to partition the province of Bengal, while made for administratively

---

[16] Sarkar (1983: 94).

logical purposes, also had definite political motivations. Bengal, with its dense concentration of urban professionals, universities, and commercial middlemen was perhaps the headquarter of Indian nationalism. During the course of British rule, the province had grown tremendously, to the point where, on the eve of Partition, it contained one-quarter of the population of British India. When the colonial decision to divide Bengal was announced in 1903, Indian nationalists correctly perceived that the real reason for Partition was, in the words of the then Viceroy, to "split up and thereby weaken a solid body of opponents to our rule."[17] The split of Bengal would have the effect of creating the Muslim-majority province of East Bengal as a counterweight to the Indian nationalist movement. Moreover, since the establishment of an alternative provincial capital would divert trade and legal business from Calcutta to the new capital of Dacca, it would have material consequences for lawyers, merchants, and landlords represented in Congress.

From the moment the partition proposal was announced, Bengal erupted in protest, charging that the government sought to marginalize and divide the nationalist movement. Anti-colonial protest for the first time included mobilization among a wider socio-economic stratum in the form of public meetings, petitions, newspaper campaigns, speeches, and distribution of various memoranda. In the first two months following the announcement, 500 protest meetings were held all over urban centers in Bengal. Numerous protest petitions, some signed by as many as 70,000 people, were submitted to the colonial government.[18] The rapid growth of protest fed on a mix of growing cultural pride in Bengal, frustration with racial arrogance of the colonial regime, and growing economic grievances.

This mass mobilization did *not* occur within the Congress Party, as the party was still controlled by Moderate leaders. But contagious, widespread, and ultimately successful agitation against Partition amply demonstrated the possibilities of mass mobilization for effecting political change. When the Partition of Bengal actually took place, the *Swadeshi* or self-sufficiency movement was launched in protest, rapidly expanding the base of nationalist agitation. Inspired partly by the successful contemporaneous Chinese boycott of American goods, the movement boycotted British goods, textiles in particular, with the aim of pressuring British textile interests into lobbying the British government in London for the

---

[17] Lord Curzon, as quoted in Chandra (1989: 123) and Sarkar (1983: 107).
[18] Gokhale's Presidential Address to Congress in 1905 in Zaidi (1990: Vol. IV, 690–701).

reversal of the Partition. Various forms of anti-colonial protest were staged, including student movements as well as spontaneous protests and speeches throughout smaller cities in Bengal. Many of these meetings attracted tens of thousands of people. The movement also achieved substantial financial success. In the year following the Partition for example, the sale of British cloth in Bengali districts fell between five and 15 times.[19] The social base of the movement included a much broader segment of the lower middle class, albeit in no consistently organized manner. Moreover, while the *Swadeshi* movement was concentrated in Bengal, it attracted attention and gained adherents across British India.[20] When the Partition was reversed in 1911, the strategy of mass political mobilization was vindicated.

The rising tide of mass politics in Bengal brought to a fore the ideological divisions between the Extremists and Moderates within Congress and resulted in its split in 1907. While both groups called for some sort of political independence or *swaraj*, and while both supported the *Swadeshi* movement, they were unable to agree on whether the Bengal movement should be elevated into wide-scale civil disobedience. This deadlock was encouraged by the British government, which used a carrot-and-stick policy to divide Congress, simultaneously repressing some of the Extremists and holding out the possibility of constitutional reforms for Moderates. This divide erupted in 1907, when at the annual session of Congress, Extremists and Moderates came to blows and hurled chairs at each other.[21] At this juncture, the British government launched a wide attack on the Extremist leadership, jailing or deporting them and effectively ending the *Swadeshi* movement by 1908. Though Moderates formally retained control of the Congress organization, colonial loyalism was no longer hegemonic within Congress.

The paltry constitutional reforms of the following decades helped to unite Congress factions behind the need for a broad-based civil disobedience movement. The reforms of 1909 created somewhat greater powers of budget discussion, allowed for the sponsoring of Council resolutions, and, for the first time, formally introduced elections with a limited franchise. But these reforms fell far short of what Congress Moderates expected at the same time as grassroots political movements such as Home Rule Leagues were launched outside of the Congress organization, extending

[19] Chandra (1989: 127).
[20] Gokhale's Presidential Address to Congress in 1905 in Zaidi (1990: Vol. IV, 690–701).
[21] Argov (1967: Chapter IV).

anti-colonial agitation to the younger generation of future Congressmen. Whereas the more conservative generation of Congressmen held out for substantial reforms through constitutional means, a younger generation of the urban, educated middle class was growing up amidst the growing popularization of communist ideas and consequently supported mobilizational politics. When major constitutional reforms were not forthcoming in the 1919 reforms, Moderate tactics were deeply discredited.

Outside Congress politics, economic grievances were multiplying as the result of World War I and creating opportunities for mass political mobilization. A large drain of resources from India through heavy war-time taxation and a steep rise in commodity prices created significant discontent among subordinate social classes who were the least economically equipped to cope with such strains. Specifically, prices of consumer goods, which had risen by 43 percent in the 40 years between 1873 and 1913, rose by 200 percent in the seven years between 1913 and 1920.[22] As the prices of industrial goods went up more than the prices of agricultural goods, the rural middle class that produced some goods for the market was among the worst-affected. While the economic needs of the war created some capitalist fortunes, trade and industry were heavily taxed to support the war effort.[23] Grievances over war taxation were compounded by uncertainty over the sterling–rupee exchange ratio, a policy critical to large-scale capitalist fortunes. All these war-related developments created both new possibilities and new obstacles for political mobilization.

Against the background of these changes, Mohandas Karamchand Gandhi assumed leadership of Congress – the fourth major change influencing Congress' turn towards civil disobedience. Gandhi's world-renowned civil disobedience technique, involving the prolonged training of disciplined volunteers who peacefully violated laws popularized as unjust, followed by the mass courting of arrests and public displays of empathy through strikes and marches, had been developed and perfected in South Africa before 1915.[24] Between 1915 and 1918, Gandhi experimented with these techniques in the context of different kinds of class conflicts in British India. In each case, the young lawyer posed himself as a mediator and managed, through some combination of personal contacts and limited, deferential civil disobedience, to achieve redress by the

---

[22] Brown (1972: 125).
[23] Sarkar (1983: 170).
[24] Brown (1972).

colonial government and promote the interests of a new, upwardly mobile rural middle class. While Gandhi's interventions received increasing publicity and attention, his interventions remained relatively confined to the resolution of quite localized issues until a civilian massacre of peaceful demonstrators protesting a series of repressive legislative acts curtailing civil liberties at Jallianwala Bagh in 1919. The massacre of many hundreds of unarmed men, women, and children became a lightning rod for anticolonial grievances and decisively drove the unification of Congressmen under Gandhi's leadership. This sea change in educated middle class attitudes is elegantly captured by future Prime Minister Jawaharlal Nehru, who describes his Moderate father's embrace of Gandhi:

> At home, in those early years [before 1915] ... Father had been closely watching my drift towards Extremism, my continual criticism of the politics of talk and my insistent demand for action. What action it should be was not clear, and sometimes father imagined that I was heading straight for violent courses adopted by some of the young men of Bengal. This worried him very much. As a matter of fact I was not attracted that way, but the idea that we must not tamely submit to existing conditions and that something must be done began to obsess me more and more. Successful action, from the national point of view, did not seem to be at all easy, but I felt that both individual and national honour demanded a more aggressive and fighting attitude to foreign rule. Father himself was dissatisfied with the Moderate philosophy, and a mental conflict was going on inside him ... The outward change in his politics came about the time of Mrs. Besant's internment [in 1917] and from that time onwards step by step he went ahead, leaving his old Moderate colleagues far behind, till the tragic happenings in the Punjab in 1919 finally led him to cut adrift from his old life and his profession, and throw in his lot with the new movement started by Gandhiji.[25]

In sum, this section has argued that the growing ranks of a new, educated, and urban middle class across colonial India instrumentally established the Indian National Congress (INC) as a means of promoting its own upward mobility. In doing so, this new middle class was advocating for limited but clearly pro-democratic reforms. While Congress leaders initially preferred elite bargaining to mass politics, the discrediting of moderate forms of constitutional agitation, the multiplication of economic grievances brought on by the World War, and the demonstrated possibilities of mass civil disobedience to redress those grievances under new leadership slowly but steadily radicalized the movement. As a result, India's eventual independence movement launched its first foray into mass civil disobedience, a subject taken up in the next chapter.

---

[25] Nehru (1945: 37–38).

II. MUSLIM LANDED ARISTOCRATS REACT TO DEMOCRATIC REFORM

Democratic reforms diminish landed aristocrats

The adoption of limited representative politics toward the end of the nineteenth century had the immediate and unintended effect of magnify-ing the influence of the educated and commercial middle class at the dir-ect expense of the (Hindu and Muslim) landed aristocracy. Congressmen, many of whom drew some income from landholdings but whose primary source of income was professional, initially maintained good relations with the landed aristocrats across British India who formed the bulwark of colonial rule. Indeed, during the 1880s, major landholders or *zamind-ars* were contributing to Congress financially and Congress opposed ten-ancy legislation for subordinate rural classes.[26]

The political interests of the educated middle classes and the landed aristocracy began to diverge as a result of the introduction of the elect-ive principle into colonial political institutions. Prior to 1892, indigen-ous representatives to colonial advisory bodies, whose powers were at any rate minimal, were nominated by the colonial government, which resulted in the heavy representation of the landed aristocracy. Between 1862 and 1888, 23 of 36 Indians on the all-India (Governor-General's) Legislative Council were landholders whereas only three members were lawyers. During the same period, 17 Indians on the Bengal Council were affiliated with landed interests while nine were in the legal professions. In Bombay, the balance of representation between landed and professional interests was roughly equal. In the North-Western Provinces and Oudh (future United Provinces), where a legislative council was only established in 1887, three of four appointed Indians were landholders.[27] In its bid to gain a foothold in colonial government, Congress lobbied for the right of urban associations to send their own representatives to these Legislative Councils, effectively demanding the right to a limited elective principle. The colonial government conceded this principle in the Indian Councils Act of 1892 with the expectation that landlords would continue to dom-inate the Councils.[28]

Contrary to government's expectations, conceding the elective prin-ciple had the effect of granting greater influence to the middle class at the direct expense of the large landowners. In Bengal, for example, of

---

[26] McLane (1977: 227).
[27] Misra (1961: 351) and McLane (1977: 234–235).
[28] Arundel Committee Report, Mss. Eur. D. 575/29, P.P. Cd. 4435 of 1908, IOL.

the ten seats reserved for non-officials on Legislative Councils, only one was now to be reserved for the great landowners or landed aristocracy. In the first Bengal Council Elections of 1893, in a franchise heavily restricted by property qualifications, two of the six Indians elected were primarily known as *zamindars*. By the second elections in 1895, not a single important *zamindar* was elected to the council – all newly elected members belonged to urban professions. This trend was echoed in other regions and at the all-India level. Between 1893 and 1907 in the district boards of Bengal and Madras, and North-Western Provinces, the 54 Indians included 36 members of the legal profession and ten landholders. The colonial government partially boosted landholder influence by nomination such that of all the 338 non-official members returned to the reformed legislative councils between 1882 and 1907, 77 or 22 percent were landowners while 123 or 36 percent were lawyers.[29] As the new educated middle class gained at the expense of large landlords, the loose alliance between Congressmen and large landlords was fractured.

Democratic reforms diminish United Province Muslims

While the political influence of landlords everywhere was weakened by electoral reform, Muslim landlords in the United Provinces were particularly threatened by such reform. On average, Muslims across British India were less likely to be educated and urban than Hindus. Twenty-three percent of the population of British India in 1882 was Muslim. Three-quarters of Muslims in British India resided in the two provinces of Punjab and Bengal.[30] Muslims in these provinces, located on the respective northwestern and northeastern wings of British India, were historically converted from the lowest socio-economic stratum and were thus under-represented among the urban, educated middle class constituting the INC.[31] Crucially, however, Muslims of the United

---

[29] McLane (1977: 232–235).

[30] Thirty-eight million Muslims of the 168 million adults in British India.

[31] Government of India (1901: 163) and Report of the Indian Education Commission of 1882: 483. Particularly in English education, there is no doubt that the educational gap between Hindus and Muslims was significant. It may reasonably be asked what lay behind lower levels of Muslim educational achievement in British India. The difference was certainly partially attributable to socio-economics, since the bulk of the Muslim population was simply poor and thus presumably was given far fewer opportunities to engage in formal education. In addition, the traditional Muslim system of education in British India emphasized religious learning as the most important component of learning and a prerequisite toward further education. Moreover, Muslims were further

Provinces (UP), where the Pakistan independence movement was created, were a marked *exception* to the broader trend toward educational under-achievement among Indian Muslims. Concentrated around Delhi, the capital of the colonial government since 1911, UP Muslims were descendants of the Mughal rulers who had also located their capital cities in Agra and Delhi. Rather than being educationally backward, they were more urban and more educated than their Hindu counterparts. In 1931, UP Muslim men were more English-literate – 14.8 Muslims for every 8.4 upper-caste Hindus among 1,000 men – and more urban – as just 14 percent of the population, they constituted over a third of the United Provinces' town-dwellers.[32]

Despite being a minority, Muslims were a powerful political force in the UP. Power in colonial India was apportioned to three main groups: landlords, traders/moneylenders, and government officials. UP Muslims were over-represented in all three categories. Muslims constituted 22 percent of UP commercial traders. Muslims owned 20 percent of the land in the province, but since much land was held in small parcels, Muslims were especially likely to be among the large landlords, particularly so in the western part of the province.[33] UP Muslims were also far more likely to be in government service than other demographic groups. In 1882, Muslims held 35 percent of all government civil service posts in the province.[34] They were even more represented in the particularly powerful positions: Muslims were 56 percent of government servants in the High Court and 42 percent of the government officers working with the deputy commissioners and commissioners (the most powerful men in the province). Yet another indicator of Muslim influence is that in one region of Oudh, Muslims were 13 percent of the population, held 20 percent of the land, and were able to elect 40 percent of the members of district boards. In the second half of the nineteenth century then, despite being a minority, United Province Muslims were disproportionately socially and politically very influential.[35]

---

disadvantaged by the necessity of intensive religious study as a prerequisite to higher educational attainment.

[32] Robinson (1993: 13).

[33] Robinson (1993: 13–17).

[34] Government civil servants, particularly in the covenanted civil services, were the local face of the British Raj. As described in the previous chapter, their power to interpret law, estimate land revenue, and carry out government policy had wide-reaching implications for most members of Indian society.

[35] Robinson (1993: 20–23).

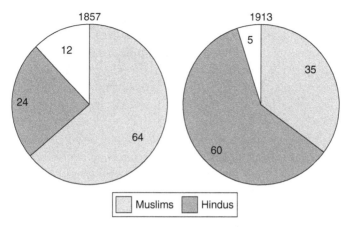

FIGURE 2.2. Composition of judicial and executive services in United Provinces. Source: adapted from Robinson (1993: 46).

The educated, urban, Muslim middle class in the United Provinces, whose position in colonial government had been historically entrenched, also experienced relative socio-economic decline as a direct result of Congress' reforms. Urban, educated middle-class UP Muslims typically maintained links to the Muslim landed aristocracy but nevertheless needed to earn a subsistence income. Due in part to their language advantage in Arabic, Muslims had historically dominated UP's urban professions by finding government jobs through family connections. They were thus threatened by political and bureaucratic reforms that rationalized access to those professions. And indeed, as Figure 2.2 indicates, Muslim representation in the United Provinces judicial and executive services had declined in both relative and absolute terms by the latter half of the nineteenth century. Despite the relatively greater influence of Muslims in the UP, however, religious cleavages were *not* politicized along religious lines during most of the nineteenth century.

Religious cleavages within the landed aristocracy of the United Provinces, and to a lesser extent the educated urban middle class, began to be strained as the government responded to demands for democratic reform and government expansion that were being propagated by Congress. In the context of growing Hindu revivalism across British India, a movement had arisen to help the so-called "Urdu-speaking elite" – composed of Hindus and Muslims alike – regain their diminishing socio-economic status. The Aligarh movement, as it became known, had promoted the use of vernacular languages in lowering barriers to

Western education. The movement's lobbying for the use of vernacular languages in government education resulted in the matter being considered.[36] But as the government explored the possibility of providing education in vernacular languages in 1867, it discussed whether the said vernacular language to be employed should be Hindi or Urdu. In response, the Urdu-speaking elite began to cleave along Hindu and Muslim lines.

The debate over which vernacular script was to be used in the government's educational facilities became intensely politicized primarily because it had major repercussions for who would be eligible for government employment. While Hindi and Urdu are broadly similar languages when spoken, Urdu uses the Arabic script and Hindi uses the Devanagari script. Arabic, initially introduced by the pre-colonial Mughal empire as the language of its court, had been adopted by the British colonial regime as it expanded across the Indian subcontinent. The introduction of the Devanagari script within the provincial government would thus seriously disadvantage Muslims, who typically had little exposure to the Devanagari script in the course of their education, as compared to the Hindu members of the Urdu-speaking elite, who were typically fluent in both scripts.

In the context of Congress-dominated agitation for political reform, the demand for vernacular languages began to break apart the Urdu-speaking elite into politicized religious groups that alternately supported and opposed democratic reforms. The Aligarh movement opposed participation in Congress because its main demand centered on the substantive expansion of Legislative Councils that would benefit English-educated upper-caste Hindus, thereby diminishing the relative influence of the well-entrenched Urdu-speaking elite. The leader of the Aligarh movement, Sir Syed Ahmed Khan, began to speak out to protect specifically Muslim interests in the context of the newfound language controversy. In 1883, as Sir Syed spoke before a Legislative Council that was debating self-governance, he articulated the widespread view among UP Muslims that representative institutions would accelerate their relative socio-economic decline: "the system of election pure and simple cannot be safely adopted. The larger community would totally override the interests of the smaller community, and the ignorant public would hold the Government responsible for introducing measures which might make the differences of race

---

[36] Robinson (1993: 96).

and creed more violent than ever."[37] In 1887, Khan clearly represented aristocratic interests when he spoke before the Legislative Council:

Would our aristocracy like that a man of low caste or insignificant origin, though he be a B.A. or M.A. and have the requisite ability, should be in a position of authority above them and have power in making the laws that affect their lives and property? Never! Nobody would like it. (Cheers). [Emphasis added.][38]

Despite the politicization of the religious differences, political alignments were still fluid and the politics of class could and did trump the politics of religion towards the end of the nineteenth century. The UP landed aristocracy was united against the advance of political reforms, even though such political reforms would be limited by property qualifications. In expounding the view that the adoption of electoral politics was undesirable, the Muslim landed aristocracy was joined by upper-class Hindus such as the Raja of Bhinga, the Maharaja of Benares and Raja Siva Prasad – who all together formed the United Indian Patriotic Association. These were many of the same Hindus who opposed Sir Syed in promoting the Devanagari script for use in government educational institutes. When the United Indian Patriotic Association (a cross-communal organization) was superseded by the Muhammadan Anglo-Oriental Defence Association of Upper India (a specifically Muslim organization), it is indicative of the class base of the latter organization that one of its key goals "aimed to discourage popular political agitation among Mahomedans [Muslims]."[39]

Overlapping threats and the creation of the anti-democratic Muslim league

The partially Muslim UP landed aristocracy, whose socio-economic influence as a class had been diminished by the 1892 reforms, as indicated by Figure 2.2, were alarmed at the prospect of additional reforms and ardently lobbied against them. A group of titled Muslim landowners, who were highly supportive of British rule that had until now secured their influence in matters political and economic, formally submitted a request to the Viceroy in October 1906 for extra-proportional Muslim

[37] Proceedings of the Council of the Governor-General in 1883 as quoted in Coupland (1945: 93).
[38] Khan (1888). Speech at Lucknow, dated September 28, 1887 in NMML.
[39] Robinson, (1993: 120–121).

representation in any upcoming reforms. The petition reminded the government that Muslims had a special relationship with the colonial government, that this relationship was steadily being eroded by mobilization and that upper-class Muslims preferred British rule to continue indefinitely. Furthermore, preventing younger, educated Muslims from joining Congress, which would considerably strengthen Congress' claim of representation and which would seriously undermine colonial charges that Congress was unrepresentative, would require the institutionalized protection of Muslim interests.[40] The deputation specified Muslims should be extra-proportionally represented in view of their loyalty to the state and Muslim electorates should be separate, meaning that only Muslims could vote for these seats. The demand for extra-proportional and separate electorates was channeled later the same year into the founding charter of the Muslim League – Pakistan's eventual independence movement.

In December 1906, a collection of landed aristocrats, dominated by the Muslim landed aristocracy, met in Dacca to found the future independence movement of Pakistan. Unlike Congress, the League was not organized by a class of individuals who stood to gain by the adoption of a social order based on meritocracy. Many highly educated Muslims across India tended to join the Congress rather than the League, including Mohammed Ali Jinnah, Pakistan's charismatic independence leader, who was until 1920 a member of the Congress movement. Moreover, the interests of Muslims from other provinces, such as the Bengali Muslim landed aristocracy, who urgently wanted a plea for the continued Partition of Bengal included in the 1906 deputation, were ignored.[41] Instead, the Muslim League was propagated by landed aristocracy from the UP which exclusively sought to protect its historically entrenched position in government from being eroded through democratic reforms.

That the membership in the Muslim League was restricted to landed aristocrats or extremely prosperous professionals is apparent from its membership requirements. The League not only limited its membership to 400 individuals, but stipulated that such individuals pay an annual subscription fee of Rs. 25 and earn a minimum of Rs. 500 annually, at a time when British India's annual per capita income is estimated to have been around Rs. 42.[42] The membership qualifications outlined in

[40] Letter from Butler to Allen, April 6, 1913, Harcourt Butler Papers, MSS F 116, IOL.
[41] Rahman (1970: 22).
[42] Muslim League Proceedings, 1907, National Archives of Pakistan (NAP).

the constitution adopted in 1907 were specifically designed to keep the League in the control of those with property and influence.[43]

That the League was dominated by the landed aristocracy of the United Provinces is evidenced by the fact that many of the most important positions in the League during its pre-independence decades were controlled by UP Muslims. At its founding session in 1906, both joint-secretaries of the provisional committee to frame the constitution were from the UP, and 21 of the 58 members of this committee were from the UP.[44] The most influential position in the League was that of the League secretary, and between 1906 and 1926, this position was *always* held by a UP Muslim. Moreover, the three permanent Presidents of the Muslim League between 1908 and 1930 were the Aga Khan (an extremely wealthy resident of Bombay and London, chosen for his political conservatism), the Raja of Mahmudabad (one of the wealthiest landowners from the United Provinces) and M.A. Jinnah (a Bombay lawyer).

The central link between the anti-democratic interests of the landed aristocracy of the United Provinces and the goals of the Muslim League was also readily apparent. Between 1906 and 1913, that is, shortly before and after the 1909 reforms, the League's pre-eminent organizational goal was the prevention of democratic reform through a claim of colonial loyalty and, to the extent that political reform would be pursued, to bargain for extra-proportional Muslim representation. The first stated goal of the Muslim League in its founding session was the fostering of a sense of loyalty to the colonial government among Indian Muslims. The 1908 proceedings of the League stated:

the best sense of the country recognizes the fact that the progress of India rests on the maintenance of order and internal peace, and that order and internal peace, in view of the conditions obtaining in our country at present and for a very long time to come, immeasurably long time to come, spell British occupation. *British occupation not in the thin and diluted form in which Canada, Australia and South Africa stand in relation to England, but British occupation in the sense in which our country has enjoyed internal peace during the last fifty years.* [Emphasis added.][45]

The proceedings of the Muslim League meetings during its first decade are replete with similar statements. As the quote demonstrates, the ideology of the Muslim League in its early years is better described as loyalist

---

[43] Rahman (1970: 52–60).
[44] Pirzada (1969: 11–12).
[45] Muslim League Papers, 1908 Proceedings, Microfiche, NAP.

and anti-democratic than as pro-Muslim. Other than negotiating at the political center with the colonial government, the early Muslim League remained limited in its aims and maintained little organizational infrastructure. Provincial Leagues were established in most major provinces across British India by 1909, but they were largely inactive save for the London and all-India branches, which were used to keep in close touch with British thinking on political reform and, where political reform was going forward, to lobby for separate, extra-proportional representation for Muslims.

In the 1909 reforms, the Muslim League achieved its goals largely due to colonial patronage. Separate electorates not only allocated a set number of seats in the new Councils for Muslims, but it allowed only Muslims the right to vote for those seats. Crucially, it guaranteed UP Muslims extra-proportional political representation. The League was quite successful in increasing the number of Muslim seats suggested in initial government proposals, especially at the all-India level, where the representation of Muslims was doubled. By granting Muslims extra-proportional representation, the colonial government bought Muslim loyalty, which it could subsequently use as a bulwark against Congress' mobilization claims. Discussing the 1909 reforms, the Viceroy wrote to the Secretary of State in India that: "I cannot see that they [Muslims] are in the least entitled to the number of seats that will now be allotted to them [under the 1909 reforms]."[46] The Secretary of State wrote a week later, "If we had not satisfied the Mahometans [*sic*] ... we should have had opinion here which is now with us – dead against us."[47] The decision to politically over-represent Muslims was directly taken to countervail Congress' growing influence.

Having succeeded in insulating themselves from the need to compete in democratic elections, the landed aristocracy had little use for the Muslim League and effectively abandoned the organization. That a new social demographic was leading the League is evidenced in the kinds of changes that were made to the constitution in 1913. The membership subscription was reduced and the size of the central League body was expanded. While the League constitution still declared its colonial loyalty and still specified the "protect[ion] and advance[ment] [of] the political and other rights and interests of the Indian Musalmans," it also added in a clause which provided for the "attainment, under aegis of the British

---

[46] Minto in a letter to Morley, 11 November 1909, Morley Papers (IV), IOL.
[47] Morley to Minto, 18 November 1909, Morley Papers (IV), IOL.

Crown, of a system of self-government suitable to India, through constitutional means by bringing about, among others, a steady reform of the existing system of administration, by promoting national unity, by fostering public spirit among the people of India and by cooperating with other communities for the said purposes."[48] Once under the leadership of the Muslim middle class, the League still aimed to protect Muslim interests, but this was no longer seen as incompatible with the goal of political reform advanced by Congress. Thus, the Muslim League joined forces with Congress in 1916, providing for the continued protection of Muslim interests through the Lucknow Pact. Thereafter, the League lay dormant for much of the next two decades, often unable to garner even a quorum for its annual meetings.

Once the principle of separate representation for Muslims was conceded, the need for political organization disappeared, the Muslim League was eclipsed by the rise of a pan-Islamist caliphate movement and the League became an irrelevant political force for much of the next two decades. Nevertheless, the legacy of anti-democratic Muslim separatism had been sown. As pan-Islamism receded, as the power of the Congress grew, and as a distant likelihood of colonial independence blossomed into an imminent prospect, the Muslim League would be reincarnated to promote the interests of the entrenched Muslim landed aristocracy in the United Provinces.

III. CONCLUSION

The primary argument of this chapter was that the independence movements of India and Pakistan were dominated by distinct social classes with opposing interests in creating more democratic political institutions, that these class interests were historically conditioned by the colonial distribution of power, and that the pursuit of class interests had a direct impact on the type of political regime each independence movement was likely to establish.

In both cases, the instrumental pursuit of class interests propelled the creation of political movements. To establish the link between the social origins of India's eventual independence movement and its political goals, I show how a qualitatively new, urban, educated middle class was emerging in nineteenth-century British India. As the ranks of the unemployed

---

[48] "Revised Constitution and Rules of the All-India Muslim League." Section 2, February 1913. Muslim League Papers, NAP.

educated elite began to swell, the educated middle class established a national organization in 1885 – the Indian National Congress – to better coordinate its demands for greater representation in colonial government. Through its monopoly of English education, the emergent educated class was uniquely situated to benefit from such demands. Nonetheless, these demands substantively advanced democratic political institutions.

Divided between loyal and radical camps, however, Congress proved unable to wrest genuine measures of democratic reform from a colonial government that decried its demands as wholly unrepresentative of the Indian population. Repeated failures to grant reform slowly began to radicalize Congressmen at the same time as the successful *Swadeshi* movement, the multiplication of war-related grievances, and the emergence of a charismatic leader engaging in limited civil disobedience all underscored the possibilities of mass politics. By the end of World War I, Congress turned to mass mobilization in order to more successfully pursue its goal of reform

To evidence the link between the social origins of Pakistan's eventual independence movement and its political goals, I demonstrate that the influence of both landed aristocrats and of a particular group of geographically concentrated Muslims was diminished by democratic reforms at the turn of the nineteenth century. These overlapping cleavages motivated Muslim landed aristocrats in the United Provinces, supported by colonial patronage, to instrumentalize a shared Islamic identity and to lobby *against* democratic reforms through a newly created organization – the Muslim League. Because the colonial government maintained a clear interest in bolstering this movement as a counterweight to Congress' claims of representation, separate, extra-proportional representation for Muslims was institutionalized. Paradoxically, this institutionalization undermined any need for political mobilization until the prospect of Indian independence loomed. At that point, the Muslim League was resurrected as Pakistan's independence movement.

3

Imagining and institutionalizing new nations
(1919–1947)

Institutionalization is, in fact, the process by which an organization incorporates its founders' values and aims … The organization slowly loses its character as a tool: it becomes valuable in and of itself, and its goals become inseparable and indistinguishable from it. In this way, its preservation and survival become a "goal" for a great number of its supporters.

(Selznick 1952)

This chapter and the next demonstrate why and how the social classes leading the Indian and Pakistani independence movements transformed these nascent organizations into the mass-based political parties that would govern each country upon independence. The core argument developed in this chapter is, *first*, that the dominant social classes in each movement imagined and institutionalized nationalisms in pursuit of narrow class goals and, *second*, that those nationalist ideologies differed with respect to the presence of positive, programmatic content and the institutionalization of this content. As Figure 3.1 suggests, this differential critically explains post-independence democratic divergence in India and Pakistan because the *presence* of programmatic nationalism would facilitate governing on the basis of agreed-upon principles, thereby explaining regime stability, while the defining *content* of each nationalism conditioned what kind of regime was likely to be created, thereby explaining regime type.

Since nationalist ideology is the central empirical focus of this chapter, it is appropriate to clearly define the concept. I employ the term *ideology* in the broadest sense of the term to mean "a set of interconnected beliefs and their associated attitudes, shared and used by members of a group or population that relate to problematic aspects of social and political

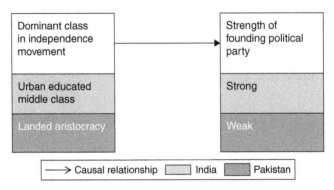

FIGURE 3.1. Argument of the chapter.

topics. These beliefs have an explicit evaluative and implicit behavioral component."[1] My use of ideology, like *Weltanschauung*, denotes a systematic set of beliefs among a population that both provides a cognitive map of the world *and* suggests actions in accordance with that map.

Ideology is herein examined within the context of a political party in which a set of beliefs are consciously created and reinforced in order to advance organizational goals. As an organization is an instrument rationally engineered to do a specific job, any *organizational* ideology is logically oriented toward achieving changes in individual behavior consistent with the job of the organization. Whether the goal is to mobilize votes for a set of candidates or to gain support for a set of social and economic policies, an organizational ideology is typically oriented toward achieving action. The key difference between ideologies of classes or individuals, which can *unconsciously* pattern social and economic actions then, and an organizational ideology, is that organizational ideology must *consciously* seek to motivate individuals to undertake actions.[2]

This study examines a quite particular kind of organization, a political party, which in this context espouses a quite particular kind of ideology, nationalism. I understand nationalism to be an ideology that, though it often builds on ethnic, racial, or linguistic distinctions, is nonetheless socially constructed. In contrast to the primordialist understandings of nationalism, this study subscribes to Gellner's definition of nationalism in which it is an ideology that "invents nations where they do not exist – but it does need some pre-existing differentiating marks to work on."[3]

---

[1] Fine and Sandstrom (1993: 24).
[2] Schurmann (1970: 18).
[3] Gellner (1965: 168).

Employing these definitions of ideology and nationalism, I show below that between 1920 and 1947, the educated, urban middle class leading India's independence movement articulated a well-developed nationalist ideology which came to stand not just *in opposition to* colonial domination, but also *in support of* political equality. In contrast, the League party articulated a vague nationalist ideology that was defined primarily *in opposition to* Congress rule and that did not otherwise stand for a set of unifying, programmatic principles. In short, India's dominant political party did and Pakistan's dominant political party did not forge substantial ideational commitment among its core support base.

I. CONGRESS POPULARIZES A PROGRAMMATIC, PRO-DEMOCRATIC NATIONALISM

The instrumental embrace of Gandhian tactics

By 1920, a newly unified educated, urban middle class began to weld its desire for political reforms to the economic concerns of rural middle and lower classes under the leadership of Gandhi, thereby helping to build a mass-based political party. The educated urban middle class initially embraced Gandhian nationalism wholly instrumentally, as a new means of achieving the same end of democratic reform that it had consistently pursued since Congress' establishment in 1885. By independence in 1947, however, the principles of Indian nationalism had become valuable in and of itself.

Gandhi's ascension within Congress was enabled by the larger political and economic developments that had rendered the party more receptive toward the adoption of radical tactics. It was in the context of growing economic discontent, unification among factions of the educated middle class, and repeated government failures to grant meaningful reform that one should interpret Gandhi's ascension within Congress. While Gandhi's personal charisma was indeed unquestioned – in the words of Gokhale, "[Gandhiji] has in him the marvelous spiritual power to turn ordinary men around him into heroes and martyrs"[4] – and while Gandhi deserves credit for doing more than any single political leader to create the egalitarian basis for Indian nationalism, Gandhi's achievements were possible because a recently unified, educated urban middle class was already casting about for a new tactic for achieving the democratic reforms that would promote their upward mobility.

---

[4] Gokhale (1967):Vol. II, 444).

Like most members of the emergent, educated middle class, Gandhi aspired to greater self-determination for colonial India, but did not immediately engage in party politics. While, as a London-educated lawyer, Gandhi was a typical member of the urban, educated elite middle class, his first employment in South Africa provided a formative experience organizing its immigrant Indian community in protest against racial injustice. It was in South Africa that he first wielded and honed the technique of civil disobedience to gain rights for Indian workers. Though his successes there earned him some fame among Congressmen and though he had periodically returned to India to attend Congress meetings, Gandhi remained a minor political figure within India.[5] When he first returned to colonial India in 1915, Gandhi devoted considerable energy to traveling the countryside and to meeting with a wide variety of social groups to better understand the nature of their various grievances. Gandhi's South African experience had taught him that creating a community for political action necessitated first building an organization which inculcates "the habit of thinking and speaking publicly about matters of public interest," which forges a service ethic among a community, and which popularizes this community through "propaganda."[6] His travels, and his accompanying exposure to the diverse social fabric of rural society, deeply influenced his understanding of how the everyday concerns and identities of Indians could be channeled into political action.[7]

Congressmen began to take note of Gandhi as a result of his successful mediations with the colonial government on localized rural grievances in 1917–18. In both of these early mediations, Gandhi pioneered the tactic of non-violent civil disobedience which later became the hallmark of the Congress movement. In the district of Champaran (in the province of Orissa and Bihar), thousands of landless, indentured laborers were forced by European planters to grow cash crops, particularly indigo, instead of food crops. In 1917, as a result of low indigo prices, these peasants struggled to feed themselves, touching off a famine. In Kheda (a district in the Bombay province), rural peasants were also adversely affected by a local famine and, barely able to feed themselves, were nonetheless being forced to pay their taxes in full. In both of these cases, severe economic dislocation had led to sporadic outbreaks of violence before Gandhi's intervention.[8] In both cases, Gandhi lived

[5] Gandhi (1993: 486) and Brown and Prozesky (1996).
[6] Gandhi (1993: 140).
[7] Gandhi (1993: Part IV).
[8] Hardiman (1981), Pouchepadass (1998), and Prasad (1949).

in the districts in question, enlisting local volunteers to create a detailed accounting of peasant grievances which were then presented to the local authorities. While Gandhi and his volunteers worked to document grievances and respectfully requested redress on specific issues such as tax remissions, they also simultaneously made substantial efforts at community-building by improving local sanitation, building schools and hospitals, and encouraging local village leaders to discard the public recognition of caste distinctions. While Gandhi accepted Congress volunteers and financial donations, he also explicitly limited the overtly political natures of his intervention, insisting that neither Congress nor other districts should involve themselves. In each case, Gandhi was successful in gaining some cooperation from the government and some accommodation on the specific issue of tax remissions.

Congressmen seized upon Gandhi's leadership because these mediations illustrated how Congress' goal of advancing political reform might be linked up with the substantive economic grievances of the rural middle and peasant classes. Gandhi's mediations took place at a time in which the urban, educated middle class had itself little understanding of the concerns of rural peasants. Jawaharlal Nehru, a rising young star within Congress and the son of the prominent Congress leader Motilal Nehru, wrote: "In 1920 I was totally ignorant of labour questions in factories and fields and my political outlook was totally bourgeois. I knew, of course, that there was terrible poverty and misery, and I felt that the first aim of politically free India must be to tackle this problem of poverty. *But political freedom, with the inevitable dominance of the middle class, seemed to me the obvious next step*" [emphasis added].[9]

Conservative Congressmen embraced Gandhi's tactics because such tactics precluded violence and promised success at a time when they grew increasingly pessimistic about the prospects for gaining political power through strictly constitutional agitation. The long-promised colonial reforms that the British implemented in 1919 granted the urban educated middle class little effective power in governing, even at a provincial level. All-India politics had effectively become the sum of provincial politics and, within each province, the combination of separate electorates for Muslims, a rural bias in electoral representation, and representation by nomination enabled the colonial government and its allies to effectively retain control of an ostensibly representative government. Since working through constitutional methods over two decades and two sets of

---

[9] Nehru (1945: 54–55).

constitutional reforms had achieved little in the way of gaining power, Moderate Congressmen began to accept the need to challenge the existing political system *in toto*. For the Congress Moderates who still controlled the levers of power within the party, Gandhi's tactics provided a means to expand the scope of conflict in a controlled and reasonable manner.

More radical Congressmen embraced Gandhian methods because such methods actually mobilized, albeit in a limited way, against the colonial regime. For example, when the Rowlatt Act suppressing civil liberties was proposed in 1919, Gandhi began to enroll volunteers who pledged to peacefully disobey the Act if it passed. He thereby gained the immediate support of the younger generation of Congressmen in particular, who were agitating for a more active approach to constitutional agitation. By proposing specific, but still limited and non-violent agitation, Gandhi gained the support of older generation Congress Moderates. And by proposing to do more than sign petitions and debate in an Assembly, he gained the support of the younger generation of Congress Radicals.

All of us admired [Gandhi] for his heroic fight in South Africa, but he seemed very distant and different and unpolitical to many of us young men. He refused to take part in Congress or national politics then and confined himself to the South African Indian question. Soon afterwards his adventures and victory in Champaran, on behalf of the tenants of the planters, filled us with enthusiasm. We saw that he was prepared to apply his methods in India also and *they promised success*. [Emphasis added.][10]

Thus, by 1920, the urban educated middle class represented in Congress embraced Gandhi as its leader not only because it was newly unified but also because Gandhian methods had proven successful in gaining colonial concessions. But if the educated, urban middle class across colonial India initially adopted Gandhian leadership instrumentally, as a means of pursuing material interests and political power, they nonetheless came to value his egalitarian principles over the course of the decades in which they practiced and institutionalized a commitment to those principles. Three of Congress' campaigns – against caste untouchability, for homespun cloth or *khadi*, and against specific colonial laws through non-violent civil disobedience – exemplify how its leaders popularized and institutionalized a programmatic and substantively egalitarian nationalism with the party. Each of these is discussed in turn.

[10] Nehru (1945).

Congress campaigns against caste untouchability

Because pervasive, religiously sanctioned differences in the social institution of caste posed formidable obstacles to the development of a unifying national identity in colonial India, creating a mass movement first necessitated forging an egalitarian public sphere where would-be citizens could come together on the basis of equality. Caste, the most developed social identity in colonial India, wholly ordered social interactions and provided for the domination of superior castes over inferior ones.[11] Before 1920, the idiom of political equality that is central to the acceptance of a democratic regime did not exist in rural colonial India.

Early Congress leaders had recognized the need for a political reform movement to be accompanied by social reform, not least because social reform movements were gaining in strength, but typically remained hemmed in by their traditional social identities. Mahadev Govind Ranade, for example, a prominent founder of the Congress movement, recognized the urgent need for social reform in Indian society to accompany demands for political freedoms. In 1896, he wrote:

> We resent the insult given by the [colonial] oppressor. We protest against the unjust judge. Here [with regards to social reform however] we are judge and jury and prosecutor and accused ourselves, and we are sometimes consciously and more often unconsciously committed to a course of conduct which makes tyrants and slaves of us all and, sapping the strength of our resolution, drag us down to our fall – to be the laughing stock of the whole world. *Till we set these matters right, it is almost hopeless to expect that we can have that manliness of character, that sense of our rights and responsibilities without which political and municipal freedom is hard to achieve and impossible to preserve.* [Emphasis added.][12]

That is, though he recognized the urgent need for social reform, Ranade was not able to resist familial pressure to marry a child bride upon the death of his wife, thus personally rejecting a core social reform issue of his time.

Congress' early acceptance of hierarchical social identities undermined its pursuit of democratic reform because the colonial regime justified its continuing rule by asserting that colonial India remained a fragmented, despotic, and feudal society that was unfit for representative political institutions.[13] The social conservatism of upper-caste Hindus in Congress

---

[11] Mines (1972: 335), Government of India (1901: Chapter IV, 372–384), Ali (2002: 593–620), and Hutton (1951: 93).

[12] Emphasis added. Ranade and Ranade (1915: 124).

[13] Metcalf (1994: Chapters 3 and 4) and Kumar (1969: 357–360).

vis-à-vis social reforms was the stated rationale for opposing political reform, namely to prevent political power from passing into the hands of a socially abusive minority. The colonial regime was often able to divide Congress ranks by playing up the issue of social reforms. In order to successfully create a unified political movement, then, Congress needed to address the question of social reform.

Limiting the pervasiveness of caste-based discrimination was particularly essential to creating a unified Indian identity that could validate Congress' claims to representing a nation. Gandhi's travels around India and his exposure to its bewildering variety of castes and sub-castes led him to understand that these deeply rooted social identities could not realistically be abandoned in short order. But such identities could be re-interpreted in such a way as to harmonize with and subordinate to a national community. Moreover, Gandhi's experience of political organizing in South Africa had underscored that creating loyalty to foundational principles among any group was a prerequisite to its ongoing organizational unity. Only a community committed to established principles and practices would not easily fracture in the course of political disputes in which opposition readily sought to divide and rule. Thus, Gandhi devoted considerable effort to forging a new public sphere in which such caste hierarchies were thought of as private and separate from a sphere in which individuals could imagine themselves as a community of political equals.[14]

Congress' efforts to halt the public recognition of 'untouchability' exemplify how the party helped to create a limited egalitarian public sphere. According to the traditional caste system, untouchables were the lowest-ranked members of Indian society. Comprising approximately 10 percent of the population, untouchables were socially ostracized in every respect. Untouchables, or *harijans*, as Gandhi called them, were denied entrance to houses of worship, use of public roads, public schools, public hospitals, public wells, and public parks.[15] Because untouchability effectively cordoned off a substantial portion of Indian society from accessing political equality, it posed a serious obstacle to the pursuit of a common political goal.

Through Congress, Gandhi tirelessly campaigned against the public discrimination of untouchables for three decades before independence. Initially, Gandhi did not advocate for the wholesale rejection of the

---

[14] Rudolph and Rudolph (2006).
[15] Literally translated, *harijan* means children of God.

caste system, which would not only have branded him a social revolutionary but would have thrown powerful segments of Indian society into opposition against him.[16] Instead, when Gandhi spoke up against untouchability, he did so by sanctioning "private" distinctions of caste as right and proper while pronouncing "public" distinctions of caste, for example, when they affected what public facilities individuals were allowed to use, as improper and in fact contradicted by the sacred texts of Hinduism.

Following Gandhi's lead, Congressmen themselves began to preach and practice equality in inter-caste interactions during the 1920s. At Champaran in 1917 for example, the *vakils* or high-caste lawyers from Congress who assisted his efforts maintained a separate kitchen commensurate with their high-caste status. "Between the agricultural clients [in Champaran] and their *vakils* [lawyers] there is a gulf as wide as the Ganges in flood."[17] Over the months spent in Champaran, Gandhi's discussions and his force of example encouraged small changes in acts of everyday living:

The curious ways of living of my companions in the early days were a constant theme of raillery at their expense. Each of the *vakils* had a servant and cook, and therefore a separate kitchen and they often had their dinner as late as midnight. Though they paid their own expenses, their irregularity worried me, but as we had become close friends there was no possibility of a misunderstanding between us, and they received my ridicule in good part. Ultimately it was agreed that the servants should be dispensed with, that all the kitchens should be amalgamated, and that regular hours should be observed. As all were not vegetarians, and as two kitchens would have been expensive, a common vegetarian kitchen was decided upon. It was also felt necessary to insist on simple meals.[18]

Such changes in behavior were not uniformly embraced by Congressmen. But top Congress leaders, almost without exception, did stop publicly recognizing untouchability and actively began to support Congress-affiliated organizations mobilizing for the elimination of the public distinctions of caste.

The rejection of untouchability was not just a matter of rhetoric but of actions that were steadily institutionalized within India's eventual independence party. While it is perhaps best known for its leadership of mass civil disobedience movements, Congress and its affiliates spent much of

---

[16] Gandhi, as quoted in Ambedkar (1979: Vol. X, 279).
[17] Gandhi (1993: 373).
[18] Gandhi (1993: 383).

their time in between these mass agitations in 1920–2, 1930–1, and 1942, on social work. In 1920, after Gandhi had assumed the leadership of Congress, he had mobilized a younger generation of nationalists, and had gained the support of much of the Muslim community through the caliphate movement, the Gandhi-led Congress passed its first resolution clearly advocating the removal of untouchability.[19] Even Congressmen who had strictly observed caste strictures began to eschew the public recognition of caste.[20] In addition, Congress established an affiliated organization, Harijan Seva Sangh, specifically to promote the abolition of public untouchability. Over the next three decades, Congress continued to promote and institutionalize a commitment to political equality by emphasizing the need for volunteer work among *harijan* communities in matters of schooling, sanitation and health. By working alongside low-caste members of Indian society, Congress leaders began to practice political equality in public interactions. Slowly but surely, if unevenly, the cause of caste equality in a public sphere became inextricably bound up with Indian nationalism.

Congressmen consistently campaigned against publicly sanctioned caste distinctions, even when their recognition may have advanced political progress, evidencing a far-sighted commitment to political equality. As Congress' sometimes official and sometimes unofficial leader, Gandhi understood that it would be occasionally possible to achieve short-term political progress by compromising on the principle of caste equality in the public sphere, but he also understood that such sacrifices would ultimately destroy the ideational solidarity of the movement. In the midst of a successful country-wide political agitation against colonial rule for example, Gandhi strenuously objected to caste distinctions being utilized *in favor* of achieving progress toward political reforms.[21] When the Communal Award of 1932 awarded separate electorates to the "depressed classes" or untouchables, Congress vociferously rejected the award on the grounds that it publicly recognized and reified the institution of caste, thereby preventing the growth of a single, common national consciousness. This decision, which was likely based on the keen understanding that accepting such compromises in the short term would

---

[19] 1920 Proceedings of the Annual Meeting of Congress, NMML.
[20] Prasad (1957: 98).
[21] *Collected Works of Mahatma Gandhi* (1958), hereafter *CWMG. Young India*, February 16, 1921.

undermine the solidarity of the movement in the long term, nonetheless advanced political equality.

Congress' programmatic commitments to the abolition of untouchability had real effects on its pervasiveness in colonial society. An example from the province of Kerala, where caste discrimination was perhaps most extensively practised, helps illustrate Congress' success in helping to create a public sphere. The Kerala Provincial Congress Committee (KPCC) first began to actively agitate in favor of the public elimination of untouchability in 1923. In Kerala, untouchables were subject not only to the typical discriminations of caste, but also to *theendal* or distance pollution, meaning that untouchables were required to maintain prescribed physical distances from members of Kerala's higher castes. Struggles against these discriminations had been waged, with very limited success, during the nineteenth century.

The KPCC, which had been formed in accordance with the reorganization of provincial Congress committees along linguistic lines in 1920, took active steps to attenuate untouchability in public places – such as on the roads leading toward temples. In 1924, employing the technique of civil disobedience, the KPCC enlisted caste Hindus to defy the prescribed distances between caste and non-caste Hindus on public roads, a cause Gandhi lent his personal support to in 1925.[22] Though the movement remained unsuccessful during the 1920s, public agitations against untouchability again arose in 1931, after the national Civil Disobedience movement reinvigorated local politics. Anti-caste agitation continued in fits and starts for the following few years, with the local KPCC wielding all the techniques employed in the national anti-colonial struggle against caste discrimination in public arenas such as roads and temples.[23]

As with regional political developments elsewhere, this movement took place against the backdrop of a rising political consciousness that was directly stoked by Congress mobilization. However, lower castes in Kerala were, in contrast to lower castes in much of the rest of colonial India, relatively well-educated and therefore sought to gain a social status commensurate with their wealth or education. In 1934, the government of this princely state relented and opened most public roads and wells to the untouchable community. Thus, though caste distinctions remained very potent in Kerala, the most obvious and public forms of caste

[22] Jeffrey (1976: 3–27).
[23] Chandra *et al.* (1989: 230–234).

discrimination were substantially attenuated in the pre-independence period, an achievement which occurred in large part due to the efforts of the regional Congress leadership under Gandhi during the 1920s and 1930s.[24]

Particularly since nationalist ideology was less well developed in the princely states than in the British provinces, the growth of a movement preaching and practicing political equality there attests to the growth of a Congress-defined programmatic nationalism during the pre-independence decades. In the words of a Keralan historian: "By 1938 'nationalism' clearly had an appeal for many citizens in princely states, and thereby a value for politicians. This nationalist sympathy allowed men who had hitherto been rivals to claim that their joining forces was for 'the national good', rather than for less high-sounding, more immediate ends."[25]

The depth of Congress' embrace of social reform varied across British India, with class, caste, and regional particularities all affecting whether and how the campaign against untouchability was advanced. In Bihar and Gujarat, where the smaller landlords or dominant peasants possessed a clear interest in advocating unity among classes and castes, Gandhian ideology was more fully embraced.[26] In Tamil Nadu, where lower castes were already politically organized and aligned with the British government against an upper-caste Congress, Congressmen had greater difficulty in pushing for caste-based reform.[27] While Congress' campaign against untouchability varied considerably by region and while this campaign can be judged as severely limited when seen against the pervasiveness of caste discriminations, it must be remembered that during the 1920s and 1930s, the campaign to abolish untouchability was rather radical. In advocating the abolition of untouchability, Congress not only helped forge an important ideological break with the past, but it institutionalized a commitment to an egalitarian public sphere.

Khadi: dress demarcates an Indian nation

A second Congress campaign that developed programmatic content to Indian nationalism was its promotion of homespun cloth, or *khadi* – the cloth which became perhaps the most potent symbol of the Indian

---

[24] Aiyappan (1965) and Jeffrey (1978).
[25] Jeffrey (2006: 464).
[26] Prasad (1957: Chapter 21) and McDonald (2006).
[27] Arnold (1977). For regional variations, see Low (2006).

nationalist movement. Politicizing clothing was an effective means of publicizing anti-colonial nationalism in Indian society because the wearing of cloth had long carried symbolic import. While the symbolism of clothing and dress is common to many societies, the complexities and subtleties of status and religiosity communicated by the wearing of cloth in India can be said to be especially important, with "transactions in cloth and the donning of new cloth or clothes attend[ing] every major life cycle ritual in preindustrial Indian society."[28] In rural Indian society, clothes not only denote caste status, wealth, and a state of mourning, but are widely believed to transfer qualities of fertility, bless marriages, and impose curses. Moreover, clothing has long held a special role in conferring religious purity and pollution. Cloth was socially understood to confer its own innate qualities – such as the quality of fabric, its weave and color, with all its variegated meanings – upon its wearers. This pervasive symbolism had religious roots in the Hindu as well as the Indo-Muslim culture.[29]

During the 1920s and 1930s, Congress utilized cloth's traditional symbolism to popularize anti-colonial solidarity in British India. Beginning in 1920, Gandhi regularly extolled the habitual wearing of *khadi* as a "sign that the wearer identifies himself with the poorest in the land, that he has patriotism and self-sacrifice enough in him to wear *khadi* even though it may not be so soft and elegant as foreign fineries nor as cheap."[30] In the years that followed, homespun *khadi* slowly but surely became the standard uniform of Congress. Congress leaders, young or old alike, discarded their English dress in favor of a white homespun uniform as their daily dress. For English-educated, urban, middle-class lawyers whose immersion in Western dress and lifestyle was nearly complete, the conscious adoption of *khadi* entailed a decided change in self-identification, a change which anchored their identity on something distinctly "Indian." Motilal Nehru, an eminent early leader of Congress who was reputed for his extravagant tastes in Western clothing, reluctantly traded in his fancy suits and top hats for the *khadi* modeled by Gandhi because he understood that this change was part and parcel of forming a broad-based national identity. Though many Congressmen might similarly have adopted *khadi* instrumentally, the process of making physical changes to mark one's embrace of the norm of political equality nonetheless involved a change

---

[28] Bayly in Appadurai (1986: 286).
[29] Bayly in Appadurai (1986: 287–288).
[30] *CWMG*, Vol. LXXIV, 224, November 11, 1938.

in ideational identification. The wearing of *khadi* was an unmistakable sign that the educated, urban middle class sought to link up with the rural masses on an ideologically equal basis.

The symbolic wearing of cloth was not just popularized but also institutionalized within Congress. Spinning of certain quantities of yarn became an eligibility condition for certain high-level Congress offices, though this requirement was later discarded.[31] In 1921, Congress resolved to investigate how homespun cloth might be produced and worn en masse. In 1925, Congress established the All-India Spinners Association (AISA) through a resolution of the All-India Congress Committee (AICC). The importance of this organization to Congress leaders is underscored by the fact that numerous top-level Congress leaders such as Gandhi, Nehru, and Rajendra Prasad were deeply involved in the AISA provincial leadership, whose goal was to systematically promote the production, sale and wearing of homespun cloth throughout colonial India. Though Congress-sponsored, AISA was consciously established as an independent and apolitical organization that could work "unaffected and uncontrolled by politics." AISA worked with Congress' support to popularize *khadi* by regularly holding exhibitions which sought to portray it as a virtuous enterprise.[32] Articles concerning the production and wearing of *khadi* production were not only disseminated internally within this organization and throughout Congress, but published every several months throughout the pre-independence decades in one of Gandhi's weekly newspapers.

Once homespun cloth became the standard choice of clothing among Congressmen, and as Congress or Congress-affiliated organizations widely urged *khadi*'s adoption, an individual's choice of clothing grew politicized. Because everyone wore clothing, because the wearing of clothing was publicly observed, and because the choice of homespun versus English clothing became imbued with distinct political values, one's own clothing was taken to be a political statement, regardless of actual intent. Consistent with modern sociological theories, Congress leaders created a national identity through narrative and symbolization. Congress forged a distinctively Indian "we" in contrast to a colonial "other" through the narrative of clothing. The economic consequences of choosing to wear British mill-made clothing were made clear through posters and propaganda.[33]

---

[31] Bayly in Appadurai (1986: 313).
[32] AISA Papers, AICC, NMML.
[33] Trivedi (2003: 11–41).

Someone who wore foreign cloth was designated as non-Indian, since "by his dress he has become a foreigner." It became "as sinful to cast covetous glances at imported cloth as it is for a man to caste lustful glances at another's wife." Playing on the popular themes of ritual pollution and purification in Hinduism, some Congress leaders spoke of the wearing of homespun cloth in moral terms. The wearing of foreign cloth was defined as "defiling," "polluting" and a violation of *dharma* or religious duty.[34] To spiritually cleanse oneself, Congress leaders advocated the burning of foreign cloth and the wearing of *khadi*, whose moral purity would be bestowed on the wearer, in turn helping to make public life "clean and wholesome."[35] In effect, Congress utilized the traditional symbolism of cloth to create a language of commodity resistance. In this way, an illiterate, uneducated rural peasant began to be systematically drawn into the orbit of Indian nationalism.

The promotion of *khadi* was thus carried to rural masses through numerous associations, training centers for spinning and weaving, the use of countryside tours to promote *khadi* production and wearing, and the picketing of foreign cloth shops, to name just the most popular. Wheels were produced and distributed to peasant communities through provincial Congress committees. Gandhi's ashrams became training centers for weavers and spinners who fanned out over the countryside to promote *khadi*. Posters and films were other popular ways of conveying the meaning of *khadi*.[36] Using portable lanterns and inexpensive slides that AISA reproduced and made available to local *khadi* organizations, lantern slideshows were organized throughout India. These slideshows, using novel technology which was seen as a form of entertainment and which consequently attracted large crowds, brought together whole village communities in ways that discouraged the recognition of caste.

Using a visual medium was particularly crucial to popularizing nationalism among illiterate rural masses because the symbolism of clothing could be easily apprehended. In other words, the wearing of simple homespun cloth was a way in which a rural Indian peasant could participate in the nationalist cause without recourse to the medium of print. Engaged in the simple labor of spinning in the dress of a poor man, the leader of the Indian independence party communicated the dignity of poverty and the equality of all Indians as well as his own saintliness in a medium that

[34] *CWMG*, Vol. XX, 433.
[35] *CWMG*, Vol. XXII, 151.
[36] Trivedi (2003: 11–41).

transcended the limitations of language.[37] The wearing of *khadi* was to Indian nationalism what print capitalism was to European nationalism.

In sum, through its promotion of homespun cloth, Congress created a culturally resonant symbol of the Indian nation. *Khadi* did not just draw a distinction between Western colonial rule and a distinctively Indian identity, but it also critically denoted clear principles and a set of actions commensurate with those principles. Most clearly, these programmatic principles included the rejection of hierarchical distinctions of caste and class as well as the simultaneous embrace of an egalitarian public sphere.

Marching for freedom

Perhaps the best known way in which India's independence party fostered a programmatic nationalism was to lead three celebrated civil disobedience campaigns against unpopular laws of the British colonial regime – movements which deepened ideational commitments to Indian nationalism. During each of these campaigns, Non-Cooperation (1917–23), Civil Disobedience (1927–34), and Quit India (1939–46), Congress leaders creatively chose symbols of resistance, all of which defined the common interest of "Indians" in opposition to the interest of British colonials *and* in accordance with a set of clearly defined programmatic principles. In doing so, they forged an ideological commitment to a national identity that was defined by the Congress Party. These nationalist agitations were successful because they capitalized upon pre-existing economic and political discontents across colonial India. Yet Congress bound together these grievances by consistently connecting local economic and political discontents to an anti-colonial Indian nationalism. In doing so, India's independence party itself became the locus of a developed ideational commitment. Upon independence, that party used this commitment to facilitate speedy compromises on a range of constitutional and social issues. Moreover, the egalitarian content of that institutionalized commitment to political equality militated towards the post-independence embrace of those egalitarian political institutions which define democracy.

The major mass mobilization campaigns led by Congress followed a distinct pattern that focused popular attention on an Indian identity and which provided for prolonged engagement in the nationalist

---

[37] Bean in Weiner and Schneider (1989: 368).

struggle. While each civil disobedience movement focused on different laws, employed different techniques, and was resolved in different manners, each mass mobilization campaign also followed a distinct eight-step pattern.[38] This pattern *first* began with Congress leaders speaking out against an unjust law or proclamation, followed, *second*, by highly publicized attempts by Congress leaders to use constitutional means of redress. *Third*, Congress and Congress-affiliated organizations meticulously prepared for civil disobedience or *satyagraha*. *Fourth*, when constitutional means of engagement were deemed to be reasonably exhausted, Congress embarked upon a mass, non-violent civil disobedience campaign to protest a narrowly defined grievance in which specific forms of non-violent protest were sanctioned. *Fifth*, a "mid-course break" ensued, wherein Congress halted civil disobedience and attempted compromise with the government. *Sixth*, after compromise failed, a second civil disobedience campaign broke out. *Seventh*, as the campaigns were quashed or exhausted, Gandhi "dramatized his own moral authority" to end the agitation.[39] *Eighth*, each agitation period drew to a close with some progress toward national political reform.

The central issues in each mobilization highlighted a way in which the colonial regime undermined the interests of a broad range of indigenous social groups. In launching the first Non-Cooperation movement, Gandhi stated:

The passing of the [Rowlatt] Bills, *designed to effect the whole of India and its people* and arming the Government with powers out of all proportion to the situation sought to be dealt with, is a greater danger ... If it [the Rowlatt Bill] means that the civil service and the British commercial interests are to be held superior to those of India and its political and commercial requirements, *no Indian can accept that doctrine*. [Emphasis added.][40]

The Civil Disobedience movement (1927–34) mobilized mass support on issues which similarly cleaved into all-Indian versus colonial interests – the exclusion of "Indians" from the Simon Commission considering constitutional reforms and an increase in land revenue taxes. But the most potent issue around which the Indian independence party mobilized mass support was through its defiance of the colonial salt monopoly. This

---

[38] Low (2006) describes parts of this pattern in the introduction to his highly informative edited volume.

[39] The exception to this was the end of the Non-Cooperation movement, which was called off by Gandhi in response to an outbreak of violence.

[40] M.K Gandhi, *Satyagraha Vow*, Manifesto published in *Bombay Chronicle*, March 2, 1919.

simple issue united the interests of all Indians, even the illiterate poor, against the British colonial regime. At its core, the colonial monopoly on salt was an economic issue because all British Indians were required to pay higher prices for salt. But this juxtaposition of economic interests assumed ideational value through the invocation of moral and legal language:

> There is no article like salt outside water by taxing which the State can reach even the starving millions, the sick, the maimed, the utterly helpless. The tax constitutes therefore the most inhuman poll tax that ingenuity of man can devise ... The necessary consequence of salt monopoly was the destruction, i.e. the closing down of salt works in thousands of places where the poor people manufactured their own salt ... The illegality is in a Government that steals the people's salt and makes them pay heavily for the stolen article. The people, when they become conscious of their power, will have every right to take possession of what belongs to them.[41]

In the third civil disobedience campaign, the Quit India movement, the central ideational issue became that of representative government itself. Though Congress leaders made fewer public statements because they were imprisoned before the movement was formally launched, Congress leaders uniformly protested against the British government's declaration of war in 1939 on behalf of India in pursuit of a freedom that the same government at the same time denied India, seeking to maintain the focus on the contrasting interests of the colonial government and India:

> India has every right to examine the implications of high-sounding declarations about justice, preservation of democracy and freedom of speech and individual liberty. If a band of robbers have among themselves a democratic constitution in order to enable them to carry on their robbing operations more effectively, they do not deserve to be called a democracy. Is India a democracy? Are the [princely] States a democracy? Britain does not deserve to win the war on the ground of justice if she is fighting to keep her African and Asiatic possessions.[42]

In each movement, Congress leaders carefully chose to mobilize on the basis of issues that would unify and eschewed issues with the potential to divide. During the Non Cooperation movement for example, the withholding of land revenues was proposed in a *raiyatwari* rather than a *zamindari* region. This meant that revenue would be withheld directly from the government instead of from other social classes, thereby evading the possibility of stoking class conflict. Congress leaders also made it a

---

[41] CWMG, Vol. XLVIII, 350–351. "Salt Tax," *Young India*, February 27, 1930.
[42] CWMG, Vol. LXXXIII, 43. "A Poser," *Harijan*, June 28, 1942.

special point to encourage tenants to specifically refrain from withholding rents from intermediate landlords and to unite to "fight against the most powerful *zamindar*, namely the Government."[43] Congress also focused on boycotts of British schools and courts and deliberately declared that labor strikes were *not* within the ambit of Non-Cooperation – thereby limiting the potential for capital–labor conflicts.[44]

Within each mobilizational campaign, Congress promoted and institutionalized an ideational commitment to Indian nationalism. Congress leaders generally allowed for local autonomy in deciding how local communities would mobilize for each movement, but this autonomy was subject to two important principles – non-violence and ideological commitment to Congress. Congress instructions to its provincial committees specified that *"every possible care should be taken to ensure that the people's elected representatives,* who will constitute the Chief Authority for each grade of centre, local and higher, with power to make laws and rules, *shall be,* not self-seekers, but *seekers of the public welfare"* [emphasis in original].[45] In each case, Congress helped establish parallel political, educational, and governmental institutions and specified the actions to be taken in support of the movement.[46] It was in large part because of these mobilizational campaigns that, by the end of World War II, India became an independent nation.

In sum, by 1947, Congress had helped delimit an Indian nation, establish its egalitarian character, and broadly popularize nationalism in the consciousness of a broad swath of colonial Indian society through costly engagement in civil disobedience campaigns. To be sure, each mass movement was able to gain substantial support because it capitalized upon growing economic grievances. Yet by also consistently underscoring the interests of a new Indian community, one that was publicly egalitarian and publicly recognizable by its dress, Congress helped disparate social groups develop a programmatic "Indian" identity. Though Congressmen embraced this nationalism instrumentally, in order to create mass support for political reforms, Indian nationalism assumed meaning independently of its capacity to advance the goal of political reform because it became widely institutionalized within the party.

---

[43] *CWMG*, Vol. XIX, 352.
[44] M.K. Gandhi, "Strikes," *Young India*, June 15, 1921.
[45] C.R. Das, "Outline Scheme of Swaraj", January 23, 1923, reprinted in full in Bamford (1925: 223–239).
[46] All India Congress Committee Non Cooperation Instructions, September 19, 1920. Bamford (1925: 220–222).

Over time, these political symbols indeed became their own form of anti-colonial grievance. The British governor of colonial India's largest province said during the earliest phase of mass mobilization in 1921, "Whereas the former [agrarian] disorders in Rae Bareli were largely agrarian in origin, the recent disorders were mainly political in origin and wholly revolutionary."[47] As even the emissary of historical school emphasizing the role of elite self-interest in developing Indian nationalism concedes: "The hillmen of Kumaon, the coolies of Assam, the headman of Oudh, the turbulent peasantries of Midnapore and Guntur, Kaira and Bhagalpur, were all using what were allegedly national issues to express their local complaints. Local grievances were chronic and narrow, but they put stuffing into campaigns which were intermittent and wide."[48] Discursively and behaviorally, a nationalism based on political equality had become an ideational cornerstone of Indian nationalism. Upon independence, the decades-long institutionalization of egalitarian ideals within Congress led the party to formalize these ideals within the Indian constitution, thereby creating India's democratic foundations.

II. LEAGUE ADOPTS VAGUE RELIGIOUS NATIONALISM

A paper party in provincial power struggles

Like India's independence party, the most consistent goal of Pakistan's independence party was the maximization of political power for a particular social class. Unlike India's independence party, however, Pakistan's independence party did not espouse a well-developed nationalism in pursuit of class goals that became meaningful in itself. Instead, until the last decade before independence, it was a paper party whose relevance to national politics was growing increasingly marginal. As such, the Muslim League was little able to articulate, much less popularize, a Pakistani nationalism. Moreover, when it finally did articulate Pakistani nationalism, this ideology remained vaguely defined, with no guiding programmatic principles.

Already a marginal political force by 1916, the United Province-dominated Muslim League grew even weaker as a result of colonial reforms of 1919, which apportioned limited political power to provincial governments and thereby necessitated electoral success in the Muslim-majority

---

[47] Sir Harcourt Butler, as quoted in Reeves (1966: 264).
[48] Seal (1973: 342).

provinces in order to validate a claim to speak for a nation of Muslims.[49] This was because the reforms necessitated electoral success in the provinces in order to claim a seat in national politics. The Muslim League was led by UP Muslims, who were just 14 percent of the population in the UP. Even with electoral weighting which gave Muslims 30 percent of the seats in the provincial council, the educated, urban Muslim middle class in the League stood no chance of gaining an authoritative political voice through provincial politics. As a result, Muslim League leaders now needed to garner the support of Muslims in one of the two Muslim-majority provinces, Punjab or Bengal, if it hoped to legitimate its claim to a place in national politics as the voice of Muslim India.

Any alliance between the UP Muslims represented in the League and the Muslims in the Muslim-majority provinces, and therefore any sort of programmatic platform that reflected shared interests, was not espoused because their interests on key constitutional issues were diametrically opposed. In Bengal, no single alliance afforded the League the opportunity to assume a prominent role in provincial governance. Not only were Bengali Muslims proportionately under-represented (as just over half the population, Bengalis were guaranteed only 31 percent of seats in the provincial Legislative Council by the 1919 reforms),[50] but they were split among three distinct socio-economic groups, none of which was politically dominant.[51] The League's best hope of accessing national political power lay in forming an alliance with Muslims in the Punjab, where Muslims were guaranteed 45 percent of the elected seats and where the Muslim landed aristocracy was already organized into a political party called the Unionists. In short, the urban, educated middle classes now dominating in Muslim League needed the support of the Muslim landed aristocrats of the Punjab to remain politically relevant in national politics.[52]

---

[49] The franchise remained highly restricted, enabling only about 3% of the population of British India to vote in 1920.

[50] See Indian Statutory Commission, Vol. I (Cmd. 3568, 1929–1930), part ii, Chapter 4, including appendices.

[51] Bengali Muslims were divided among three politically salient groups (the small landed Muslim aristocracy in eastern Bengal, the large Muslim peasantry in eastern Bengal, and the educated middle class Muslim elite in western Bengal), none of which commanded the loyalty of a majority of Bengal's Muslims. Class interests typically formed the lines of political cleavage between these groups – whereas the landed aristocracy collaborated closely with the colonial regime, the Muslim peasantry often opposed the colonial regime, and the Muslim middle-class elite joined forces with the Hindu middle-class elite in demanding political reforms. See Page (1999: 41–42). For a typology of the social structure of Bengal, see Bose (2007: Chapter 1).

[52] Jalal (1985: Chapter 1) and Page (1999: Chapter 1).

But UP Muslim and Punjabi Muslim leaders were not able to agree on a shared approach to promoting Muslim representation in national politics. For example, the interests of the Punjabi landed aristocracy and the UP Muslim middle class on both the desirability of reforms and the extent of provincial power in the course of additional reforms were at odds with one another. The Punjabi landed aristocrats were uniformly opposed to national-level political reforms, preferring the maintenance of British colonial rule which allowed them to protect their social and economic dominance unhampered by any political interference from the center. One of the most powerful Punjabi politicians of the day, Firoz Khan Noon, wrote in 1928 that "Muslims fear overcentralisation ... because in the Central Legislature the Hindus will always be in an overwhelming majority and if they have the power to legislate for the provinces also, then the Muslim majorities in Bengal, Punjab, North West Frontier Province, Sindh and Baluchistan will be entirely imaginary."[53] To the extent that political reforms were inevitable however, the Punjabi landed aristocracy strongly preferred provincial autonomy in the context of a weak federal center.

In direct contrast, as a provincial minority with entrenched and disproportionate political influence, the UP Muslim middle class opposed reforms which granted strong provincial autonomy in which their political voice would invariably be trumped but welcomed reforms which created a strong political center in which, through their extra-proportionate political reservations and their relatively advanced educational status, UP Muslims could expect to retain a dominant influence. As a result, the League split into two factions, one dominated by the educated, urban middle class – the Jinnah faction – while another was dominated by Firoz Khan Noon and Fazli Husain, members of the Punjabi landed aristocracy.

With the interests of its primary supporters in direct opposition throughout the 1920s and early 1930s, the Muslim League was unable to espouse a clear set of organizational goals, much less a consistent set of principles and symbols to propagate a Muslim nationalism. Because of this deadlock, the League was eclipsed by other Muslim organizations and effectively faded into political oblivion. As the Governor of the Punjab wrote of the Punjabi landed aristocracy in 1927, "They [Punabji Muslims] see that they can never quite have the same interests as Muslims in the provinces with large Hindu majorities and they think seriously of breaking away from the All-India Muslim League and starting a federation of

[53] Noon (1928: 182).

their own."[54] The ineffectiveness of the League during this time is witnessed by the fact that between 1928 and 1935, the pre-eminent political voice for Muslims was *not* the Muslim League, but the All-India Muslim Conference, an organization committed to extra-proportionate political representation for Muslims.[55] As a consequence of the 1919 Reforms, the League found itself dangerously irrelevant to national politics and representative of no clear set of goals or principles.

Communal conflict and the continued lack of programmatic Pakistani nationalism

Tension between Hindus and Muslims, or communalism as it is commonly referred to in South Asian historiography, grew and assumed wider political resonance during the course of political reforms at the beginning of the twentieth century in areas where Hindus and Muslims were in close competition for employment. Only after the 1919 reforms introduced the electoral principle at the provincial level did religious cleavages began to assume consistently political dimensions. Before 1919, educated, urban Muslims had on the whole possessed an incentive to align with educated, urban Hindus to lobby for constitutional reforms which would provide both communities with greater employment opportunities and political power, though Muslims still had an interest in pursuing this through separate Muslim electorates. Over the course of Hindu–Muslim cooperation in the Congress–caliphate alliance between 1920 and 1922, there was little to no communal conflict, demonstrating how closely political interests defined the extent of communal conflict. After 1922 however, when the Congress–caliphate alliance had collapsed for geopolitical reasons and when Congressmen began to compete for access to government positions in local elections, the invocation of religious rhetoric began to prove an effective tactic for undermining the hegemony of secular Congressmen.

The desire for political gain was the primary driver of the rising communal conflict in the United Provinces and the Punjab.[56] To be sure, the United Provinces had witnessed growth in Hindu reform movements

---

[54] Hailey to Hirtzel, December 15, 1927. Hailey Papers, 11B, IOL.
[55] *Civil Military Gazette*, November 1, 1933.
[56] Leaving aside three riots that were confined to Calcutta, over 50 per cent of the communal disturbances in India between 1923 and 1927 were accounted for by injuries and deaths in these two provinces, which account for slightly over a quarter of the population. Report of the Indian Statutory Commission, Vol. iv, 108–110. Cmd 3572. Population figures taken from Government of India (1931).

over the course of the nineteenth century. A rise in the consciousness of Muslim identity as a result of the caliphate movement, particularly in instances where such consciousness had led to direct attacks on Hinduism, provoked orthodox counter-reactions on the part of these Hindu reform movements and also led to a rising popular consciousness of a Hindu identity. After the Congress–caliphate alliance collapsed and the 1919 reforms provided for elections to municipal councils, the invocation of communal rhetoric became a convenient means of rallying political support away from secular Congressmen in urban elections. In Allahabad in 1924, for example, the Malaviya family exploited religious sentiment for political gain at the expense of the politically dominant Nehru family. The Malaviya clan is widely thought to have arranged the exclusion of Muslim musicians from bands hired to celebrate a Hindu religious ceremony. The Muslim musicians had typically been included and had long ensured that music was not played before the Islamic mosque during prayertime. The combination of music played before the mosque at prayertime, in the context of a previously provocative demonstration by Hindus before the same mosque, led to a riot in which a dozen individuals were killed and over a hundred injured. British investigations into this incident lay the blame squarely on the interests of the Malaviya family in political gain.[57] Similar incidents occurred across the UP as conservative Congressmen sympathetic to the reactionary Hindu movements stoked religious issues for political gain. These trends were also at work in the Punjab, though the extent of violent religious conflict was not as severe as it was in the United Provinces. The Deputy Commissioner of Amritsar wrote to the Commissoner of Lahore in 1923 that "it is notorious that [religious] excitement has deliberately been fanned by interested men of position, principally by prospective candidates at the next elections."[58] During the 1930s, despite the growing politicization of religious identities, itself a consequence of political competition between Congress factions, communalism remained primarily confined to those urban cities in which elections were fought closely.

It was in this context of rising communalism that the Muslim League, already marginalized by the growth of Punjabi dominance in Muslim politics, faced the prospect of political extinction in 1937. The Government of India Act of 1935 provided for the first meaningful reform of colonial

---

[57] Page (1999: 81).
[58] DC Dunnett to Lahore Commissioner, Government of India Home Poll. 125/1923. India Home Political Records, NAI.

government. The Act provided for provincial elections under an expanded electorate, the participation of elected officials in the full governing responsibilities of the provinces, and the eventual devolution of power at a federal level. As a consequence, any organization claiming a legitimate role in the negotiations over national political reform now unquestionably needed to marshal electoral support in the provinces during the upcoming 1937 provincial elections. Initially, the League, whose goal had always been to secure an authoritative role for UP Muslims in such constitutional negotiations, initially attempted to secure this goal by direct conciliation with Congress.

As the pursuit of political power did yet not entail a demand for a separate state, the Muslim League had formulated no programmatic nationalist ideology by 1937. Before this time, the League's rhetoric made little reference to Islam or Islamic ideals. Instead the League's discourse consistently described Muslims as a minority whose rights needed protecting within a united India.[59] In 1933, for example, the League President Hafiz Hidayat Husain stated in his address at the annual League meeting that "The idea of *political* Pan-Islamism, in the sense of unifying Muslims into one State, never existed … It has never meant that the Indian Musalman has turned his face to Mecca and his back to India. It must be distinctly understood that the interests of Musalmans of India are centered on affairs relating to India, and not on those outside India, and that *the Musalman is as much a part of the Indian nation as any other people* living in this land of ours" [emphasis in original].[60] In the early 1930s then, the Muslim League was clearly *not* positioning itself as the purveyor of a nationalism which sought an independent Muslim state.

Even as the coming of the Government of India Act of 1935 motivated some unification among the League's factions to contest provincial elections, the Muslim League's rhetoric still remained primarily political (rather than religious). The need for unity led the UP Muslims to recruit M.A. Jinnah, reputedly the most eloquent Muslim orator and in his time the highest paid lawyer in India, to return from England to galvanize the League for the upcoming elections.[61] Even as he sought to unify the League, however, Jinnah did not invoke a separatist religious ideology as a means of validating the Muslim claim to political power. To the contrary, the leader of the Muslim League sought conciliation with the party

[59] Annual Meeting Minutes, All India Muslim League, Microfiche, NAP.
[60] Twenty Third Session of the All India Muslim League, Microfiche, NAP.
[61] Hasan (1993: 8) and Wells (2006: 235).

of Indian independence. In his Presidential address to the League the same
year, Syed Wazir Hasan emphasized that "I have already shown that ...
the ultimate object of the constitutional advancement of the Muslims of
India, as represented by their several political associations, is the attainment of responsible government *for our motherland*, and I have also
shown that in its essentials the object of the Indian National Congress is
the same" [emphasis added].[62] Moreover, the programmatic platform on
which the League contested the 1937 elections, with the exception of the
bid for separate electorates for Muslims, differed in no substantive way
from that of Congress. Scarcely more than a decade before independence
then, the League had formulated no coherent set of principles, set out
no distinct programmatic platform and espoused no nationalist rhetoric
based on religion.

1937: the turn toward religious nationalism

The pivotal change in the League's ideology, from conceptualizing
Muslims as a minority in need of reserved representation within a sovereign India to setting forth a demand for an independent and sovereign Muslim state, came about as a direct result of the 1937 provincial elections in which the League failed to garner widespread electoral
support among Muslims. Whereas Congress had won outright electoral
majorities in much of the country, the League won a popular majority
in no province and gained just 5 percent of the vote in reserved Muslim
constituencies. Predictably, given that its primary constituency was UP
Muslims, the League had polled well in the United Provinces but had
performed very poorly across the rest of colonial India. In the UP, the
League had won 29 out of 35 Muslim seats. In the crucial Punjab, however, it won just one of the seven seats it contested, meaning that there
was one League representative among the 88 reserved seats for Muslims
in the most important Muslim-majority province of colonial India.[63] In
the other Muslim-majority province of Bengal, the League won 39 of 117

---

[62] Presidential Address of the Twenty-Fourth Annual Session of the Muslim League, Muslim
League Papers, Microfiche, NAP.
[63] In Bengal, it won 39 of 117 reserved Muslim seats. In Assam, it won nine of 34. In the
other Muslim-minority provinces of Bombay and Madras, the League had done well.
Still, the League had won only 109 seats in British India and had a weak or non-existent
position in the Muslim-majority provinces. United Kingdom House of Commons,
Parliamentary Papers 1937–38, XXI (Accounts and Papers VI), Cmd. 5589, "Returns
Showing the Results of Elections in India, 1937," IOL.

Muslim seats, giving it fewer seats than the peasant-supported Praja party or a group of independent Muslims. From the perspective of Congress, then, the League remained representative of a privileged group of urban, educated Muslims in a Hindu-majority province in which Congress had won an outright majority. Seeing little need to accommodate the claims of a party which was unrepresentative of the crucial Muslim-majority provinces, Congress rejected the League's demands to reserve one-third of the seats in the Central Legislative Assembly and over a quarter of the UP Provincial Assembly seats for Muslims. Shut out by Congress, the League had to rally the support of Muslims in the Muslim-majority provinces to legitimately claim leadership of Muslim interests at the all-India level, or else face political extinction.

The Muslim League was able to rally the support of the Muslim-majority provinces because the latter's strategic perspective had changed. Before the 1937 elections, the parties in Muslim-majority provinces saw little need for national political representation when they were politically dominant in their provinces and the colonial government brooked little interference. After the 1937 elections, however, the Muslim-majority provinces came to realize that Congress' overwhelming electoral success probably presaged the departure of the colonial regime and an independent India ruled by Congress. Consequently, whereas provincial leaders had previously been content to ensure their political dominance within their own province in the context of colonial guarantees of non-interference, the organized political groups in the most powerful Muslim provinces – i.e. the landed aristocracy in Punjab and the peasant movement in Bengal – now began to understand that colonial guarantees would mean little if India became politically sovereign. In the interest of protecting their social and political dominance, the Muslim-majority provinces formed alliances with the League for the latter to bargain on their behalf at the all-India level. Support for the League in Muslim-majority provinces was achieved because key Muslim leaders saw support for the League as a means of advancing their political interests at the political center.

The Muslim League's claim for extra-proportional political representation for Muslims within an independent India was validated by espousing a Muslim nationalism but by keeping the specifics of this claim vague. Stating that Indian Muslims were a nation, but not clearly conceptualizing in what ways a Muslim state would differ from a Congress-dominated state struck the right balance between allowing the League to claim conceptual parity with Congress in constitutional negotiations on the one hand and keeping the Pakistan demand from delving into the kind of specifics which would have fractured the League's fragile unification of divergent social bases on the other hand. Specifying what Pakistan stood for in terms of constitutional arrangements or in terms of addressing concrete social or economic issues would have exposed the very different economic and political interests in the two Muslim provinces whose support the League needed.[64]

The League demand for Pakistan and the content of Pakistani nationalism was thus primarily defined negatively (by opposing the procedure of majority-rule with constitutional protections for minorities advocated by Congress) rather than positively, in terms of what specific programs a Pakistan state would embody. A review of the League's annual meetings between 1940 and 1947 reveals that while a considerable portion of these meetings was devoted to maligning Congress or the colonial regime, less than a tenth of these meetings was devoted to defining the League's vision for an independent state in any substantive manner.[65] In the crucial years before the League would be responsible for governing Pakistan, there was, for example, no discussion of the basic rights which a Pakistani constitution would protect, of the basic power-sharing agreement between its constituent units, and no clarification on the role religion would play in the state. This contrasted markedly with a Congress leadership that, for at least two decades before independence, was thinking very seriously about the economic and social policies that a future India would adopt.

The ideational embrace of a religious nationalism thus followed immediately upon the heels of the League's failed rapprochement with Congress. In 1938, just after the elections showed the League's hollow base, Jinnah still described Muslims as a minority with organizational equality to Congress.[66] By 1940, however, Jinnah elaborated a demand for a sovereign state based on the idea that Muslims formed a separate nation. In his oft-cited Lahore declaration, the first speech in which he clearly embraced the demand for a separate state of Pakistan, Jinnah said:

If the British Government are [*sic*] really in earnest and sincere to secure the peace and happiness of the people of this Subcontinent, the only course open to us all is *to allow the major nations separate homelands by dividing India into autonomous national states* ... [Islam and Hinduism] are not religions in the strict sense

---

[64] Jalal (1985) and Sarkar (1983).
[65] Muslim League Papers, NAP.
[66] Proceedings of the Muslim League Special Session at Calcutta, April 1938. Pirzada (1969: 294–295).

of the word, but are, in fact different and distinct social orders. *It is a dream that the Hindus and Muslims can ever evolve a common nationality.* [Emphasis added.][67]

This conception of Hindus and Muslims as incompatible national communities was instrumental, however, for it was wholly contradicted by Jinnah's speech to the Pakistan's Constituent Assembly in 1947, when the rationale for conceiving Muslims as a separate nation had already served its purpose. So while Jinnah stated in 1940 that Hindus and Muslims could never evolve a common nationality, a few days before Pakistan's independence in 1947, he said that in the state of Pakistan, "You may belong to any religion or caste or creed – that has nothing to do with the business of the State ... *You will find that in course of time Hindus would cease to be Hindus and Muslims would cease to be Muslims*, not in the religious sense, because that is the personal faith of each individual, but in the political sense as citizens of the State" [emphasis added].[68] That the foundational claim for Pakistan, namely that a sovereign state needed to be created because Muslims formed a separate nation, was being contradicted by the Muslim League's dominant leader on the eve of national independence attests to the lack of a serious commitment to the religious basis for the Pakistan state.

By 1940, League leaders claimed that Indian Muslims were a nation in order to put the organization's claims to extra-proportional representation within the constitution on an ideologically equal footing with Congress' claim to represent the Indian nation. Indeed, Jinnah was, as were most Muslim League leaders, largely secular and by public manner or custom little committed to Islam. Whether it was by dress, by prayer, by habits, or customs, Jinnah could not be described as a practicing Muslim. Jinnah drank freely and ate pork. There is evidence that Jinnah lived off of interest income, thereby violating Islam's prohibition against charging interest.[69] Jinnah and the League's core bases of support did not experience an ideological conversion to Islamic ideals or an overwhelming pressure to respond to the grassroots growth of communal sentiment. Instead, they espoused Muslim nationalism in the form of the demand for Pakistan because doing so provided the League with an opportunity to extract maximal concessions in the course of constitutional negotiations.

---

[67] Presidential Address of M.A. Jinnah, Twenty-seventh Session of the Muslim League (Lahore, March 1940) in Pirzada (1969: 337–338).

[68] M.A. Jinnah, Address to the Constituent Assembly of Pakistan, August 11, 1947. Accessed at: www.pakistani.org/pakistan/legislation/constituent_address_11aug1947.html.

[69] Wolpert (1984: 171).

Between 1940 and 1947, even as the Muslim League was promoting Pakistani nationalism, the League leadership set out no clear principles or actions in pursuit of principles that would give programmatic content to Pakistani nationalism. Nor could such a set of principles be articulated, for the claim to a Muslim state was embraced primarily in the hopes of maximizing the share of power allotted to allied Muslim groups (e.g. the landed aristocracy of Punjab, the urban, educated middle class of the UP, and the peasantry of Bengal) in the course of constitutional negotiations. In the 1943 annual meeting, for example, Jinnah stated that Muslim Leaguers are "opposed to any scheme – nor can we agree to any proposal which has for its basis any conception or idea of a Central government – federal or confederal; for it is bound to lead in the long run to the emasculation of the entire Muslim nation – socially, educationally, culturally, economically, and politically – and to the establishment of Hindu majority raj in this subcontinent."[70] In each of the League's annual meetings or working sessions between 1940 and 1947, for example, the League leadership called for Muslim unity and for "social uplift." Yet in none of those meetings or sessions was a specific program laid out or organization formed for the implementation of this vision. Indeed, the League's demand for a separate state had to be left vague because any specification of a program of education and support for downtrodden groups was likely to simultaneously be supported by Bengal and opposed by Punjab. For example, the Praja party of Bengal demanded the abolition of *zamindari* or landlords, while the Unionist party of Punjab, which was in fact a landlord party, was naturally opposed to this demand. Pakistani nationalism was unlikely to be programmatically defined because, at least until 1946 and quite possibly through independence, it was little more than a tactic for achieving constitutional concessions for the Muslim minority and its leader within the framework of a united India.

That there was scant ideational commitment to the demand for Pakistan is further evidenced by the fact that the League leadership was willing to drop the demand for a sovereign state just a year before independence. In 1946, when the British Cripps Mission offered independence to India on terms that would have kept a sub-federation of Muslim states within the sovereign state of India, this offer was accepted by Jinnah on behalf of the League,[71] clear evidence that the state of Pakistan was being demanded

[70] Pirzada (1969: 427).
[71] Jalal (1985: 189–190).

not out of a conviction to Islamic nationalism, but in order to strengthen the political power of particular groups of Muslims in the negotiations over constitutional reforms.

Moreover, to the extent that the Pakistani nationalism did have content, that content was anti-democratic in the sense that it rejected a defining process of democracy. Given that a democracy is substantively defined by the *process* of competitive elections for executive or legislative offices, then a "minority" in the electoral process is only defined as a minority by virtue of having voted with the losers in that process.[72] The protection of minority rights is first and foremost a constitutional problem. The League charge against Congress of a "tyranny of the Hindu majority" in an independent India could have been meaningful if the League were seeking to protect specific religious rights or if the League was seeking specific constitutional guarantees for particular religious rights. Yet neither of these was the case. The League was not seeking constitutional guarantees for religious rights. Indeed, as early as 1931, Congress had agreed that it would adopt no constitutional decision to which a majority of either the Hindu or Muslim community disagreed. Nor, despite its rhetoric after 1940, was the League committed to national sovereignty for the Muslims of India. Instead, the League was demanding that Muslims, as a quarter of the population, be guaranteed one-third of the seats in a central legislature and effective veto power over the electoral *process*.

A demand for veto political power to be reserved to a minority group is fundamentally at odds with a defining process of a political democracy, namely that one individual possesses one vote and that winners are defined by a plurality of the vote, subject to certain fundamental guarantees of civil, political, and religious freedom. In this sense, League-defined Pakistani nationalism effectively rejected the process by which an electoral majority was created. In 1940, for example, when Gandhi called Jinnah a brother, Jinnah responded: "the only difference is this, that brother Gandhi has three votes and I only have one vote!"[73] In rejecting the process by which freely cast votes determined outcomes, the League was rejecting the very process by which a democracy selects its representatives. Thus, League leaders propagated a nationalism that was not only vaguely articulated but whose core demand was also fundamentally inconsistent with a constitutive characteristic of electoral democracy.

[72] Sartori in Blaug and Schwarzmantel (2001: 194–195).
[73] Proceedings of the All India Muslim League, Twenty-Seventh Session (March 1940, Lahore). Pirzada (1969: 332).

In sum, groups of Muslims threatened by Congress' electoral success in 1937 instrumentally united under the banner of Pakistani nationalism, ostensibly based on the claim that Islam was endangered, in order to either maximize their claim to power in all-India politics or to protect their writ of power in provincial politics. Unlike Indian nationalism, the Muslim League as the institutional incarnation of Pakistani nationalism did not become more than a means of accessing or maintaining power for disparate groups. League supporters did not develop an ideological commitment to the party beyond their short-term interest in accessing political power. Whereas India's independence party had developed an economic and social content to its nationalism at least a decade before independence, Pakistan's independence party propagated only vaguely Islamic slogans a year before independence. These slogans gained support among broader social groups and impelled independence because the League provided organized Muslim groups with a direct means of maintaining their social and political dominance. But after independence, when invoking Islam as a unifying ideology no longer served the goal of accessing state power, Muslim League supporters quickly abandoned the party. In the absence of a developed programmatic commitment, Pakistan's dominant political party would be unable to broker key regime-building conflicts.

III. CONCLUSION

In the decades before independence, both Indian and Pakistani nationalisms were instrumentally adopted by distinct social classes pursuing their interests in the historically specific circumstance of a colonially imposed state seeking to maintain its grasp on power. Both of these nationalisms were imagined by defining a nation in contrast to an "other" – against the British colonial Raj in the case of India and against a Hindu Raj in the case of Pakistan. Despite these apparent similarities however, the nationalisms of India and Pakistan were substantively different in two ways which were causally germane to their divergent regime outcomes.

First, whereas Pakistani nationalism was wholly anti-Hindu in character, Indian nationalism was not just anti-British in character. During the course of a protracted anti-colonial struggle, India's independence movement defined its nationalism through the sometimes costly practice and institutionalization of core principles. After independence, India's ruling party was able to impose unpopular decisions and achieve compromises on difficult issues of state-building in part because its supporters had agreed upon and often mobilized for key principles, such as public egalitarianism and economic self-sufficiency. The absence of a similar ideational glue which bound together its party members meant that the Muslim League was considerably less able to achieve consensus on key issues of state-building upon independence. Instead, when Pakistan's ruling party sought to achieve compromises on similar state-building issues, the Muslim League was quickly deserted by its fair-weather supporters. Thus, the presence of ideological commitment to the party would help to foster regime stability in the case of India while its absence would contribute to regime instability in Pakistan.

Second, the content of each country's nationalism rendered its dominant party more or less amenable to democratic decision-making upon independence. Indian but not Pakistani nationalism involved institutionalizing a prolonged and practiced commitment to political equality. Before independence, India's ruling political party had separated the private identities of religion, region, and language from that of national citizenship, thereby creating a public sphere. Within that public sphere, political equality was embraced, both in terms of rhetoric and to some degree in terms of practice. Pakistan's ruling political party espoused a nationalism which did little to alter hierarchical authority patterns and which therefore did little to habituate its members to accepting the governing compromises that define democratic decision-making. The substantively egalitarian content of its nationalism habituated Indian but not Pakistani governing elites to the process of democratic compromise before independence. Thus, the content and character of national ideologies, though instrumentally espoused, mattered because they ultimately impacted whether each country's ruling political party was able to govern effectively and democratically in the post-independence decade.

4

Organizing alliances (1919–1947)

While the substance of politics has no doubt to be perceived beneath formal institutions ... political-institutional forms assume a primacy and a dynamism of their own, define society's goals and means, and bring more of the social reality under their area of control.

(Kothari 1970)

This chapter is the second of two that examines the transformation of the independence movements for India and for Pakistan into multi-class political parties in the decades before their twin independences. This chapter demonstrates *who* joined the respective independence movements for India and Pakistan, *why* they did so, and *how* the participation of these social groups was institutionalized. The two core claims developed herein are, *first*, that each independence movement created coalitions which varied dramatically in terms of their distributive coherence and, *second*, that each independence movement varied dramatically in terms of its intra-party organizations. As Figure 4.1 suggests and Chapter 5 demonstrates, both the distributive coherence and the robustness of its intra-party organization critically impacted the likelihood of regime *stability* in each country upon independence.

I. CONGRESS ORGANIZES A COHERENT DISTRIBUTIVE COALITION

The urban, educated, and predominantly upper-caste segment of the middle class across British India came together during the last decades of the nineteenth century and created the Indian independence movement in

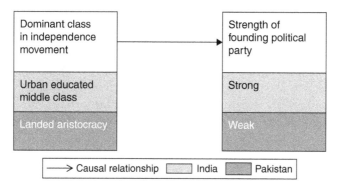

FIGURE 4.1. Argument of the chapter.

order to achieve upward mobility in the historically specific context of a developed, expanding state apparatus and an under-developed economy. By the 1920s, historically specific events had led this class to radicalize and embrace civil disobedience methods as a means of harnessing rural discontents and knitting together a broad-based anti-colonial movement.

Below, I show that the educated urban middle class leading Congress broadened the anti-colonial alliance to include myriad social groups, but especially the rural dominant peasantry or India's "rural middle class." Congress thus came to represent a coherent distributive coalition, composed of members of the middle class that shared an interest in, on the one hand, more favorable treatment at the hands of the colonial government and, on the other hand, preventing downwards redistribution towards subordinate social groups. Congress was able to do this in two ways. First, mass mobilization campaigns heightened the salience of shared distributive interests vis-à-vis the colonial regime and thereby helped to overcome barriers to collective action. Members of the rural middle class joining Congress possessed grievances with the colonial regime, grievances which had developed independently of the anti-colonial Congress movement. Congress' accumulating successes in gaining colonial concessions motivated the rural middle class to view the Congress Party as the appropriate vehicle for expressing their discontents. Second, any perceived risks associated with joining the anti-colonial movement were minimized by the non-violent nature of Congress nationalism, which intentionally minimized class conflict. In short, the creation of a multi-class coalition was facilitated both by shared distributive goals as well as by the content of Indian nationalism.

The rural middle class: the pivotal Congress alliance

The central alliance that Congress leaders forged was with the rural middle class across British India. This alliance not only gave Congress a rural base, one which successfully refuted the colonial claim that Congress represented a "microscopic minority," but it meant that Congress came to represent a broad spectrum of the middle class which desired redistribution away from the colonial state and its collaborators but which also wished to prevent downwards redistribution towards subordinate classes.

Forcing the colonial government into acknowledging that the Congress Party represented broader popular sentiment in British India required, first and foremost, the cultivation of support in rural India, which represented a large majority of colonial India's population. Between the beginning of mass mobilization in 1920 and independence in 1947, Congress successfully mobilized this rural support by mobilizing on the basis of grievances which clearly divided the interests of the British colonial regime from that of the indigenous population and by *rhetorically* centralizing the plight of the poorer peasantry. An egalitarian yet non-violent nationalism enabled the poorer peasants and dominant peasantry alike to join the anti-colonial movement. The poorer peasantry joined Congress both because of its rhetorical centralization within Congress and because it faced pressures to do so from the dominant peasantry. The dominant peasantry, in turn, joined Congress both because Congress substantively advocated its interests and because the non-violent nature of its nationalism minimized the risk of downwards redistribution.

Before describing the alliance between Congress and the dominant peasantry which formed the rural middle class of British India, it is necessary to describe who the dominant peasant is and how he fits into the rural social structure. Village India was complex and typically highly differentiated by region, rendering difficult the task of generalizing social categories. One broad generalization helping to distinguish social structures is that the colonial government's land revenue collection cleaved into two systems. Under the *zamindari* system, which generally predominated across northern India, taxes were paid by larger landlords known by the general term of *zamindar*, who were vested with ownership rights to land, as well as juridical and executive functions over the local population. *Zamindars* were a heterogenous group however, with some, typically absentee, landlords (which I refer to as the large, landed aristocrats) owning vast tracts of land and others (which I refer to as dominant peasants) owning smaller parcels of land who were firmly entrenched within village social and economic life. Under the *ryotwari* system, which predominated in southern India, smaller peasant cultivators were themselves vested with propriety rights to the land and paid taxes directly to the colonial government. Regardless of whether the land tenure system was *ryotwari* or *zamindari*, however, dominant peasants existed across colonial India and typically stood at the apex of a village's economic and social structure.

Dominant peasants were often upper-caste owners of land who sat at the apex of an extensive and deeply hierarchical village-based patronage network which effectively controlled the political allegiance of a subordinate network of poorer and landless tenants. Dominant peasants typically owned between 10 and 50 acres of land, constituted approximately 20 percent of the landowning population, and owned over half of the cultivated land of British India. Unlike the large landed aristocracy, the social and economic life of the dominant peasant was firmly entrenched within village society. These individuals held the proprietary rights over land in one or several villages and cultivated this land themselves or with the help of hired labor. Through their control over land, dominant peasants wielded an enormous amount of influence over village politics. Where the caste hierarchy did not perfectly correspond to the hierarchy of land ownership, for example, social status tended to be accorded primarily by land ownership and not by caste. In some cases, the social status and political power associated with land ownership was attenuated or exacerbated through historical custom, caste sanctions, and control over credit. Though internally differentiated and regionally dispersed, dominant peasants were nonetheless socially and politically distinct from large-scale regional rulers who typically owned extremely large tracts of land, or the variety of super-imposed intermediaries that the pre-colonial Mughals, these chieftains themselves, and later the British employed to extract wealth from the village economy.

Beginning in the 1920s, the urban, educated middle class in Congress began to champion the specific grievances of the rural middle class, channeling its discontents into a broader anti-colonial agitation demanding more representative political institutions. While the poor landless peasants were rhetorically centralized in Congress campaigns, Congress' first party-sponsored, fully fledged anti-colonial agitation in the Bardoli area of Gujarat exemplifies *how* Congress leaders were able to successfully

mobilize dominant peasants. In the Bardoli *satyagraha* or freedom struggle, Congress leaders organized the withholding of land revenue in a
region where a large landed aristocracy did not exist, meaning that land
revenue would be directly withheld from the government instead of from
a landlord class, foregoing the possibility of provoking an indigenous
class conflict.

Congress leaders had already linked up with local political activists
and social reformers in the Bardoli *taluq* and had made preparations with
local leaders for the dominant peasantry to withhold its land revenue tax
as part of the 1920 Non-Cooperation movement. The remission of higher
land revenues, the essence of the Bardoli *satyagraha*, was clearly an issue
of importance primarily to those who actually owned land and were
therefore responsible for remitting taxes, i.e. the dominant peasantry. In
1926, when the regional colonial revenue officer recommended a 30 percent increase in the *taluq*'s land revenue demand, a senior Congress leader
formally launched a civil disobedience campaign. Mobilizing thousands
of volunteers, a top Congress leader, Vallabhbhai Patel, drummed up support for the boycott of government land revenue taxes through meetings,
speeches, and the publication and distribution of a daily paper set up for
the purpose. Intelligence networks as well as village sanctions were used
to prevent individuals from paying their taxes, with remarkably successful results. By 1929, the regional colonial government effectively relented
and allowed the cultivating peasantry to pay the pre-assessment amount
of land revenue.

A stress on non-violence and "village uplift" work were core to the
success of the Bardoli protest, particularly in the face of colonial tendencies to play up class conflicts to divide anti-colonial protests.[1]
Programs of "village uplift" were implemented before, during, and after
the anti-colonial agitation. Networks of ashrams were created, schools
were built, and inquiries into the abusive nature of upper-caste social
practices were held, all of which gradually helped to create more har-
monious relations between lower-caste cultivators and the upper-caste
dominant peasantry. Village uplift work undertaken by Congress for the
decade before the Bardoli mobilization helped maintain unity between
castes and prevented the lower castes from rising up against the small,
upper-caste landowners when the colonial government made predictable
attempts to divide the Congress movement.

[1] Patel (1990: 265), Shah (1974), and Chandra *et al.* (1989: 204–205).

Attempts such as Bardoli to forge an alliance with the dominant peasantry were aided by the worldwide economic depression beginning in 1929. Consequently, Congress involvement in limited agitations during the 1920s grew into a more widespread national tendency during the 1930s, as dominant peasant communities saw the increasingly visible Indian national movement as an appropriate platform in which to express their grievances. The strategic interests of the urban middle class thus combined with historical circumstances to facilitate the making of an alliance with the rural middle class. Despite its rhetorical emphasis on the plight of the rural poor, Congress substantively championed the interests of the rural middle class. When Congress launched its next mobilization campaign in 1930 – the celebrated boycott of salt – in the midst of this economic dislocation, rural support was far more extensive than in 1920. Critically, this agitation was not a campaign to stop paying land revenue taxes, which would threaten the financial foundation of British colonial regime, but a symbolic violation of colonial legitimacy. Congress leaders regularly stressed that their only condition for participation in the national movement was non-violence. Because the costs of participating in the defiance of the salt monopoly were low (compared to the boycott of taxes, in which peasants were faced with the prospect of losing their land) and because participation in what was a symbolic anti-colonial agitation minimized the risk of exposing deep class and caste fissures within Indian society, Congress leaders rightly calculated that rural peasantry and middle class alike could participate in this anti-colonial protest without invoking a class conflict.

The great spurt in Congress membership during the 1930s represented growth in the members of rich peasants and small landowners with urban linkages. During and after this mass demonstration, which gained the Congress extraordinary national and international visibility, many more upwardly mobile dominant peasant groups sought to link up their local grievances with the Congress movement. Though some of the areas which had been mobilized during the 1920s were actually less involved during the 1930s, peasant involvement generally intensified in the hopes that mobilization would facilitate the accommodation of their demands. In Gujarat, segments of an increasingly educated dominant peasantry of Kheda were radicalized by an ongoing economic crisis and joined Congress. By 1940, the United Province Congress had become a party of wealthy cultivators. In Bihar, where the large, landed aristocracy remained loyal to the colonial government, Congress support grew strong among smaller landlords who were increasingly sending their sons to be educated in Western educational institutions. The Bihar Provincial Congress Committee thus came to be dominated by both small landlords and educated, urban professionals. In Punjab, local student organizers formed *kisan sabhas* [peasant organizations] which were associated with yet separate from Congress, and which demanded reductions in land revenues, in the rates of canal water use, and in existing debt, with the main targets of peasant mobilization being the large *zamindars*.

In southern regions of British India, such as Andhra, Congress was most successful in mobilizing in those *ryotwari* districts in which smaller landlords were typical, where higher land revenue taxes were to be implemented in 1930, and where economic pressures were growing due to falling grain prices, rising levels of debt, and a growing population. In the Central Provinces and Berar, an urban lawyer from the city of Nagpur with established connections to the small landowning community served as the organizer of Congress' rural outreach, which made Congress the most successful rural party in the 1937 elections. In what later became the Indian state of Tamil Nadu, local Congress leaders, initially wholly upper-caste Brahmins, so dramatically expanded their rural support by recruiting urban students who came from small landowning families that they won 85 of the 93 seats they contested in the 1937 regional elections.[2]

Expanding rural participation in the Congress agitations put India's independence party in a position to legitimate its claim of representing a single Indian nation. The salt boycott affected not just coastal areas and urban cities, but was in fact adapted to a wide variety of local contexts, including a defiance of forest laws in Maharashtra, Karnataka, and Central Provinces and the Red Shirt movement in the North-West Frontier Province. Though Muslim support for Congress was waning as a result of rising communal tension throughout the 1920s, middle-class Muslims were still participating in the Congress movement, particularly in the North-West Frontier Province and Bengal. By the time that the Gandhi–Irwin Pact of 1931 negotiated a halt to the movement, over 90,000 people had been jailed and imports of cloth, cigarettes, and liquor had fallen dramatically.[3] Congress had effectively juxtaposed "Indian"

[2] Arnold in Low (2006: 259–288).
[3] Chandra *et al.* (1989: 282).

interests with those of the British colonial regime. It had also *rhetorically* focused on the adverse consequences of the tax on the very poor while *practically* carefully protecting the interests of the upwardly mobile rural peasantry.

All across colonial British India then, the 1930s witnessed a burgeoning though by no means universal trend toward the integration of upwardly mobile peasants who adopted anti-colonial nationalism to local contexts, as evidenced in its overwhelming success in the colonially sponsored elections of the 1930s. In the 1937 provincial elections, based on a newly expanded franchise of approximately 11 percent of the population, Congress won dramatic victories in seven of the 11 British provinces. The colonial government, who had gambled that an extension of the franchise would help British allies win these elections, were surprised by the extent of Congress support. What the dominant peasantry was not given by the colonial government, and what won them over to the Congress cause, was a voice in how much land revenue was extracted from dominant peasant communities. After the 1937 election results, the Viceroy and much of the British colonial government accepted the need to work with Congress at the all-India level.

Several caveats about the growing alliance between Congress and dominant peasant communities in British India are worth emphasizing. First, the depth and breadth of the alliances varied greatly across space and time. Second, growing support for Congress was not always linear and in fact actually retracted in some areas as independence neared. Third, the development of communal politics as a local, regional, and national phenomenon meant that large parts, but by no means all of the Muslim peasantry abstained from supporting Congress agitations and joining the Congress movement after the mid 1920s.

Peasants across most of the British Indian subcontinent were drawn into the orbit of the Congress Party during the 1930s and 1940s. While local, regional, and even national peasant organizations were not always successful in getting their demands accepted, either by the colonial government or even fully within the Congress movement, poorer and wealthier rural cultivators alike had learned that by attending meetings, rallies, demonstrations, conferences, and membership drives, they could gain limited recognition if not redress of their demands. Serious differences between peasant organizations and Congress leaders in some regions not withstanding, the rural peasantry of British India had become accustomed to associating with and compromising within the Congress Party. While it is undoubtedly true that many of the conflicts upon which these peasants initially agitated were local in origin, Congress leaders were able to nationalize local peasant struggles such as the salt *satyagraha* and graft newly "national" struggles back into local contexts. Consequently, the national movement took on a political significance apart from the narrow economic grievances which provided the initial impetus for these agitations.

Committed *bania* support

Small-scale business support for the Congress Party, already significant by the turn of the twentieth century, grew steadily stronger as independence neared because of a growing perception of shared interests. Traders, merchants or *banias*, and a variety of middlemen formed the bulk of the commercial classes in British India until World War I, when the Indian industrialist community was still in its infancy. Though this group was internally differentiated and could not be said to have formed a coherent "class for itself," many of these small businessmen tended to be early and consistently staunch supporters of Congress for both economic and social reasons.

British India's merchant communities grew in strength, cohesion, and wealth during the eighteenth and nineteenth centuries, coming to be dominated by certain Hindu castes from the northwestern desert regions of modern-day Gujarat who, through pre-colonial specializations in commerce, colonial linkages, and distinct migration patterns, successfully monopolized small-scale business networks across northern and to a lesser extent southern colonial India. Particularly because of the relatively recent spread of these merchant networks, small-scale businessmen exercised little direct control over rural production networks, tending to be superimposed onto rather than integrated within the rural economy. In areas where colonial rule was well-established, these merchants provided for seasonal credit, the storage and marketing of goods over long distances, and banking services.

An important motivation for these merchants to support Congress was its opposition to income taxes. Already by the latter half of the nineteenth century, these merchant communities were active in the politics of larger cities and smaller towns across British India, with a sizeable section of smaller merchants well-represented Congress within. As a senior colonial official from the United Provinces already noted in 1889, "the class which is more inclined than any other to identify with the claims of the literary and law class is the trading section of the community, especially the retail trader caste of the large towns."[4] This generalization did not hold true for all small-scale middlemen however. Since the patronage of the colonial regime was in many cases responsible for the financial success of these communities, commercial middlemen varied considerably in their Congress support, even as they began to directly conflict with the colonial regime on specific issues. By the end of the nineteenth century, indigenous business communities were cautious Congress supporters, with mercantile castes forming half of the members attending annual Congress meetings in India's most populous province.[5]

New economic grievances at the end of World War I exacerbated economic discontent among merchant communities and intensified small business support for Congress' anti-colonial agitations. During the war, the government imposed a series of taxes that were important in alienating the small-scale business community, including customs taxes, excise duties, and income tax. The British themselves understood that the trading community principally supported Congress demands for economic motives, namely to gain remission from British taxes. British District Magistrates in the 1930s invariably echoed the sentiment that "the small shopkeeper class ... is always resentful of taxation and hopes to gain remission of taxation through Congress."[6] During the 1930 Civil Disobedience Movement, the Governor of Bombay wrote to the Viceroy that the movement won the "support of practically whole of the very large Gujarati population of Bombay, [the] great majority of whom are engaged in business trade or as clerks."[7] There was profit to be gained from supporting the Congress Party, since a central plank in the Congress platform was the support of domestic cloth or *swadeshi*, which the merchants of northern India were responsible for trading.

In addition to economic gain, small-scale business communities would stand to benefit socially from the ideational transition away from a traditional caste society that Congress promoted. Many trading communities, especially the powerful Marwaris, were devout Hindus who had joined religious reform movements during the nineteenth century in part because these movements advocated that caste status not be determined by birth. In the context of their desire for upward mobility, the brand

[4] Sir Auckland Colvin, Note on Provincial Councils, June 11, 1889, Home Public A, August 1892, pp. 237–252, NAI.
[5] Hill (1967).
[6] Low in Low (2006: 141).
[7] Sykes to Irwin, June 20, 1930, Irwin Papers, IOL.

of Indian nationalism which Gandhi promoted, with its promotion of caste equality, therefore opened up the possibility for these trading communities to improve their social status. This was especially true because Gandhi himself originally came from a trader caste and became the newly adopted leader of an upper-caste movement. Gandhi himself thus became a symbolic embodiment of the desire of successful merchant communities for upward mobility.

For economic and ideological reasons alike then, small business communities increasingly lent Congress their political and financial support, particularly after Gandhian ideology became dominant in 1920. Economic grievances with the colonial regime were important in motivating this alliance, as was compatibility between the socio-religious goals of these newly affluent small businessmen and the political goals of the urban, educated middle class in Congress. Overall, small-scale businessmen were often very active in local politics and supportive of Congress in regional cities, but their energies were typically channeled into municipal and regional politics. While small-scale business support formed an important reason for Congress conservatism, these urban merchants were not organized into all-India organization and therefore rarely exerted a coordinated influence upon national-level Congress politics.

Capitalists, a fair-weather ally

While neutralizing capitalist opposition to Congress was important to the ultimate success of the party, large capitalists in India allied with Congress only a few years before independence. Indian capitalists grew into a sizeable political force during the 1930s, at a time when the Indian National Congress was already a well-established political movement. Despite its growth, Indian capital was rarely characterized by a common approach toward political affairs, tending instead to be divided along regional and sectoral dimensions. Indian capital was generally ambivalent about the cause of independence because, while it possessed some incentive to support an independent Indian government instead of a colonial regime which tended to protect British industry, it also feared Communist radicalism within Congress. During the 1930s, the combination of the colonial government's introduction of progressive taxation, the increasing likelihood of Congress' dominance in a politically sovereign India, and Congress' aloof attitude toward organized labor induced Indian capitalists to more decisively support the Congress movement.

During the early twentieth century, large capital effectively organized into a "class for itself." Big Indian capitalists, identified by the breadth and depth of their business enterprises, their organizational depth, and the sheer scale of their financial resources, were located almost exclusively in a few urban centers across British India, namely Bombay, Calcutta, Ahmedabad, Cawnpore, and Coimbatore, where large-scale mechanized factories existed. Large Indian capital grew tremendously during the 1920s and 1930s, such that by 1944, Indian private capital controlled 62 percent of the large industrial units employing more than 1,000 individuals, an especially impressive figure when compared with British capital, which correspondingly controlled 27 percent of large industrial units.[8] Indian captains of industry on the whole did not have very good links with the rural elite, however, and tended instead to form a distinct, urban social class. A growing awareness of common interests among large capitalists had led to the organization of India's first national organization for commercial, industrial, and financial interests in 1927 – the Federation of Indian Chambers of Commerce and Industry (FICCI). Despite the presence of FICCI, however, Indian capitalists rarely acted as a unified political actor toward the Congress Party and consequently exerted little influence over India's independence movement before the early 1930s.

By 1930, Congress and Indian capital began a gradual rapprochement for two reasons, the first being economic. The onset of the worldwide depression and the colonial protection of the British textile industry progressively alienated Indian capitalists, who began to cultivate relationships with Congress leaders. Congress' nationalist platform also became demonstrably beneficial to certain sectors of the Indian capital. Indian industrialists were particularly irked over what they perceived to be an over-valued exchange ratio throughout the 1920s and 1930s, an issue which Congress began to take up by 1920. Congress' central emphasis on the boycott of foreign cloth had unambiguously positive affects on the market position of textile capitalists. For example, during both the Non-Cooperation and Civil Disobedience movements, the value of foreign textile imports fell by half in the space of one year.[9] Though Congress leaders advocated that individuals spin their own cloth, they also made it clear that textile magnates had an important role to play in furthering independence. Writing in 1930, Gandhi stated: "In my opinion, the

[8] Mukherjee and Mukherjee (1988: 532).
[9] Sarkar (1983: 207 and 293).

purest form of *swadeshi* [economic independence] to the extent it is prac-
ticable is *khadi* [handspun cloth]. If this is not possible then swadeshi
should mean cloth made in mills owned and controlled by Indians out
of yarn spun in those mills."[10] Congress leaders thus carefully carved
out a contributory role for Indian capital within the fold of the Indian
independence movement and thus provided for the possibility of capital-
Congress rapprochement.

A second reason for the gradual rapprochement between Congress
and Indian capital during the 1930s was the desire of large capital to
strengthen its legitimacy within and the moderation of what it increasingly recognized would be the future governing party of an independent
India. As the younger generation of Congressmen grew more powerful and the socialist wing of the Congress Party consequently gained
strength, Indian capitalists sought to countervail the tendency toward
political radicalization by strengthening the more moderate elements
within Congress. One of Congress' biggest financial supporters among
the industrialist community was G.D. Birla, who cultivated a particularly close relationship with Gandhi. Writing in a manner that was representative of capitalist feeling toward the Congress movement, Birla
wrote in 1932 that "Gandhiji is the greatest force on the side of peace
and order. He alone is responsible for keeping the left wing in India
under check."[11]

Indian capital still maintained only cautious support for Congress
throughout the 1930s, however, most probably because of the latter's
(existent but by no means all-embracing) support for labor in the view
of rising labor militancy, witnessed in Gandhi's mediation between the
workers and owners of textile mills in Ahmedabad in 1919 and in the
limited accommodation of labor demands in the 1931 Fundamental
Rights and Economic Programme at Karachi. The lukewarm nature of
collaboration between Congress and the Indian captains of industry is
witnessed in the National Planning Committee (NPC), a consultative
body formed by Congress to determine the economic policy of an independent India. The NPC, founded in 1938, consisted almost exclusively
of large capitalists along with a few Congressmen who were close to
the business community.[12] In two brief years in existence, this body

[10] *CWMG*, Vol. XLIX, April 6, 1930.
[11] G.D. Birla to Hoare, March 14, 1932, enclosed in Hoare to Willingdon, April 8, 1932,
Mss. EUR. E. 240 (I), IOL.
[12] Markovits (1985: Chapter IV).

agreed on very little in the way of real policy coordination and business leaders sought to distance themselves financially and politically from Congress whenever disagreements arose, as they did on the role of the state ownership in planning India's industrial development. By 1940, as these disagreements over the role of the state in economic development grew, business contributions to Congress concomitantly declined considerably.[13]

During the early 1940s, as the prospect of a sovereign Indian state under Congress stewardship appeared ever more likely, the Indian industrial community began to more vigorously cultivate a relationship with Congress leaders in an attempt to strengthen its standing with what would now likely be the future government of India. This outreach is witnessed in the announcement of the 1944 Bombay Plan, created at the behest of the large capitalist community to outline the economic agenda of an independent India. A glimpse of the writings of the large industrialists who primarily authored the Plan reveals that they were motivated to create and announce the Bombay Plan as a means of insuring their continued economic profitability in an independent India. In 1942, for example, the key drafter of the Plan wrote a note to one of the more prominent industrialists in the country, Purshotamdas Thakurdas:

The most effective way in which extreme demands in the future may be obviated is for industrialists to take thought while there is yet time as to the best way of incorporating [in the capitalist system][14] whatever is sound and feasible in the socialist movement.[15] [Emphasis added.]

Additional evidence of the late-developing relationship between Congress and large businessmen is seen in both the press statements put out by the business community in the decade before independence and in the assessments of the relationship between Congress and industry by the colonial government, which was deeply concerned with any developing link between Congress and big industrialists. When the last mass civil disobedience movement had been initiated by Congress in 1942 for example, FICCI issued mildly worded calls for social peace and negotiation between Congress and the government, hardly a ringing

---

[13] National Planning Committee, Report of the Sub-Committee on Industrial Finance (Delhi: Government of India, 1948).

[14] "In the capitalist system" was penned in.

[15] Note from John Mathai to Purshotamdas Thakurdas. December 8, 1942. *Proceedings of the First Meeting of the Committee on Post-War Economic Development*, PT Papers, File 291, Part I, NMML.

endorsement of the Indian independence movement.[16] Moreover, secret government inquiries, both in 1939 and in 1943 into the nature of business support for Congress concluded that while the business community kept abreast of the Congress activities and were in some cases in close communication with its leaders, it gave little direct financial assistance to Congress.[17] While Indian capitalists extended ever clearer and more open support to Congress during the 1940s and while they were not ideationally opposed to economic planning, they nonetheless continued to hedge their bets and maintain ties to the colonial government until the eve of independence.

For their part, Congress leaders were interested in developing a congenial relationship with India's indigenous industrial community because Congress hoped to forge as broad and successful an anti-colonial coalition as possible. Nineteenth-century Indian nationalists had already built their political nationalism on a foundation of economic nationalism, citing the British drain of wealth out of India. Even the earliest progenitors of Indian nationalism saw the development of an indigenous capital community as being a central task in advancing the Indian nationalist cause and few Congress leaders felt that an independent capital base within India would be inconsistent with the spread of nationalist sentiment. At the same time, Congress leaders viewed mass engagement as the most important pillar of the anti-colonial movement, irrespective of capitalist support. Already in 1922 as he launched Congress' first civil disobedience movement, Gandhi as Congress President wrote, "whether they do so or not, the country's march to freedom cannot be made to depend on any corporation or groups of men. This is a mass manifestation. The masses are moving rapidly towards their deliverance and they must move whether with the aid of the organized capital or without." Thus, though Congress leaders desired a working relationship with Indian capital and made every effort to cultivate affable relations, they were prepared to and in fact did expand the Indian national movement without the explicit support of Indian capital.

All the same, Congress leaders recognized that gaining the support, or at least neutralizing the opposition of Indian capital in their independence bid would be critical. This was certainly true of the more moderate Congress leaders, such as M.K. Gandhi and Vallabhbhai Patel. Even the more left-leaning Congress leaders such as Jawaharlal Nehru, however,

---

[16] FICCI Press Statement, dated September 13, 1942. PT Papers, File 267, NMML.
[17] Home Political Department, F. no. 4/14-A, 1940, NAI.

recognized that industrialization would play a critical role in achieving social development goals. As described below, Congress was also careful to not cultivate so close a relationship with organized labor that it would alienate Indian capital. When it assumed control of several regional governments between 1937 and 1939, Congress regularly sided with business interests rather than with labor interests, though this was not an indication of a developed ideological or institutional link between these communities. Rather, it was an indication of the pragmatic approach that Congress leaders and Indian capital took toward cultivating mutual support. A secret British intelligent report of the time confirms this: "As to the relationship between big business and Congress, the available evidence does not appear to justify any assumption that 'Big Business' has been secretly using Congress as an unsuspecting instrument towards the achievement of its own ends, or vice-versa, but rather that the two have been working together in a partnership of convenience with no illusions on either side."[18]

Congress leaders created and institutionalized election-winning alliances with segments of the rural and urban Indian middle class *well before* Congress gained the unequivocal support of India's capitalist class. Still, the organization of such support along non-violent and economically conservative lines, as well as the recognition of key Congress leaders that an indigenous capitalist class played an important role in advancing Indian nationalism, slowly but surely encouraged Indian capital to ally with Congress. At a minimum, this alliance neutralized the opposition of a powerful social class to growing Congress hegemony.

Labor, a distant Congress ally

Though industrial labor formed a relatively small sector of the colonial economy, urban labor consistently, if unevenly, sought the support of India's independence party. Sizeable industrial labor populations had sprouted in Calcutta and Bombay during the last decade of the nineteenth century, resulting in several dozen important strikes over factory conditions. Concurrently with the growth of industrialization in the post-World War I period, the Indian labor movement grew into an organized national force with the formation of the All-India Trade Union Congress in 1920, a movement which was closely associated with the communist movement in India.

[18] British Intelligence Bureau. April 3, 1944. L/P&J/117 C27 MA, IOL.

During the 1920s, India's nascent labor movement strove to remain broadly united with Congress, opposing it only on specific, well-defined issues. The growing labor militancy of 1928, which resulted in organizational tension between Congress and labor, was dampened down by the arrest of prominent trade unionists in the Meerut case and several organizational splits that resulted in the emergence of rival labor organizations. Consequently, labor strike activity in 1932 reached its lowest level since 1920.[19] By 1935, however, the labor movement was again growing in strength due to the economic hardship accompanying the Depression. During this time, the labor movement experienced limited success in getting its political goals recognized by Congress.

For its part, Congress' attitude toward labor, though changing over time, was generally one of cautious and limited support. Early Congressmen largely ignored labor conditions. After 1920, Congress leaders accepted some demands of labor, as witnessed by the promises made to labor in the Fundamental Resolution at Karachi in 1930. Nevertheless, Congress was careful to eschew too close an alliance with the labor movement as the latter grew stronger under Communist leadership during the late 1920s. Congress' repeated civil disobedience campaigns during that time pointedly disavowed labor strikes as a means of nationalist agitation, though labor was encouraged to participate in other Congress-sanctioned nationalist activity.[20] When the All-India Trade Union Congress (AITUC) made several attempts to organizationally link up with Congress, Congress demurred, though prominent Congress leaders such as Nehru still chaired several sessions of the AITUC. None of the labor movement leaders were closely affiliated with Congress, and top Congress leaders, including Gandhi, made efforts to set up separate labor organizations that would operate directly under Congress leadership.

The policies of Congress ministries between 1937 and 1938 provide a clear window into how Congress reconciled the conflicting demands of labor and capital while in power. During electoral campaigning in 1936, Congress manifestos had made promises to labor regarding both working conditions and the right to organize and, consequently, garnered successfully half of the electoral seats reserved for labor. Congress ministries with the power to legislate over labor issues were formed in seven of the 11 British provinces. How these ministries legislated, and in particular,

---

[19] Revri (1972: 183–185).
[20] Revri (1972: Chapter 4). Also, *CWMG*, Vol. LI, "Speech to Labour Union at Ahmedabad," March 11, 1931.

how they adjudicated between the oppositional interests of capital and labor, is indicative of how Congress encouraged both groups to moderate their demands.

Overall, Congress ministries sought to satisfy some worker demands while not wholly alienating the capitalist community. During the running of their ministries, Congress alternately placated the demands of capital and labor. Initially, pursuant to its electoral promises, Congress passed resolutions in October 1937 which sought to improve labor conditions, though it set up no timeline for implementing these resolutions. Specific committees and sub-committees were set up in regions with industries to investigate the question of wages. On the whole, these committees, which included representatives of both employer and labor associations, eventually recommended wage increases that were substantial but that only partly compensated for Depression-era wage cuts.

These moderate proposals reflected that Congress ministries were genuinely trying to forge a middle road between the interest of capital and labor. In most regional governments save for the United Provinces, Congress was able to reach compromises between labor and capital on wage increases by using the threat of a general labor strike (which Congress could rightly argue was not under its control) and the benefit of its future governing power to induce the capital community to reach a compromise. In Bombay, for example, "mill-owners, in heated interviews, pointed out that they had supplied in the past a large part of the Congress funds and that they were now receiving in return very heavy burdens to bear. They extracted from the [Congress] Ministers and from Sardar Patel [a prominent member of the All-India Congress Committee] a promise that further legislation providing sickness benefit and old-age pensions for the workers, the cost of which would be mainly borne by the millowners, should not be put into operation for at least a year."[21] Early Congress ministries made a show of extracting concessions from the capitalist community while still working to make the capitalist community amenable to such concessions.

After initially placating labor interests in 1937, Congress ministries changed course and made attempts to placate the capitalist community. In 1938, capitalists rightly argued that compromises with labor had not resulted in diminished labor unrest, in part because Congress did not

---

[21] Lumley, Governor of Bombay, to Viceroy Linlithgow, Report no. 12, dated March 15, 1938, Linlithgow Papers, Vol. LI, IOL.

directly control labor organizations. It was during this time that Congress attempted to create Congress-sponsored labor unions with the hope of bringing the labor movement more firmly under its control. Moreover, the Congress Ministry in Bombay introduced legislation, the Bombay Trade Disputes Act, which institutionalized a forum for policy compromise between labor and capital. The Act, which introduced a compulsory delay before either strikes or lockouts could begin, was introduced into the Legislative Assembly with an unequivocal condemnation of labor strikes, met with the general approval of capitalists. In response, organized labor protested considerably, erupting into strikes which were firmly put down by the Congress Ministry.

Other Congress ministries similarly sought to balance the interests of capital and labor, thereby developing both the experience with and the institutional mechanisms for reconciling conflict. Though they were generally unsuccessful in dealing with labor unrest during the two years that they governed between 1937 and 1939, Congress ministries did demonstrate that they would genuinely seek some form of compromise between capital and labor. While it tried to placate segments of these different class groups, Congress likely also alienated segments of both. Nonetheless, it is important to note that, in this period, Congress was forced to grapple with the reconciliation of competing urban interests and gradually evolved a set of policies for doing so.

In addition to institutionalizing compromises on the contradictory distributive interests of capital and labor, Congress leaders also evolved ideational justifications for compromise. Congress leaders, particularly Gandhi, emphasized that organized, non-violent labor movements as well as responsible capitalists were both necessary components of a successful nationalist movement. For example, speaking to labor in 1938, Gandhi urged mutual accommodation by conceptualizing capitalists as trustees:

[C]apital and labour will be mutual trustees and both will be trustees of consumers. *The trusteeship theory is not unilateral and does not in the least imply the superiority of the trustee. It is, as I have shown, a perfectly mutual affair, and each believes his own interest is best safeguarded by safeguarding the interest of the other.* [Emphasis added.][22]

At the same time as Congress' leader actively urged the organization of labor as a part of the nationalist movement, however, his central emphasis on non-violence allowed him to reassure property owners that

---

[22] *CWMG*, Vol. LXXIII, June 25, 1938.

Congress would not seek radical redistribution policies: in speaking to landowners, Gandhi clearly stated: "But supposing that there is an attempt unjustly to deprive you of your property, you will find me fighting on your side."[23]

Gandhi's positioning of capitalists as potentially benevolent trustees of India's wealth, though not uncontroversial even among Congress leaders, nonetheless enabled capital and labor to see themselves as collaborators in a shared anti-colonial project. Though these ideas often failed to happily unite capital and labor in compromise, this ideological perspective allowed both groups to perceive themselves, at least in part, as partners in the independence movement.

In sum, multiple social groups had by independence signed onto the Congress movement, though for different reasons and unevenly over space and time. Congress had created a coalition that was relatively unified in its bid for colonial independence and that reflected, above all, the interests of upwardly mobile peasant communities. Congress was able to build this coalition *in part* because it shared distributive aims with the rural middle class and *in part* because the non-violent nature of Indian nationalism diminished the radicalism of the movement. Upwardly mobile groups in both rural and urban areas with multiplying economic grievances and a desire for upward social mobility signed onto the Congress cause either because they saw within Congress participation the possibility of gaining recognition for their own desired set of social and economic reforms or because they wanted to gain influence with an organization which was gaining political power. In most cases, both were true.

The organization of influence

A final reason for the electoral and governing success of the Congress Party in the pre-independence decades was that Congress leaders created and honed an organizational basis for these alliances, providing for the direction of a movement through complex leadership structures from above as well as some expression of manifold grievances from below. Between 1920 and 1947, the Indian National Congress gradually grew to become *the* institutional incarnation of Indian nationalism. It was able to forge this dominant political position because Congress leaders both evolved a nationalist ideology that coherently critiqued colonial rule and

[23] Gandhi as quoted in Nehru (1941: 325).

agreed on specific social and economic reforms that provided a focal point for disparate sets of anti-colonial grievances. Moreover, Congress strengthened this position by effectively forging loose but regionally specific alliances with commercial traders, emerging capitalist barons, the poorer peasantry and, most crucially, the rural dominant peasantry across British India.

Congress' intra-party organization, particularly its small executive and the graduated representation between party levels, provided an effective template for channeling grassroots support into a relatively streamlined but democratic party leadership. According to the party constitution adopted by Congress in 1920, Congress' organizational structure consisted of a President, three General Secretaries, and an All-India Congress Committee, which was elected by Provincial Congress Committees, who were in turn elected by District Congress Committee.[24] Each party level was elected by the level below it, and already in 1920, began to extend its reach downwards into colonial India's 700,000 villages via District, Taluka, and Town Congress Committees. While the position of Congress President carried great prestige, it was largely a figurehead, and the most important bodies in Congress were the All-India Congress Committee (AICC), which effectively served as a Parliament, and the Congress Working Committee (CWC, created in 1921 and composed of 15 members), which effectively possessed the executive decision-making capacity of a Cabinet. Almost all decisions taken by Congress were effectively taken by a vote of either the AICC or CWC, bodies which were elected by constituent bodies at annual or ad-hoc Congress sessions.

The 1920 reorganization also introduced a number of important changes that enabled the party to more effectively attract financial and grassroots support. Provincial Congress Committees were henceforth to be organized into 21 linguistically homogenous provinces that were encouraged to conduct party business in local languages. The all-India Congress was now conducted in Hindustani inasmuch as it was possible, which was thought to make Congress participation more accessible to the less-educated. Paid membership was also introduced, though at such a low level that it enabled all but the very poorest to join. Non-paying members were allowed to join Congress as long as they

---

[24] *Indian National Congress 1920–1923* (Allahabad, All-India Congress Committee, 1924): 38–51, NMML.

pledged to uphold the Congress creed, but only paying members could have a say in the workings of the local and provincial Congress bodies. With these changes, Congress' President Gandhi hoped "to give the Congress a representative character such as would make its demands irresistible."[25]

In addition to its structural reorganization, Congress also drastically improved its financial position after 1920. Annual membership dues provided a regular source of income. The Tilak Memorial Swaraj Fund, launched by Gandhi to solicit funds from the business community in Calcutta and Bombay, collected ten million rupees in 1921, representing large contributions from industrialists as well as numerous contributions from small-scale traders. From its rural membership drives, Congress raised over 13 million rupees.[26] The approximately 25 million rupees raised between 1921 and 1923 amounts to approximately $250,000, at that time, a very substantial amount of money when one considers that, with substantially higher costs, American President Calvin Coolidge spent just over four million dollars and his opponent just over one million dollars on their contemporaneous election campaigns.[27] These funds enabled Congress to extensively popularize the anti-colonial cause through *khadi* tours, "village uplift" work, the campaign against untouchability, national education drives, famine and flood relief, and a variety of other election propaganda.

These changes, in combination with alliances made and mass agitations led, greatly expanded Congress' membership during the pre-independence decades. While it is difficult to establish the reliability of these numbers, Congress primary membership reached two million people during the height of the Non-Cooperation movement in 1921.[28] In 1938, Congress membership stood at four and a half million members.[29] In 1945, Congress membership was estimated at over five and a half million individuals.[30] Moreover, this growth in membership largely came from growth in rural regions of India. In 1919, 59 percent of the AICC members came from towns whereas 41 percent came from rural districts. Already by 1923,

[25] *CWMG*, Vol. XVIII, July 2, 1920.
[26] *Indian National Congress 1920–1923* (Allahabad, All-India Congress Committee, 1924): 331–338, NMML.
[27] Wayne (2008: 34) and Balachandran (1996: 137).
[28] Various Congress membership lists, AICC Papers, G-24, 1921, NMML.
[29] File 4/7/1941: 8, NAI.
[30] AICC Papers, File 4–50, 1946, NMML.

Congress had more members in rural areas, 35 percent then coming from towns whereas 65 percent came from rural districts.[31] Of course, these numbers were almost certainly inflated. Particularly after Congress began governing in 1937, the growth in membership likely represented an opportunistic conversion to the Congress government. Nevertheless, since Congress possessed large membership rolls already in 1921, when joining Congress was a politically risky thing to do, these earlier membership figures also genuinely reflect the growing popularity of Congress at grassroots level.

Not only was Congress increasingly able to mobilize and represent a cross-section of Indian society, but the party itself possessed a not insubstantial degree of downwards and upwards coherence. Congress' leadership could not always control regional and local agitations, but Congress' leadership clearly linked up with and gave some expression to demands from below. For example, when Congress ministries and their allies assumed control of seven provincial governments between 1937 and 1939, they did in fact initiate ambitious legislation on land reform in many provinces, legislation which indicated that regional Congress ministries were responsive to their rural constituents.

Crucially for the purposes of showing the independent causal impact of the party, Congress leaders were also able to effectively discipline provincial governments when keeping the party line contradicted narrowly defined short-term interests. In Punjab, for example, where Congress represented primarily urban moneylenders, all-India Congress leaders gave strict orders that provincial Congress organizations were not to oppose bills which restricted moneylending because it was crucial for Congress everywhere to be seen as representing the interests of the small peasantry. Congress leaders were also able to prevent Punjabi and Bengali Congressmen from openly condemning the 1932 Communal Award, over vehement internal dissension.[32] While Congress members needed only to sign the party creed, pay dues, and spin *khadi*, the decisions and orders of Congress leaders were binding on all Congress office-holders, who were expected to fully execute Congress policy.[33] The fact that the national Congress leadership was able to keep its provincial members from opposing policies that contradicted their own short-term interest evidences that the party itself came to be identified with the pursuit of their interests.

---

[31] Krishna (1966: 423).
[32] AICC Papers, G-24, 1934–1936, NMML.
[33] Krishna (1966: 428).

II. MUSLIM LEAGUE COBBLES TOGETHER COALITIONS OF CONVENIENCE

At the beginning of the twentieth century, a geographically concentrated, colonially entrenched, Muslim landed aristocracy created a movement to lobby for Muslim extra-proportional political representation, effectively invoking religious identity as a means of legitimating class privilege. Once extra-proportional representation for the Muslim minority had been granted by the colonial regime in 1909, the League movement, without a *raison d'être*, faltered for the better part of two decades. As late as 1934, the Muslim League "was dominated by the titled landed gentry, *Nawabs*, Landlords, and *Jee Huzors* who were generally well-meaning gentlemen but wanted to serve the Muslim cause *only so far as it did not affect their position either socially or in Government quarters*" [emphasis added].[34]

As mentioned above, the key turning point in revitalizing the Muslim League was Congress' striking electoral success in the 1937 elections, presaging as it did the imminence of colonial independence under Congress leadership. Those elections underscored that a Congress-led government promoting land reform and the broader adoption of Hindustani posed a clear threat to a Muslim landed aristocracy that was well-entrenched in both government services and political institutions. This sense of threat, perceived in ways both economic and social, motivated the revitalization of the Muslim League under the leadership of a single charismatic leader who forged alliances in the two crucial Muslim-majority provinces of colonial India – Punjab and Bengal. Given a relatively short window to drum up support, the League was forced to turn to organizations which already existed in the Muslim-majority provinces. In the Punjab, the Muslim League gained electoral support by gaining the support of landed aristocrats, who opposed any economic redistribution. In Bengal, the League created electoral support by vaguely promising economic redistribution to the peasantry. In neither province did the Muslim League create a grassroots or an organizationally integrated party. Nor could it, in large part because these social bases fundamentally lacked a shared political agenda. While the League-sponsored politicization of religious cleavages did justify the creation of an independent state in Muslim-majority provinces, these alliances fractured shortly upon independence and spurred on regime instability in an independent Pakistan.

---

[34] Khaliquzzaman (1961: 137).

In the future geographical core of Pakistan – western Punjab and eastern Bengal – the League's organizational infrastructure was weak to non-existent. The absence of shared distributive interests and the organizational or ideological means with which to sustain these interests made it extremely unlikely that these regional elites would stay committed to the governing political party after independence. Consequently, Pakistan's dominant political party was unable to forge compromises on key issues of governance. The lack of a shared distributive agenda and the inability of the League's nationalism or organizational infrastructure to provide a roadmap for reconciling these contradictions effectively meant that the League was unable to provide for regime stability in Pakistan.

United Province Muslims and the invocation of Islam

Upon independence, the region which led the Pakistan independence movement remained geographically within India. Since the Muslim League leadership in the United Provinces was largely responsible for the creation of the sovereign state of Pakistan, an assessment of Muslim League politics in this region is necessary to understanding why the Muslim League was upon independence composed of an unsteady alliance between a landed aristocracy and a peasant movement. Despite the rise in localized communal conflict throughout colonial India, regional League leaders remained politically marginal throughout the 1937 elections even in the United Provinces, and the Muslim League was "primarily representative of *nawabs* who met annually and adjourned for the remainder of the year."[35] The 1937 provincial elections effectively amounted to a struggle between Congress and the National Agriculturalist Party [NAP], or in other words, between the urban, educated, and predominantly Hindu middle class that stood to gain from more representative government and the disproportionately Muslim rural landed aristocracy that sought to lose from more representative government. Rather than setting up an independent organizational infrastructure, however, the Muslim League's new leader, Mohammed Ali Jinnah, brought the League's virtually non-existent political organization firmly under his own personal control.

Even in a reorganized form, the Muslim League in its ostensible stronghold was weak and highly centralized in the hands of its single charismatic leader. Jinnah began to monopolize the leadership of the League in

[35] R/3/1, Haig to Viceroy, dated October 29, 1936. Linlithgow Papers, IOL.

a variety of ways. Jinnah set up a central executive committee, the party's Central Parliamentary Board, which he wholly controlled. Candidates were selected to run on a Muslim League ticket by the UP Provincial Parliamentary Board, whose members were in turn chosen by the Central Parliamentary Board, all of which was tightly controlled directly by the one person who retained the position of Muslim League President from 1938 until independence, with no internal elections.[36] While provincial League organizations existed, local Leagues for the most part did not. Relying almost exclusively on donations, moreover, the Muslim League offered almost no financial support to candidates. When there was a dispute over how the candidates to the UP Parliamentary Board were to be selected between Choudhry Khaliquzzaman and Liaquat Ali Khan, it was resolved by appealing to the final authority of Jinnah, rather than to regularized procedures.[37]

The 1937 elections, reflecting as they did the overwhelming success of the Congress Party, starkly threatened the existence of an old social order dominated by Muslim landed aristocrats and, with it, the political viability of the Muslim League. The legacy of Congress' governance during this time impressed upon the colonially aligned landed aristocracy that it could no longer rely on colonial patronage for continued economic and social dominance. Contesting as it had under a platform which strongly opposed any expropriation of private property – a platform which reflected its social base of support, the Muslim League did relatively well in the United Province provincial elections, but performed very poorly in the Muslim-majority provinces of Punjab, Sindh, North-West Frontier Province (NWFP), and relatively poorly in Bengal. Congress leaders, who had won an absolute majority in the UP, offered UP League leaders Ministry positions under the precondition that the League disband as a separate political party. Given that the League was shown to be very weak in other provinces, which belied its claim to be the sole spokesman of Indian Muslims, and given that the foremost organization of Muslim clergy, the *Jaimat-ul-Ulema-i-Hind*, had recently withdrawn its support for the League in favor of Congress, this was perhaps not an unreasonable demand. But Jinnah, the now all-powerful League leader, rejected the demand and, for the first time in nearly two decades, a UP regional government was formed without representation of the Muslim League.

---

[36] Sayeed (1968: Chapter 6). Also Khaliquzzaman (1961: 192).
[37] Khaliquzzaman (1961: 145).

The detrimental effect of being cut out of power was immediately perceived by the upper-class Muslims represented in the League and drove
the organization to seek alliances with Muslims elsewhere. A committee which examined the local structure of government in 1938 suggested
abolishing separate electorates for Muslims, which would have effectively diminished their proportional over-representation.[38] Congress' post-
election establishment of parallel administrative structures at the district
level, which were to effectively serve as the local government and which
thereby outranked the colonial administration in the districts, further signaled to League members the erosion in their regional authority. Muslim
representation in the higher ranks of government service began to decline
as the result of the introduction of reservations of lower classes and the
introduction of the Devanagari script as the medium of English-school
instruction. Muslim landlords charged that Congress Ministry's pro-ten-
ant legislation was "destructive of the culture of the minority community, sustained by the patronage of the Muslim landed aristocracy,"[39] even
though the colonial governor interpreted that such tenancy legislation
would primarily affect only the largest landlords. Wrote the UP Governor
of the Muslim reaction:

[The big landlords] are in varying degrees bewildered, frightened, and angry. They
put great efforts into the electoral campaign and spent money freely. The result is
a complete reversal of all their anticipations. They are very apprehensive of what
the Congress may do to them. There is also a good deal of resentment against the
attitude of the Government. One cannot help understanding their feeling. Their
argument is as follows. We have for generations been loyal to the Government
and the Government have supported and encouraged us. In this election we have
been fighting not only our own battle but the battle of the Government, for the
Congress have throughout made it clear that they are attacking the whole system
of Government and the British connection. But the Government have stood by
indifferent and allowed us to be beaten.[40]

Under threat, upper-class UP Muslims gave Jinnah free rein in revitalizing the all-India Muslim League, a position from which he portrayed
himself as the single authoritative spokesman of Muslim interests in
colonial India. Congress attempts to cultivate the support of lower-class
Muslims, which was initially somewhat successful in urban areas, deeply
threatened League leaders. Muslims, wrote the provincial governor, are:

[38] Brennan in Hasan (1993: 350).
[39] Das (1969: 187).
[40] R/3/1, Haig to Viceroy, dated October 29, 1936, Linlithgow Papers, IOL.

disintegrated and completely uncertain of their policy ... Muslims are frankly alarmed at the Congress attempt [to gain the support of] the Muslim masses and it may be successful. In the absence of a strong and united Muslim policy some are inclined to wonder whether it is wise to oppose such a powerful body as the Congress. On the other hand, the majority I believe, are determined to oppose the Congress, and are only waiting for a lead. This they seem likely to get from Jinnah [the leader of the all-India Muslim League].[41]

Though Muslims were still extra-proportionally represented in the UP regional government, upper-class Muslims rallied to the League because they foresaw the diminution of their political, economic, and social power. In many cases, the loss of Muslim access to privilege was not because Congress Ministry directly discriminated against Muslims, though such cases also existed, but rather because the introduction of merit-based appointments and the abolition of separate electorates advantaged a Hindu majority in a province at the expense of an entrenched Muslim community (landed aristocracy and government servicemen alike) which had effectively ruled the United Provinces for centuries. So while the UP Congress did appoint two Muslim ministers to its Cabinet, for example, Congress was bound to appear as though it were favoring Hindu interests when it responded to an increasingly vocal Hindu majority for a representation of their interests.

The move toward representative government by the majority Hindu community, in the context of an age-old and colonially legitimated social order dominated by Muslims, provoked a reactionary backlash which bolstered the Muslim League's sagging political fortunes. The decline in the socio-economic status of UP Muslims thereby bolstered the League movement. Educated, urban middle-class Muslims, who stood to both gain and lose, depending on their positions, were effectively "torn between two loyalties."[42] In an atmosphere of communal distrust and a divided Muslim middle class, threatened upper-class Muslims turned to the League and "conservative Muslims" subsequently regained control of the UP Muslim League.[43]

The League's popularity grew as a result of its ability to cast the protection of UP Muslims' economic interests in religious rhetoric. Between

---

[41] R/3/1, Haig to Viceroy, dated October 29, 1936, Linlithgow Papers, IOL.
[42] Khaliquzzaman to Nehru, June 29, 1937, AICC File G-61, 1937, NMML.
[43] R/3/1, Haig to Linlithgow, April 7, 1937: 37–75. Even in 1939, the colonial governor of the UP felt that most Muslims in the UP were opposed to the communal rhetoric and that many were "in general outlook much nearer to Congress" than the Muslim League, though Muslim landlords in the UP were the exception. Haig to Linlithgow, June 10, 1939. Linlithgow Papers, IOL.

1937 and 1938, those years in which the Congress Ministry controlled the regional legislature, the leaders of the UP Muslim League spoke out on substantively economic issues – against the tenancy legislation which Congress was introducing and for the rights of Muslims to be represented in regional government services for example.[44] For its part, Congress' reaction to the Muslim desire for reserved representation in government was that proportionate religious representation was appropriate. "[I]t [is] not wise on the part of Muslims to lay undue stress on the question of communal proportion in services. Their attitude in this matter is already creating a reaction among the Hindus. We are now receiving representations to the effect that there is no reason why the Hindus should have less than what they are entitled to on a population basis."[45] In the context of these differences over access to government employment, the League devoted itself to cataloguing, often in inflammatory language, the "atrocities" of Muslims in the Hindu-majority provinces.

Thus, UP Muslims felt that Congress rule effectively translated into a decline in Muslims' economic and social status, spurring on the embrace of a religious ideology in reaction to their declining economic, political, and symbolic status. When contrasted with British rule, which had deliberately sought to socially elevate and politically over-represent Muslims in the UP, the fears of the Muslim upper class of cultural and economic decline under a Congress government can be clearly understood. The marked decline in UP Muslims' social and economic status, as well as the prospect of further decline under a sovereign Congress government, led this regionally concentrated Muslim community, consisting of large landowners and some section of the urban, educated middle class, to rally behind the Muslim League and support its bid to carve out a position for itself in all-India politics. The League leadership, by publicizing cases of communal conflict under Congress governance and by connecting these grievances to religious identities which the colonial regime had long recognized, sought to legitimate the claim that Muslims formed a separate nation whose interests needed to be advanced by the Muslim League.

Consequently, the League turned to the task of cultivating alliances in the Muslim-majority provinces of Punjab and Bengal.[46] For the League's

---

[44] Liaquat Ali Khan in UP Legislative Assembly debates on, for example, March 22, March 28, and August 10, 1938. U.P. LAD, IOL.

[45] Pant Address is quoted in Brennan in Hasan (1993: 355).

[46] There were, in addition to Punjab and Bengal, three additional provinces, Sindh, Baluchistan, and NWFP, which eventually joined to form the state of Pakistan. Because

claim to be the voice of Muslim India to be taken seriously, it needed to show it also represented the Muslim-majority provinces, a claim that rung hollow in light of the League's meager 1937 election results. The successful mobilization support in those two provinces during the next decade made the creation of the sovereign state of Pakistan possible. Upon independence, when the United Provinces remained in India, the League's demographic support in the Punjab and Bengal came to determine the coherence of the League as a political party.

The alliance with Punjabi landed aristocrats

Gaining electoral support in the Punjab was the single most important task for the Muslim League if the League was to legitimize itself as the organizational spokesman of Muslim interests in the remaining decade before independence. This was not only because the Punjab was one of two major Muslim-majority provinces, but also because it, through its geographical position, agricultural wealth, and dominance of military recruits, was a strategically pivotal state in colonial India. Punjabi politics was wholly dominated by a (Hindu and Muslim) landed aristocracy that was loosely organized into the Unionist party. Until just a few years before independence, this party had little interest in allying with the League. Just a few years before independence however, when colonial independence was imminent and when influence with the national Muslim League organization was consequently crucial for protecting provincial autonomy, Muslim segments of landed aristocracy in the Unionist Party began to support the League as a means of protecting their economic interests and political influence at the all-India level.

Gaining support for the Muslim League in Punjab was perhaps the crucial turning point in enabling the independent state of Pakistan to be created. As a key organizer of the League wrote at the time: "No one can deny that without this action on the part of Sir Sikander [Unionist leader, who threw his support behind the Muslim League] the Muslim League fight would have been confined to [Muslim] minority provinces alone and sooner or later they would have had to go under."[47] To gain a Punjabi base of support, the League reinforced the writ of

their provincial politics were less important to legitimating the demand for Pakistan and because, together, they possessed less than 10 percent of the Pakistan population, they are not discussed here.

[47] Khaliquzzaman (1961: 290).

the landed aristocracy and religious leaders (*pirs*) instead of creating an independent party infrastructure. The consequent lack of provincial support for the party and the direct conflict of interests between the landed aristocracy in Punjab and the peasant interests in Bengal most directly explained the League's inability to effectively govern Pakistan after independence.

Before explicating the nature of the Muslim League's alliance with the landed aristocracy in the Punjab, it is worth briefly outlining the agrarian social structure of western Punjab, or that part of Punjab which acceded to Pakistan in 1947. In the last decades of the nineteenth century, the social structure of Punjab was profoundly transformed when approximately nine million acres of wasteland in colonial India's northwestern corner was irrigated through the creation of massive canals, at its time one of the largest infrastructure projects in the world.[48] Through the granting of land, water rights, and honorific titles, the colonial state had effectively populated this newly fertile area with a large landed gentry that came to be considered the bulwark of colonial rule in the Punjab. These large landlords were Muslim, reflecting the fact that Muslims not only formed 55 percent of the Punjab population but tended to be geographically concentrated in the western portion of Punjab that became Pakistan.

A second important political group was the hereditary rural Islamic religious leaders known as *pirs*. *Pirs* rather than landlords often possessed the most direct political influence over cultivating and landless peasantry. *Pirs* had historically been granted political authority under Mughal rule and had essentially developed into local tribal chieftains as the Mughal state collapsed. The colonial state, as it annexed Punjab, had entrenched some of the more important *pirs* through a combination of lucrative land grants, low taxes, and honorific ranks and titles. For most *pirs*, however, the basis of their social and political influence was primarily religious, and the *pirs* of western Punjab were particularly involved in supporting a religious revival movement during the nineteenth century which emphasized Muslim identity as a way of consolidating their support in the absence of central religious authority.[49] The colonial regime also skewed the distribution of representation in the Punjab provincial Legislative Council, created in 1897, heavily in favor of landed interests. Together, the twin forces of the landed gentry and

[48] Ali (2003: Chapter 2).
[49] Hassan (1987: 552–565).

local religious leaders effectively provided a stable system of colonial control in rural Punjab.

The third politically important social group was an urban professional class that had typically served in the government bureaucracy or was involved in a variety of other educated professions. For a variety of historical reasons, this urban, educated middle class was predominantly Hindu and through their caste-based communities, served as moneylenders throughout the Punjab. Moreover, many of these urban Hindus were particularly involved with the Hindu revival movements such as the Arya Samaj at the turn of the century.

At the end of the nineteenth century, tensions which arose between the cross-communal landed gentry and Hindu urban moneylenders began to threaten the stability of British rule and to slowly assume political significance. As a result of rising agricultural and land prices, the landed gentry found it easy to assume debt at the hands of urban moneylenders. When they were subsequently unable to service these debts, land was appropriated by moneylenders. These land transfers were occurring at such an alarming rate that the provincial assembly, composed mostly of British colonials and the landed aristocracy, passed a law rendering it illegal for "non-agricultural" castes to acquire land.

Despite their increasingly precarious financial position, the landed aristocracy was the linchpin of British colonial rule in the Punjab. Landowners' connections with the British regime intensified during World War I, when the landed families assisted in procuring military recruits from the Punjab. As provincial autonomy began to be introduced under Congress rule in other provinces, the colonial regime continued to try and protect the influence and prestige of the landed community which supported ongoing colonial rule. For their part, the cross-communal cohort of landowners sought, through a combination of colonial patronage and links with religious leaders, to effectively ensure colonial loyalty in the Punjab.

When the Jinnah-dominated Muslim League sought to create electoral support in Punjab in time for the 1937 provincial elections, it did so by cultivating the support of the Unionist Party. The Muslim League had made overtures to the Unionist Party as early as 1936, but Unionist Party leaders, firmly in control of their provincial politics and secure in British patronage, rejected any need for outside interference in provincial politics.[50] The 1937 elections were a clear reflection of the

---

[50] Talbot (1988: 86).

resounding rural support of the Unionist Party, which won 95 of 175 seats, the largest single party by far. This compared with 18 seats for Congress, which came from mostly urban areas, and just one urban seat for the Muslim League.[51] Having failed to gather any support at all in what was widely considered to be the most important Muslim-majority province in colonial India, the League initially turned toward mass organizing.

Resounding Congress victories in 1937 quickly changed the political landscape of colonial India and ultimately led Unionists to bandwagon with the Muslim League. For the League, the lack of Muslim representation in Punjab posed a major problem and immediately motivated a mass mobilization drive. For the first time, the Muslim League sent workers to form village-based branches of the League with the goal of enrolling tens of thousands of new members.[52] For the Unionist Party, which had been guaranteed unimpeded control over provincial politics before 1937, the Congress victories made clear Congress would politically control a sovereign Indian state. Unionists were particularly concerned at the possibility of Congress control because it probably portended the loss of both provincial autonomy and of an important source of wealth and prestige, namely the Punjabi dominance in the colonial army. This new political reality drove Unionist leaders to ally with the Muslim League. By the terms of the Jinnah-Sikander Pact in 1937, all Muslim members of the Unionist Party were encouraged to become members of the Muslim League. Both the Unionists and the British government essentially understood this alliance as enabling the Unionists to remain in control of provincial politics and enabling the Muslim League to represent Muslims at an all-India level.

But the fact that the secular Unionist Party, which also represented a minority of Sikh and Hindu landowners, aligned themselves with a communal party began to drive Hindus away from the Unionist party. Whereas the early decades of the twentieth century had seen cross-communal alliances between rural interests, the effect of the 1937 elections was to begin to break apart the Unionist Party along communal lines.

The Muslim League's alliance with the Unionist Party leader also halted the League's mass mobilization campaigns in the Punjab, meaning that no grassroots presence for the League was organized there. Indeed,

---

[51] *Parliamentary Papers 1937–1938*, XXI (Accounts and Papers VI), Cmd. 5589, "Returns Showing the Results of Elections in India, 1937": 80–93.
[52] *Civil and Military Gazette*, May 4, 1937.

arresting the League's mass mobilizational campaign was part of the reason that the Unionists acquiesced to a League alliance in the first place.[53] In 1938, the Punjab Muslim League was actually dissolved and subsequently reconstituted with a plurality of its new leaders being members of the old Unionist Party. The All-India Muslim League Council found the Muslim League Organizing Committee in the Punjab, set up for the task of enrolling League members at the grassroots levels, so ineffective that it was dissolved by November 1939.

By 1941, the League had enrolled just 15,000 members in its six active districts of Punjab, whereas in ten districts, no League organization existed at all.[54] Instead of creating its own organizational infrastructure then, by the terms of its alliance, the Muslim League in Punjab essentially agreed to forgo mass mobilization attempts in the province and rely on the large landowners to marshal political support for the League. The Unionists themselves, moreover, possessed little party infrastructure of their own, having relied on their traditional social authority to win votes in the 1937 elections. Writing just before those elections, the Punjab Governor wrote: "The general position at the moment is that everyone with political ambitions is thinking in terms of votes. *Except among the urban Hindus and the Congress Party*, the elections will be fought on personal and tribal lines rather than on Party creeds" [emphasis added].[55] To the extent that any party organization did exist before the elections, it quickly dissipated after the elections. The Governor of the Punjab wrote just after the 1937 elections:

Previous to and during the elections the organization of the Unionist Party was very good, and their agents and supporters were very active in the villages. Since Government took office there has been a very marked falling off in this respect ... There have been very few meetings indeed organized or addressed by supporters of Government other than the Ministers and there is no comparison between the number of meetings organized by the Congress or communists and those organized in support of Government. District officers frequently comment on this, and unless the ministerial party wakes up, it is likely to lose ground.

Foregoing the creation of organizational infrastructure for the Muslim League in Punjab was the price that Leaguers paid in order to gain Unionist support, since the League's primary goal was to retain significant political power for Muslims at the all-India level. But in addition to the League essentially eschewing the creation of an independent party

[53] Daultana to Jinnah, November 13, 1937, Muslim League Papers, Microfiche, NAP.
[54] Talbot (1988: 90).
[55] Emerson to Linlithgow, October 19, 1936, IOR R/3/1/1, p. 10, IOL.

infrastructure, the League–Unionist alliance meant that the existing rural hierarchy, with large landowners and religious authorities together wielding extraordinary economic and social power over small landowners and the landless, remained fully in control of provincial politics until the eve of Pakistani independence.

Between 1937 and 1943, the landlord-dominated Unionists controlled the Punjab Muslim League. In 1941, Unionist influence over the provincial League is indicated by its leader's ability to convince all the important landlords to threaten to leave the League if needed:

[Unionist leader] Sikander had a most successful meeting at Lahore of Muslim members of the Unionist Party. Over 60, including Nawab of Mamdot, President of Provincial Muslim League, have handed him their resignations from the Muslim League to use if necessary [as he prepares to meet with Jinnah]. Remaining members (about 12) who were absent from Lahore have been asked by letter whether they wish to follow this lead and a favourable response is expected.[56]

Though the League leadership wished to have a great deal more control over provincial politics in the Punjab, the interests of the Unionists in protecting their political domain from encroachment, as well as the cross-communal nature of the Unionist party, prevented an all-India alliance of Muslims from emerging. Until 1943, Unionists were little motivated to do more than pay lip service to the Muslim League.

The ascent of communal politics at an all-India level enabled the central Muslim League to more definitively assert itself in the Punjab by 1943, particularly in light of the death of the Unionist leader Sikander Hyat Khan in December 1942. Upon Khan's death, factional rivalries for Unionist leadership began to weaken the Unionists' colonially sponsored unity. Moreover, heavy army recruitment, the wartime requisitioning of food-grains, and heavy inflation had strained the relationship between the colonial regime and the Unionists on the one hand and between the Unionists and the smaller landlords and peasant cultivators on the other hand.[57] In this context, the Muslim League began to stoke anti-Unionist sentiment on the issue of food-grains requisitioning and link the solution of the peasant's economic and social problems to a vaguely defined "Pakistan." By April 1943, the Punjab Governor wrote that: "There is no doubt that the 'Pakistan' slogan is gaining volume, and I fear that there are a fair number of politicians in the province who would sell the

---

[56] Telegram from Punjab Governor to Viceroy, April 16, 1941. Wavell Papers, IOL.
[57] Talbot (1988: 73).

Unionist fort for their own personal advantage."[58] Just a few weeks later, the Viceroy reported that the Unionist leader was "profoundly uneasy at the Punjab position so far as Pakistan is concerned, and told me that Pakistan, deeply tinged as it was with religious prejudice, was getting to a point at which it could not be resisted."[59]

Given the imminence of independence, the landed aristocracy began to increasingly calculate that their material interests were better served by an alliance with the Muslim League than by relying exclusively on colonial sponsorship. Slowly but inexorably, landlord-dominated politics in the Punjab crumbled under the communal logic at work in all-India politics. In 1944, talks between the Unionists and the League broke down over the issue of whether a new Ministry coalition should be named Unionists or Leaguers and the Unionist leader was expelled from the League. Though some leading landlord families stayed with the Unionists, a number of important large landlords also stayed on with the League, signaling the weakening of the Unionist grip over Punjabi politics. As World War II drew to a close and colonial independence loomed, many more landlords turned to the League for political protection at an all-India level. Though the League's religious rhetoric undermined the Unionist's cross-communal alliances, Islam was now the most convenient way of protecting socio-economic interests.

By 1945, most of the most important landlords had defected from the Unionist party to join the Muslim League. Many members of the Muslim landed aristocracy of Punjab were already reckoning that their interests were better served by allying with the League for political influence in all-India constitutional negotiations in 1944, but this calculation was thrown into stark relief in July 1945, when Jinnah insisted that no non-League Muslims be allowed on the Viceroy's Executive Council, which guided negotiations over the constitutional future of colonial India. Making sure that non-League Muslims were excluded from all-India constitutional negotiations was imperative to Jinnah's claim that the League was the exclusive legitimate voice of Muslim India. But it also made unambiguously clear to the Punjab Unionists that future access to political power, either in a united India or an independent Pakistan, could only be had through the Muslim League. Consequently, many of the Unionist landlords quickly converted to the Muslim League, which

[58] Glancy to Linlithgow, April 23, 1943, IOL.
[59] Linlithgow to Secretary of State, May 4, 1943, IOL.

therefore began to possess a solid but hardly committed political base in the Punjab.

Thus, the Muslim League won the support of both the landed aristocracy in Punjab as well as the Muslim religious leadership known as *pirs* through last-minute coalitions of convenience. Traditionally, *pirs* had loosely supported the Unionist party, which protected the economic interests of the rural landed aristocracy. In addition to being interested in protecting their material interests, however, *pirs* were also interested in extending the basis of their own social influence by injecting religion into politics. Though these *pirs* were tied in with the Unionist party leaders then, they were also generally dissatisfied with the secular organization of Punjabi politics.[60] These religious leaders saw in the League an opportunity to boost the influence of Islam in politics, particularly as rural landowners defected from the Unionist party to the League.

In the years before independence, many *pirs* rallied to the Muslim League because League leaders made vague promises of Pakistan being run by Islamic law. For example, a prominent League leader sought to cultivate the support of a prominent *pir* by declaring that Pakistan would be run by a government "of the Quran" and that, as such, every Muslim must support the jihad.[61] Though there was no indication that all-India Muslim League leaders intended to constitute Pakistan as a theocratic state, these appeals were sufficient to induce *pirs* to cast their own votes (as well as to use their influence to convince other landed peasants to do similarly) for the Muslim League in the 1946 elections.

In sum, the League gained a rural base in Punjab, one of two crucial Muslim-majority regions of British colonial India, by reinforcing the writ of large landlords and traditional religious leaders. This strategy proved successful in validating the League's claim to be the organizational representative of Muslims in constitutional negotiations since the Muslim League was the single most successful party in the provincial elections. It won 33 percent of the vote, as compared with 23 percent and 20 percent for Congress and the Unionists respectively.[62] But this electoral support was gained neither through the creation of a programmatic commitment to the League nor was such support organized within a robust party infrastructure. Both the landed aristocracy

---

[60] Gilmartin (1979: 502).

[61] Sardar Shaukat Hyat Khan, as quoted in Hasan (1993: 223).

[62] *Return Showing the Results of Elections to the Central Legislative Assembly and the Provincial Legislatures in 1945–1946*, 1948, NAI.

and religious leaders who joined the League in the mid 1940s were primarily interested in maintaining a hierarchical system of rural control, a goal that was diametrically opposed by the organized political group in the other crucial Muslim-majority region of Bengal. Upon independence, the conflicting nature of these interests quickly led to the disintegration of the Muslim League party and, with it, the likelihood of a stable regime in Pakistan.

Mobilizing the Bengali tenantry

The other Muslim-majority province in which the Muslim League needed to evince electoral support was Bengal. Like in Punjab, the Muslim League's strategy of coalition-building in Bengal can only be understood when keeping in mind that the League sought above all to position itself as the sole voice of Muslim interests in colonial India. This overarching goal had to be reconciled with the demographic realities of Muslims in colonial India. In Bengal, the vast majority of Muslims were poorer cultivators whose interests were not readily compatible with the League's constituency (landed aristocracy) in the United Provinces and Punjab. Since the support of this Muslim-majority province was nevertheless critical in legitimating the League's demand to be treated as the authoritative organizational voice of Muslim India, the League attempted a variety of strategies to gain the support of the poorer Muslim cultivators of East Bengal during the late 1930s and early 1940s. The Muslim League was ultimately able to gain a social base by playing upon the close coincidence of economic and religious cleavages. The Muslim League thus gained the support of the small cultivating peasantry of eastern Bengal by loosely equating the amelioration of their economic condition with the demand for Pakistan. Here, as in the Punjab, the Muslim League did not develop the institutional capacity to reconcile political factions and accommodate demands through regularized rules and procedures. Upon independence, neither the League's appeals to religious nationalism or its tenuous organizational infrastructure would prove capable of reconciling the opposing distributive interests of the dominant social groups which came to constitute Pakistan.

Before explicating the creation and organization of the Muslim League's support in Bengal, it is necessary to first briefly outline the agrarian social structure of eastern Bengal, that is, the part of Bengal which eventually became Pakistan. As a legacy of patterns of conversion and British patterns of land revenue extraction, Muslims formed a bare popular majority in the eastern half of Bengal, where they were primarily poorer, cultivating tenants. Hindus formed a bare popular majority in western Bengal, where they were both landowners and the cultivating tenants. The socially dominant strata in both urban and rural areas across western and eastern Bengal tended to be Hindu. In eastern Bengal, which later became East Pakistan, the cultivating peasantry possessed strong customary tenurial rights and was bound together by an Islamic identity. Despite overlapping economic and religious cleavages, however, religious conflict in rural eastern Bengal was rare before 1920. In other words, though religious symbols were often used to express economic grievances, political engagement did not assume an overtly religious dimension.

During the early decades of the twentieth century, historical developments helped to politicize religious conflict in Bengal, thereby facilitating an alliance between the Bengali peasantry and the UP-dominated Muslim League. The first of these was an economic crisis that adversely impacted the cultivating peasantry of east Bengal. Centuries of British colonialism had witnessed a slow but steady fragmentation in landholdings. As many of the landholdings became too small even to produce subsistence crops, the predominantly Muslim cultivators increasingly engaged in the cultivation of specialized cash crops such as jute, enabled by a landlord-provided credit market. During the nineteenth century, relations between the predominantly Hindu landlords-cum-moneylenders and their Muslim tenants, characterized by social norms that encouraged lending in times of scarcity, remained relatively free of religious conflict. The worldwide economic recession beginning in 1929 translated into extreme new economic pressures. This was not only because of a direct drop in peasants' standard of living resulting from a steeper drop in jute prices than in rice prices, but also because rural credit, the traditional source of financing in times of hardship, also effectively ceased to exist.[63] The "disruption in the system of credit robbed these groups [landlord-moneylenders and traders-moneylenders] of their social and political clout."[64] As the result of an exogenous economic shock, the norms of mutual obligation and credit linkages which had long stabilized landlord–peasant (and at the same time, Hindu–Muslim) relations in east Bengal began to give way. At this time peasant organization in

[63] Burdwan Fortnightly Report to Viceroy on July 10, 1941. Confidential File 13/41, Wavell Papers, IOL.
[64] Bose (2007: 177).

the form of *krishak samitis*, which were formed during the early decades of the twentieth century in Bengal to express economic discontents and lobby for tenurial security, surged.

These developments – the rupturing of social bonds between Hindu landlords and Muslim tenantry as well as the increasing politicization of the peasantry – provided fertile ground for an all-India Muslim League to gain a provincial base of support in Bengal. Initially, Congress leaders were closely involved with peasant organization in east Bengal, with many peasant organizers simultaneously being Congress organizers. But linkages between the all-India sphere of politics and the provincial politics had already begun to be felt during the 1920s. Though the League–Congress alliance at an all-India level collapsed in 1922, it was not until 1926, when new economic grievances appeared in the form of weakening demand for Bengal's primary cash crop (jute) and a tightening credit market, that peasant violence against landlords and moneylenders manifested itself under the guise of religion. In 1926, peasant agitations began to target not just Hindu-dominated markets, clear symbols of economic exchange, but for the first time, Hindu religious festivals as well.[65]

The Muslim League's goal of seeking organizational parity with Congress at the all-India level in constitutional negotiations necessitated its mass electoral mobilization of Muslims. In Bengal, this motivated the invocation of religious identity for political gain. Since the League's alliances in Bengal were predominantly dictated by the need to marshal *Muslim* support rather than by the pursuit of a distinct platform or program, a shifting constellation of alliances based on mutual convenience was the League's modus operandi. In 1936, having just acceded to the leadership of the Muslim League, Jinnah was initially able to gain a League foothold in Bengal by allying with the United Muslim Party, a party of Muslim landlords and urban business interests who simply adopted the League's name at Jinnah's behest. When given a choice, the national League organization initially allied with the same social class of Muslims in Bengal that it represented in the United Provinces and the Punjab, namely titled Muslim aristocrats who were uninterested in championing radical redistribution.

In Bengal, this landed Muslim aristocracy was quite small and uninfluential however. Since the League needed to evince large-scale Muslim support in the upcoming provincial elections, Jinnah also made earnest

[65] Chatterjee in Guha (1994: Vol. I, 9–38).

efforts to create an alliance with the far more popular peasant movement (the predominantly but not wholly Muslim) Krishak Praja Party (KPP), nominally unified under the charismatic leadersip of Fazlul Huq. Since the need for Muslim unity trumped all other needs, Jinnah attempted to subordinate both the KPP and the United Muslim Party to Jinnah's League Parliamentary Board, an all-India organizational platform from which Jinnah sought to directly control the selection of provincial candidates running on a League ticket. Unsurprisingly, since the KPP advocated the abolition of the *zamindari* system without compensation in direct contradiction of UMP interests, the League's efforts to create a united Muslim front of these two organizations were largely unsuccessful before the 1937 elections.[66]

The provincial election results reflected the still-fluid nature of political alignments among Muslims in Bengal just a decade before independence. The Muslim League played up communal identities and sought to portray the non-communal, peasant-oriented KPP as aligned with Hindu interests. Given the coincidence of economic and religious cleavages in Bengal and the changed economic circumstances described above, this strategy was partly successful. But still only partly, as the 1937 elections still saw the Muslim vote in Bengal relatively evenly tied three ways between the landlord-dominated Muslim League, the KPP, and a variety of independents, while Congress swept the general constituencies. That the KPP first attempted to form a coalition government with Congress rather than the League is indicative of the fact that Congress and the KPP shared more in the way of distributive goals. But Congress' delay in office acceptance at the national level, combined with the League's offer of the Chief Minister position to the KPP leader Fazlul Huq, led the KPP to form a governing coalition with the League between 1937 and 1941. Because this coalition was essentially composed of classes who shared little in the way of distributive interests, however, the radical electoral demands of the KPP, such as the abolition of landlord holdings and stronger tenurial rights, did not translate into policy.[67] When the Ministry did relatively little to follow through on election promises, many of the local peasant movements which had supported Huq as the KPP leader disassociated themselves from the Huq Ministry.[68] For its part, the League had entered into

---

[66] Rashid (1987: Chapter 1), Sen (1976: 50), and Zaidi (1976).
[67] Sen (1976: 88–93).
[68] Bose (2007: 206–207) and Governor-General to Governor, June 23, 1937. L/P and J/5/141, IOL.

the KPP–League coalition government because it urgently needed a popular base of support in Bengal to substantiate its national claim of Muslim representation, particularly given the League's dismal electoral performance elsewhere across colonial India.

The workings of provincial politics in Bengal for the next decade – between 1937 and independence in 1947 – was a microcosm of the Congress–League struggle for electoral support at a national level. The governing League–KPP coalition had effectively been captured by landed interests and governed by regular recourse to communal propaganda, which had an effect in large part because the religious cleavage so clearly coincided with the economic one.[69] The Muslim League provincial government did take measures to ameliorate the socio-economic position of the Muslim peasantry and middle class between 1937 and 1941, though it also deliberately sought to magnify the salience of religion. Hindu higher castes, because they typically came from higher socio-economic backgrounds and because they historically enrolled in colonial educational institutions at far higher rates, had traditionally dominated the government services. By 1939, however, half of the government service seats were reserved for Muslims. The Bengal Provincial Muslim League also set up an Employment Bureau, which kept records of unemployed Muslims and helped them to find jobs. A young Muslim League leader wrote that the Muslim League Ministry "for the first time opened avenues of employment [for] the educated middle class Muslim young men. As a matter of fact, Muslim League movement became strong due to this competition and rivalry between the Hindu and Muslim middle classes."[70] The League coalition Ministry also provided some agrarian relief, such as the Tenancy Act amendment of 1938, the Agricultural Debtor's Act of 1938, and the Bengal Moneylenders Act of 1940.[71] These accomplishments popularized the Muslim League and simultaneously heightened Muslim solidarity in contradistinction to Congress. The KPP leader Huq now spoke of the "atrocities which Congress has committed on Muslim minorities" and authored a pamphlet called "Muslim Sufferings Under Congress' Rule."[72] Any Muslims who supported Congress (and a faction

---

[69] The composition of Fazlul Huq's Cabinet is indicative of who was represented. In an 11-member Cabinet, eight were large landlords. Whereas four members of the Ministry were Muslim Leaguers, there was just one member of the KPP. Governor to Governor-General, R/3/2/2, IOL.

[70] Ahmed (1970: 44).

[71] Sen (1976: 110–115).

[72] Aziz (1978: 388–419) and interview with K.K. Aziz on March 28, 2005.

of the KPP did) were branded as "traitorous self-seekers," "pawns of Congress," and "wreckers of Muslim solidarity."[73] Muslim solidarity was also supported by the British colonial regime, which was keen to avoid any breakdown in the League–KPP coalition government which might bring Congress into government.

Overall, the League Ministry presided over a marked rise in Muslim solidarity through polarizing communal rhetoric. Political competition between the Congress and the League coalition Ministry in Bengal now regularly assumed the form of communal propaganda. Reflecting the Congress' all-India platform, some Congress leaders, in alliance with some KPP deserters rebelling against the dilution of the KPP pro-peasant platform, criticized the governing Ministry for not going far enough to advance tenant interests in provincial legislation. But Congress' ability to position itself as the sole champion of peasant issues was undermined by the League Ministry's ameliorative legislation.

During its coalition government, the League created very little in the way of regularized rules or procedures constitutive of party institution- alization. Much like the Unionists in Punjab, the KPP alliance with the League effectively meant that the KPP ceased to function as a separate party organization. While the KPP had started to create grassroots sup- port in the run-up to the 1937 election, this emergent party unity had been fractured by the KPP alliance with the League, which had meant that some KPP factions left the party. Moreover, since the League coali- tion, the party leadership held only annual elections and spent very lit- tle time on matters of party organization. Writing in 1941, a Muslim League report to Jinnah stated that "Mr. Huq's Praja Party exists only on paper with no office, no organization, no branch, no party fund and no paper."[74] Party organization was little better in the Bengal Provincial League itself, which functioned largely to serve the interests of Jinnah. Suhrawardy, a top leader of the Bengal Muslim League, did undertake some party organization during the coalition government, but the domin- ant trend was one of Jinnah increasingly centralizing power in the League Presidency.

Obedience to the Muslim League's leader, rather than party service, thus became the chief characteristic of those who rose to positions of power in the party during the 1940s. The new Muslim League constitution of

[73] *Star of India*, July 12, 1938 and August 6, 1938.
[74] Letter from Raghib Ahsan to Jinnah, June 3, 1941. File 204: 173–178. Muslim League Papers, NAP.

1938 formulated a Working Committee whose members were nominated by the President. This President was Jinnah for every year in the decade before independence.[75] After 1938, a series of resolutions passed by the Council or the Working Committee further empowered the President at the expense of provincial decision-making apparatuses. The leader of the All-India Muslim League wrote that "the time has come when there should be only one party and that is the Muslim League as far as the Muslims are concerned."[76] At the end of 1939, when a member of the Working Committee criticized Jinnah for announcing the League's "Day of Deliverance" without consulting the League's Working Committee, a resolution was passed prohibiting a standing member of the Working Committee from publicly criticizing the President.[77]

A steady concentration of organizational powers in its leader both reflected and exacerbated the lack of internal party organization. The Bengal Muslim League was consistently cut out of the all-India League, both in terms of decision-making and representation. Bengal was already marginalized in the all-India Muslim League before Jinnah centralized the powers of the League leader. Of the eight annual sessions of the Muslim League held between 1936 and 1943, none were held in Bengal and, after 1943, no annual sessions of the League were held. Moreover, the Muslim League's most important decision-making organ – the 23-member Working Committee – included just three members from Bengal, despite the fact that Bengal was the most populous (of four) Muslim provinces – with roughly one-third of the Muslim population of colonial India. These three Bengali members (Nazimuddin, Akran Khan, and Hasan Ispahani) were intensely loyal to Jinnah and it is notable that some of the most powerful and popular Bengali leaders (Hashim or Suhrawardy) were never nominated to the Working Committee.

No meetings of the Muslim League's central decision-making apparatus (Council) were held in Bengal in the decade before independence. During the same time, the three most important positions in the Muslim League were always held by the same persons: Jinnah (from Bombay), Liaquat Ali Khan (from the UP), and the Raja of Mahmudabad (from the UP). While the Muslim League constitution of 1938 provided for much centralized power within the Working Committee over the

---

[75] Pirzada (1969).
[76] Letter from Jinnah to Ispahani, dated April 20, 1939. Zaidi (1976: 123).
[77] Rashid (1987: 113).

provincial Leagues in, for example, the selection of League candidates, "over and above the central organs [of the League] stood the august and awe-inspiring personality of the Great Leader, who controlled the central organs. The Working Committee was his creature. He more or less nominated the Central Parliamentary Board. The Committee of Action carried out his wishes and the Council, with some minor protests here and there, put a stamp of its formal approval on his behests."[78] The Bengal Governor also spoke of the League as "Jinnah's autocracy" in a communiqué to the Viceroy.[79]

The lack of genuine political representation in the top League leadership eventually led to a breakdown in the League's governing coalition in Bengal in 1941. Strains between Jinnah as the President of the all-India Muslim League and Huq as the League Chief Minister of Bengal were already apparent over League support for the British war effort. When the coalition government in Bengal wanted to pass a motion of support for the British declaration of war on Germany in 1939, Jinnah and his League loyalists protested on the grounds that such a decision should only be taken by Jinnah, lest his prestige as the League leader be diminished. Huq, aware he was losing his ability to make any decisions independently, entered into discussions with the Viceroy about the possibility of forming a national government of a united Bengal if and when independence came.[80] Strains between Jinnah and Huq finally erupted in earnest over the Viceroy's appointment of Huq (among other provincial League leaders) to his National Defence Council in July 1941.

Jinnah used his position as the chief representative of the Muslim League in all-India politics to cut his political opponents out of power. Jinnah wanted the national Muslim League to be the sole institutional representative of Muslim interests and he protested against the Viceroy not consulting with him before making such appointments. The League Working Committee immediately passed a resolution directing Huq to resign from the Council or enabling the President to "take such action as he deemed appropriate" should Huq refuse. Insofar as any provincial leader within the Muslim League was able to independently negotiate with the colonial government, he would pose a threat to Jinnah's efforts to subordinate all Muslim voices to the League's command. Huq

---

[78] Sayeed (1968: 196).
[79] Herbert to Linlithgow, October 1, 1941, "Bengal Political Situation in Formation of New Government." L/P&J/5/548, IOL.
[80] Herbert to Linlithgow, May 20, 1941, L/P&J/5/148, IOL.

resigned from the Muslim League "as a mark of protest against the arbitrary use of powers vested in its President" and decried that Jinnah was a "political dictator" for whom "Bengal does not count much."[81] The resignation of the one leader who represented a substantial portion of Bengali Muslims reflected the sidelining of Bengali interests in the all-India Muslim League.

The breakdown of the League coalition led the Bengal Chief Minister, newly exiled from the League, to seek rapprochement with Congress. But by now, Huq, who just a few years earlier had urged his followers to "follow the policy and programme of the Muslim League fanatically" had by now lost much of his support to the Muslim League.[82] Moreover, the rise in religious identification which the League government had intentionally cultivated was by now no longer easily controlled by the weakened KPP. Intent on bringing down any non-League Muslim government, Jinnah and the national League leaders worked hard for the dissolution of the Ministry by branding Huq a traitor to Islam. Simultaneously, League leaders stepped up local propaganda for Pakistan, propaganda which had been popularized by Huq while he was still in the League coalition.

Even in this context of growing religious polarization, the demand for an independent state of Pakistan was portrayed by Bengali League leaders primarily as a means of bettering the material conditions of the Muslim masses in Bengal. With Huq's ultimate resignation in 1943, the political defeat of the KPP was complete and the Muslim League, with its regular invocation of religious identity, was left the chief political force in the province. Since only parties supporting the British war effort (in Bengal, the Muslim League, KPP, and the Communist Party) were allowed to freely operate after 1942, the League was free to propagate communal rhetoric with the tacit support of the British government. In 1942, as the fall of Huq's Ministry neared, the British Viceroy wrote to the British Secretary of State, "Jinnah's dictatorship is complete, and I see no one in the Muslim fold who is in a position to resist it for very long, certainly no one who is in a position to revolt against it successfully."[83]

---

[81] Letter from Fazlul Huq to Liaquat Ali Khan dated September 8, 1941. Zaidi (1976: 614–615).

[82] Rashid (1987: 137).

[83] Private letter from Linlithgow to Amery, July 11, 1942. Formation of a New Government, part 2, "Bengal Political Situation in Formation of New Government." L/P&J/5/548, IOL.

Jinnah's centralization of power within the League left it with minimal organizational infrastructure as late as 1943. This changed when
a group of young Dacca students, led by the socialist-influenced Abul
Hashim, effectively won control of the provincial Muslim League organization and ousted the Dacca landlords who had heretofore dominated
it. Hashim understood that Pakistan "was not a communal demand but a
political objective" and that party leaders who popularized Pakistan had
"no idea of what Pakistan concretely stands for" while for non-Muslims,
"Pakistan stands for the pogrom of all those who are outside the Muslim
pale."[84] By 1945, these younger leaders pushed the League toward a more
strongly anti-landlord stance, a political position which the devastating
1943 Bengal Famine helped to popularize.

After 1943, the Bengali Muslim League for the first time began to
represent a genuine grassroots movement. The League successfully
recruited and organized support in rural areas, pulling in many local leaders of peasant movements that had sprung up in the 1930s. Membership
fees were lowered to two annas, annual elections were instituted, and the
provincial Bengal League Working Committee met regularly, even frequently in some years. By the time of the 1946 elections, the Muslim
League had enrolled over a million members.[85] Before independence, then,
the Bengal Provinical Muslim League stood alone among the provincial
Muslim League organizations in having developed a grassroots organization. Yet the provincial Muslim League organization in Bengal was
disconnected from the Muslim League leadership at an all-India level,
which it will be remembered was monopolized by a leader who brooked
no dissent. A relatively robust party infrastructure that was built *within*
the Bengal Muslim League during the mid 1940s thus had to contend
with very different economic and political interests represented within
the national parent organization.

Any powerful provincial leaders who threatened Jinnah's authoritative
writ were consistently marginalized within the party before independence.
Neither of the two most important Muslim leaders in the most populous Muslim province were appointed to the all-India Muslim League
Working Committee. Instead, Jinnah appointed yes-men, such as Ispahani
and Nazimuddin, who were loyal but unrepresentative of Bengali sentiment. For example, while the socialist-leaning Hashim–Suhrawardy

---

[84] Annual Report of the Bengal Provincial Muslim League, 1944, as cited in Rashid (1987:
    176).
[85] Hashim (1974: 172).

faction clearly controlled the Bengali arm of the party, nominations to the Central Parliamentary Board in 1945 included nominees only from the Nazimuddin faction, typically landed aristocrats. Jinnah urged these factions to unite and abide by this decision, since unity above all was needed to achieve Pakistan. These intra-organizational differences were thus papered over long enough to win the 1946 elections and to legitimate the demand for Pakistan, but there was no working out of shared political principles, much less specific programmatic goals. Once Pakistan was created and the League was charged with the task of running an independent state, a call for Muslim unity no longer sufficed to resolve such disputes.

The last pre-independence provincial elections were fought and won on the one demand for a sovereign state of Pakistan. Jinnah called the creation of Pakistan the only issue for the Muslim League while never specifying exactly what Pakistan stood *for*. Actually defining Pakistan in concrete terms could have fractured the fragile Muslim unity which was so important to legitimizing the League as an equal claimant in power-sharing arrangements at the center. The Lahore Resolution of 1940, which first introduced the concept of Pakistan as a League goal, called for fully independent "states" rather than "state," which left it possible for Bengali leaders to imagine that they would have their own independent state within a united India.[86] In fact, the two most popular leaders of the League in Bengal – Hashim and Suhrawardy – envisioned that the creation of Pakistan entailed an independent Bengal. As soon as a partition of Bengal was seen as a likely outcome of the demand for Pakistan, the Bengal Muslim League leadership made a desperate bid for a united state of Bengal independently of Pakistan, evidencing how little commitment there was to Pakistan per se. But at that late hour, without the support of the central Muslim League leadership, of Congress, or of the colonial regime, this was too little too late.

In the run-up to the 1946 elections as the concept of Pakistan was popularized, top League leaders deliberately avoided any discussion of "a cut and dried scheme for Pakistan" since doing so might "create dissensions in the Muslim camp."[87] Liaquat Ali Khan, the most prominent leader of the Muslim League after Jinnah, also regularly referred to Pakistan using the word "states" while Jinnah regularly refrained that there should be "no difficulty understanding Pakistan" without

[86] Pirzada (1969).
[87] AIML session at Delhi, April 24 to 26, 1943 in Mansergh (1982: Vol. III, 921–922) (hereafter *TP*).

elaborating further.[88] When called upon by the British or Congress to define Pakistan, Jinnah responded that Pakistan – and the League as its exclusive arbiter – should first be accepted in principle by both the Congress and the British, after which point its details would be worked out.[89] This strategic ambiguity was consciously cultivated by League leaders because it allowed different kinds of Muslims to imagine the Pakistan they wanted – whereas concretely defining what Pakistan meant would undermine the fragile Muslim unity Jinnah had worked so hard to create.[90] In other words, while the League stood *against* the Congress domination of constitutional negotiations at the all-India level on the basis that Congress represented Hindu rule, what the League stood *for* was never clear, even insofar as the basic form of the Pakistani state.

If Pakistan was so poorly defined, how did the League manage to win elections with it? The demand was popularized among the Bengali voters in the 1946 elections primarily because the concept of Pakistan was equated with economic betterment. As the newly organized League absorbed the remnants of the peasant movement, the League election manifesto in Bengal incorporated a number of socio-economic measures for the first time, e.g. rural electrification and intensive agricultural reforms, but it notably still did not promise *zamindari* abolition. The posters and placards which were sent out from the provincial Muslim League contained such slogans as "Land Belongs to the Plough," "Abolish Zamindari without Compensation," and "Pakistan for Peasants and Labourers."[91] When touring Bengal for the elections, a key League leader stated that Pakistan "will mean raising the standard of living for the poor, the oppressed, the neglected; more food, wealth, resources, work, better living conditions and more joy and happiness for the common."[92]

Even the Governor of Bengal at the time wrote that Pakistan, to most of the Muslims in the League, meant that they, rather than the Hindus, would own the stores.[93] Thus, the change in the social basis of its provincial leadership, the Bengal Pakistan Muslim League's revitalized organizational infrastructure, and especially the linking of Pakistan to economic betterment for Bengali Muslims was directly responsible for the League's

---

[88] Pirzada (1969: 423).
[89] Jinnah (1947: Vol. II, 359–360).
[90] See Governor Casey's discussion with Nazimuddin in Casey's *Personal Diary*, Eur 48/4, IOL and Jalal (1985: 119).
[91] Ahmed (1968: 248).
[92] Rashid (1987: 206).
[93] Casey, *Personal Diary*, Eur 48/4, pp. 320–322, IOL.

overwhelming victory in the 1946 provincial elections, which saw the Muslim League winning 115 of 123 Muslim seats. The League victory in Bengal validated its claim to representing the Muslim nation in colonial India and enabled the partition of Bengal into two halves, the eastern half becoming East Pakistan in 1947.

The pre-independence introduction of provincial elections, combined with the Muslim League's incentives to heighten religious sentiment for national political gain, effectively transformed substantively class-based conflicts in the eastern Bengali countryside into an overtly religious conflict. Between 1935 and 1943, myriad coalitions were created and dissolved, with no one political organization staying dominant. In 1943, the new leadership of the Bengal Muslim League mobilized and organized on a platform that was vaguely linked with Pakistan. While a substantial organization linking village and districts to the provincial Muslim League also emerged, this organization remained at odds with a national organization which was dominated by a single autocratic leader who did not brook dissent and who was not amenable to the creation of regularized party rules. The League's sweep of provincial elections in Bengal was politically interpreted as a clarion call for Pakistan. But the different social bases of the Muslim League, as well as the lack of an institutional or ideational means of reconciling those social bases, was to pose serious problems for a party which after August 1947 grappled with the task of governing an independent nation.

In sum, the sovereign state of Pakistan was created through the efforts of the Muslim League, which successfully positioned itself as the exclusive and authoritative spokesman of Muslim interests in British India. This goal was only achieved through alliances with the Punjabi and Bengali Muslims. As a key organizer of the Muslim League mused:

What would have happened if the Punjab and Bengal Premiers had not agreed to come to the rescue of the Muslim League organisation in the United Provinces? ... Briefly, it would have remained merely the Muslim League of the Minority provinces and in time to come would have had to surrender to the Congress. Sir Sikander [leader of the Unionist Party in Punjab] and Fazlul Huq [leader of the Krishak Praja Party in Bengal] saved Muslim India by throwing their full weight at the crucial hour behind the Muslim League.[94]

This goal of accessing power in constitutional negotiations was partially derived from class interests – since a Muslim League that was considered the guardian of Muslim interests would better enable UP Muslims

---

[94] Khaliquzzaman (1961: 171).

to strike an advantageous constitutional bargain. But under Jinnah's leadership, the Muslim League assumed organizational primacy of its own, serving mostly to augment Jinnah's personal power and not always in ways that represented the interest of those UP Muslims who had first empowered him. It is indeed supremely ironic, UP Muslims themselves were actually made worse off by the creation of Pakistan, since most of them remained behind in an India characterized by heightened religious tensions.

Overall, two classes with diametrically opposed economic interests united under the banner of the Muslim League in order to maximize their claim to power in national politics. Many Muslim League supporters were not necessarily interested in creating a fully sovereign state and support for the Muslim League and its ill-defined Pakistan was little more than a means of accessing power for disparate groups of Muslims. Most groups supporting the League did not develop an ideological commitment to the organization beyond this short-term interest in accessing power. Nor were such elites or groups well-institutionalized within an organizational infrastructure that was effectively capable of reconciling or aggregating their interests. After independence, when invoking Islam no longer served to unify such elites, the League was unable to draw on an ideological commitment or substantive political organization to effectively resolve elite conflict. Amid intensifying deadlock, the bureaucracy and eventually the military intervened to govern, setting Pakistan on a path of regime instability by 1958.

III. CONCLUSION

In the decades before their twin independences, the classes represented in both the Indian and the Pakistani independence movements mobilized mass support as a means of instrumentally advancing their interests. The kinds of coalitions which each movement built, however, varied markedly in distributive coherence and in organizational complexity. These had direct effects on India's and Pakistan's democratic divergence. The urban, educated middle class leading India's independence movement sought to advance its interest by winning provincial elections and by mobilizing for national sovereignty throughout the pre-independence decades. To do so, these leaders primarily allied with the rural middle class. Consequently, India's political party predominantly came to represent class groups interested in the redistribution of economic and political power away from the colonial regime and its collaborators, but also in maintaining the hierarchical patronage-based economic and political order over which it presided. India's dominant political party upon independence represented a *coherent* distributive coalition because the distributive interests of its core coalition partners were relatively aligned. After independence, this distributive coherence enabled the party to broker state-building and governing compromises with relative ease.

In contrast, the landed aristocrats founding Pakistan's independence movement mobilized a mass base in the two Muslim-majority provinces of Punjab and Bengal in order to stay politically powerful. The organized political groups in these two provinces shared no distributive interests, though they did share an interest in promoting Muslim power in national negotiations over colonial India's constitutional future. Pakistan's dominant political party thus came to represent landed aristocrats in northwestern British India who stood to lose by any sort of economic or power redistribution as well as peasants in northeastern British India who stood to gain significantly from such redistribution. This was a relatively *incoherent* distributive coalition because the distributive interests of its core coalition partners were nearly in diametric opposition to each other. After independence, this distributive incoherence frustrated the party's attempts to govern because its two core support bases found it difficult to forge compromises.

In their bid to forge and maintain these alliances, the leaders of India's independence party built a robust and internally democratic party organization, partly because the shared distributive interests of its coalition made it more possible to create consensus around policy platforms and partly because a demonstrably non-violent and egalitarian nationalism encouraged property-owners and landless peasants alike to join a broad anti-colonial movement. During the decades before independence, the Congress Party therefore developed into an internally differentiated, loosely integrated organization with several tiers of leadership that reflected local and regional interests and that had developed mechanisms for reconciling those interests. Upon independence, the fact that India was governed by a political party possessing this kind of party organization meant that it was far more able to address key state-building challenges, thereby brokering regime *stability*.

In contrast, the national leaders of Pakistan's independence party did not create a similarly robust institutional infrastructure. The leaders of Pakistan's dominant political party were less able to create a complex party organization primarily because doing so would have required working out power-sharing arrangements between organized groups with contradictory distributive interests. The League leadership thus eschewed the building of regional and local party organizations altogether, instead nominally merging regional parties under a single national banner. The fact that Pakistan's dominant political party did not possess a robust party organization which effectively aggregated local and regional interests within the national party meant that, upon independence, this party was far less capable of reconciling competing interests, directly driving regime stability.

5

Freedom at midnight and divergent democracies (1947–1958)

At the stroke of midnight on August 14 and 15, 1947, Pakistan and India respectively became fully sovereign members of the British Commonwealth. These newly independent countries came into existence with, relatively speaking, similar opportunities and challenges. Yet the democratic trajectories of each country, in terms of both regime *stability* and *type*, quickly assumed contrasting characters. This chapter shows how these divergent regime trajectories are primarily explained by the class compositions and strength of their dominant political parties, the differences established in the previous three chapters. Though this chapter focuses on the variation in the strength of the political party as the most proximate cause of the differential democratic trajectories in question, it also establishes that the institutional strength of the political party itself reflected, and was only enabled by, an underlying class logic.

In this chapter, as Figure 5.1 indicates, I trace the causal impact of party strength before independence on the establishment of regime type after independence. The creation of two institutions – the drafting of a constitution and the adoption of an elected chief executive in each state – illustrates how the existence of an ideationally valued and organizationally regularized political party, reflecting but not reducible to an analytically prior class logic, explains the variation in post-independence regime type and regime stability in India and Pakistan. In particular, this chapter makes two claims: *first*, I claim that the variation in each country's ability to adopt a working constitution (regime stability) was a reflection of the governing party's ability to effectively forge compromises while the democratic character of that constitution in India is primarily explained

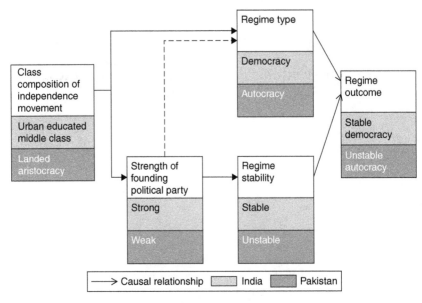

FIGURE 5.1. Argument of the chapter.

by the democratic practices already institutionalized within its dominant political party prior to independence. *Second,* I claim that the variation in the adoption of an elected chief executive, the *sine qua non* of any democratic regime, is explained by the variation in each independence party's organizational centralization.

This chapter proceeds in four sections. The first section briefly reviews the legacies of independence that directly bear on explaining the divergent regime trajectories of India and Pakistan. The second section examines how the newly created states grappled with the constitutional questions of federal power-sharing and national language, explaining the contrasting outcomes through two factors – the class composition of its independence coalition and the (organizational and ideational) strength of its dominant political party. The third section investigates the installation of a democratically elected chief executive in India and its absence in Pakistan, explaining this variation through the organizational prowess of its dominant political party. A brief fourth section concludes.

I. FREEDOM AND FRATRICIDE

On August 14 and 15, 1947, British India formally transferred the sovereignty of the British Crown over colonial India to two sovereign successor states, Pakistan and India respectively.[1] How did this come about? Unfavorable economic conditions facing post-war Britain and the growing influence of an American foreign policy promoting decolonization were important factors impelling Britain's decision to open genuine constitutional negotiations for independence with the primary political parties in colonial India, Congress and the Muslim League. But Congress' mass mobilizations in favor of independence – which had for decades consistently undermined British colonial rule in India by demonstrating its internal contradictions and moral illegitimacy – was probably the single most important factor in motivating the British to grant British India's independence at the conclusion of World War II. An inclination to move toward Indian independence, already apparent in 1944, was strengthened in July 1945 by the overwhelming victory of the opposition Labour Party in Britain. This victory brought to power politicians who were more amenable to the cause of Indian independence. In 1946, the Viceroy of India described the initiation of discussions aimed at transferring power of colonial India as necessitated by the desire to "avoid the mass movement which it is in the power of the Congress to start, and which we are not certain we can control."[2]

Once the British government had generally accepted the need to cede Indian sovereignty, it tried in vain during the post-war period to broker a settlement that would transfer power to a single, united Indian state.[3] After long promoting the Muslim League's demands as a way of thwarting Congress' demands for sovereignty however, a succession of British negotiators were unable to get Congress and the League to come to mutual agreement on a general framework for a united Indian government in the years preceding independence. Indeed, the British colonial government's recognition of the Muslim League as the organizational voice of Indian Muslims was itself a critical factor in preventing a united India from emerging.

---

[1] The colony of British India in its entirety included the modern-day states of India, Pakistan, and Bangladesh. At the time of independence in August 1947, however, British India was dissolved into two sovereign successor states, India and Pakistan. Pakistan itself was geographically discontiguous and comprised of West Pakistan (northwestern British India) and East Pakistan (northeastern British India, which subsequently became Bangladesh in 1971).

[2] Wavell (1973: 232), *TP*, Vol. VII, 151.

[3] The British attitude seemed to be weakly in favor of a united India, though a divided India with common defense and security arrangements would also be a satisfactory outcome. *TP*, Vol. VII, 197–198.

During the first constitutional conference over the transfer of power in 1945, for example, talks broke down because the leader of the Muslim League refused to participate in any conference which included Muslims who were not members of the Muslim League. Given the terribly weak position of the Muslim League at this point in time – the top Congress leadership included a few Muslims; Congress was in power in one Muslim-majority province as well as a large number of Hindu-majority provinces; and the League itself controlled neither crucial Muslim-majority province of Punjab or Bengal – this was a fantastic claim which could legitimately have been dismissed by the British as unreasonable. Instead, the conference was adjourned, effectively capitulating to the League's demands that it alone represent the Muslims of colonial India. Having affirmed the League's representational claims for decades and having encouraged the communalization of politics, the British colonial regime now found it difficult to reverse its pre-war policy and undercut the League's separatist claims.

During the first two sets of failed negotiations over the transfer of colonial power, disagreement between the independence parties of India and Pakistan centered on two issues which revealed their respective priorities at the time, the first of which was Muslim representation in the central legislature of a united and independent India. The Congress' position was that Muslim representational demands could be accommodated only *after* the British transferred sovereignty, since Congress claimed to represent the whole Indian nation on secular terms and did not recognize the right of the British colonial regime to broker questions of communal representation. The Muslim League, however, wanted the British to recognize it as the *only* legitimate representation of Muslim interests and to recognize the parity of the Congress and the League at the national level *before* any sovereignty was transferred. Once the British departed, League leaders understood that all guarantees of extra-proportional political representation for Muslims in a central legislature would by the definition of national sovereignty be subject to revision. While India's independence movement was proactively seeking political independence from Britain, thereby facing strong incentives to construct a political party that could wrest political sovereignty through extra-constitutional and constitutional mobilization, Pakistan's independence movement was primarily a defensive movement interested in retaining privileges that could only be guaranteed by the retention of the colonial regime. The core political goals of the respective movements, defined by their respective class goals, created varying incentives to engage in organizational and ideational party-building.

The second core area of disagreement was over the form of an independent federal government, as the Muslim League was still open to acceding to a united Indian state. Given the desire of the two key Muslim-majority provinces for maximum provincial autonomy within the framework of a united India, the leader of the Muslim League was beholden by his coalition of provincial support to lobby for a weak federal government, even though he himself almost certainly desired the creation of a strong central government with guaranteed extra-proportional Muslim representation. Congress leaders, who for their part wanted to implement a variety of social and economic reforms and who thus greatly preferred the creation of a strong federal government, were willing to tolerate a weak federal government only if this government controlled all of the territory of British colonial India.

Though these talks ultimately failed, it is worth stressing that a mere year before independence, the leaders of Pakistan's dominant political party embraced a plan which did *not* create a fully sovereign Pakistan and accepted provincial autonomy within the framework of a single, sovereign, and united India. Thus, while the Indian independence movement was preparing itself organizationally to assume the governance of a sovereign country in the lead-up to independence, the Pakistan independence movement was not making similar preparations, simply because the movement was not fully committed to national sovereignty as late as a year before independence.

The inability of the Muslim League and Congress to come to a mutually satisfactory agreement on the format of a shared independent state led to explosive communal violence which probably rendered inevitable, from the summer of 1946 onwards, the partition of colonial India into two rather than one sovereign successor states.[4] The last set of failed colonial negotiations in early 1946 over the format of independence took place against a backdrop of ever-greater religious tension as a result of the 1945–6 elections, in which League politicians in particular had benefited from the politicization of religious tensions. The League's sweeping success in the separate Muslim electorates of those elections was widely seen as legitimating the League's demands to represent Muslim India in constitutional negotiations, thus providing Jinnah, the Muslim League's leader, with much-needed bargaining power in all-India negotiations over the transfer of sovereign power. By the time the Cabinet Mission

[4] Jalal argues that it was still conceivable that Mountbatten could have finagled a joint settlement in 1947. See Jalal (1985: 247–250).

came to India during the spring of 1946 to engage in such negotiations, these religious tensions were not wholly, if they ever were, controlled by the League or Congress. The cost of politicizing religious identities to win elections before independence was that the fragile veneer of social order superimposed by colonial rule was increasingly threatened by religiously motivated violence.[5]

These next set of negotiations deadlocked over the same issues as in 1945, namely, the degree of Muslim representation in the central legislature and the extent of powers to be apportioned to a federal government. The failure of the Mission talks and the growing threat of communal and labor violence led the British colonial government to invite Congress to form an interim government at the center on August 6, 1946 in the hopes that doing so would get Congress to "realise that firm control of unruly elements is necessary" and to bring in the League at a later point in time.[6] Jinnah's reaction to being cut out of power altogether was to call on all Indian Muslims to engage in a day of mass demonstrations, a day he termed Direct Action Day, on August 16. The result of Direct Action Day was a large-scale outburst of rioting across colonial India, in which an estimated 4,400 were killed, 16,000 injured, and 100,000 made homeless in the city of Calcutta alone.[7] This horrific communal violence, which spread to many parts of colonial India to varying degrees during the fall of 1946, and the inability of the Congress and the League to effectively work together led both the British government and Congress to effectively accept the principle of a partition of colonial India into two successor states. Consequently the British set a firm June 1948 deadline for the transfer of sovereign power.

Though Partition was now accepted as the operative solution to League–Congress differences, disagreement still abounded over the precise format of the successor states. The Muslim League had consistently argued for a Pakistan which included *all* of the territory of the two crucial Muslim-majority provinces, Punjab and Bengal. But both the British colonial government and Congress responded that those Muslim-majority provinces should be divided into Hindu-majority and Muslim-majority regions with the right to join either state on the very same principle of self-determination that the League used to argue for the division of India into two sovereign states. Since both the provinces of Punjab and Bengal

---

[5] *TP*, Vol. vii, 150–161 and AICC File G26/1946, NMML.
[6] *TP*, Vol. viii, 154.
[7] *TP*, Vol. viii, 323.

possessed large Hindu minorities, including substantial contiguous areas where Hindus were in the majority, the applicability of this argument could not be denied. Jinnah, who preferred to keep the League in power within the framework of a united India, vehemently opposed the partition of these provinces. Jinnah's preference for a united Bengal and Punjab to join Pakistan was overridden in the June 3 plan for the partition of India, the eventual basis for independence.

By the formal act of independence, each of the provincial assemblies in Muslim-majority provinces as well as the nominally independent princely states chose to accede to either the dominion of Pakistan or the dominion of India. The Hindu members of the Punjabi and Bengali (the two Muslim-majority provinces with substantial Hindu populations) provincial assemblies were given the right to meet separately and vote for accession to India. The provincial assemblies split along religious lines, with the Hindu-majority eastern Punjab and western Bengal both joining the sovereign state of India while the Muslim-majority western Punjab and eastern Bengal both cleaved off to join the new sovereign state of Pakistan. The Pakistan which emerged from this plan was, in the words of Jinnah, a "mutilated" and "moth-eaten" shadow of the state that the Muslim League had initially intended to create, to the extent that it had intended to create a separate state at all.

Pakistan and India legally became fully sovereign, independent states by the Indian Independence Act on August 14 and August 15, 1947, respectively. The twin births of these two new states from the erstwhile fabric of colonial India was celebrated in jarring contrasts – on the one hand with speeches and parades rejoicing in a hard-won independence struggle and, on the other hand, with immense communal bloodshed as Hindus, Muslims, and Sikhs living on the "wrong" side of the border migrated to states were they would be in the majority. Given the decision of its provincial assemblies to partition Bengal and Punjab, the precise territorial boundaries of India and Pakistan were not clear at independence and the boundary awards were only made on August 17.[8]

Moreover, the process of cleaving one colonial state into two independent states was a complex and fraught process, involving the challenges of dividing the colonial Indian army and bureaucracy as well as integrating over 500 nominally independent princely states that had heretofore

---

[8] The Punjab and Bengal Boundary Commission, both headed by Sir Cyril Radcliffe, had sat through July and August 1947, announcing its decisions on August 17. Chatterji (1999) and Jeffrey (1974).

operated independently within the framework of British colonial rule.[9] The Indian Independence Act charged the Constituent Assemblies of India and Pakistan, in turn elected by the provincial assemblies, with the tasks of drawing up the constitutions governing the two new states, both of which were formally committed by the Act to becoming parliamentary democracies. How precisely this was to be done was left to those sovereign Constituent Assemblies, both of which were overwhelmingly dominated by their respective independence parties.

II. POWER-SHARING AND LANGUAGE CONFLICTS IN FEDERAL CONSTITUTIONS

The creation of respected rules for sharing power between social groups and the elites who represent them, often within a constitution, is a hallmark of a *stable* regime. The task of writing each constitution, which laid out how power was to be formally shared and transferred, was itself an important reflection of how the respective national political parties were able to reconcile elite conflicts (where they did, providing for regime stability) and into whether such resolution was achieved in a representative fashion (where it was, providing for democracy). This section thus describes how constitutions were adopted in each sovereign state after independence, with particular attention to the resolution of each state's most difficult political issues. I posit that the variation in the core class coalition for independence and the strength of the governing political party – defined by coherent class interests but also by a shared ideational commitment to the party and regularized party rules – most directly caused the variation in the resolution of constitutional conflicts over power-sharing between the federal state and its sub-national units in India and Pakistan. In each country however, a national "interest" and a party "interest" could only be created when groups of elites with similar distributive interests had already come together and created an institution capable of articulating these interests.

Indian constitution-making by consensus and accommodation

Upon independence, India's relatively speedy adoption of a democratic constitution is primarily explained by the organizational development of and ideational commitment to India's dominant political party, the

[9] Menon (1956).

Indian National Congress. In the decades prior to independence, urban, educated, middle-class elites had created a centralized party organization operating on the basis of meritocratic internal elections that effectively created political power by aggregating yet still subordinating individual preferences.

Congress was the predominant organizing force within the Indian Constituent Assembly. Individuals elected on the Congress ticket formed over three-quarters of the 300 plus members of the Constituent Assembly. The Assembly's representatives also included 14 of the 18 members of the Congress Working Committee – the highest echelon of Congress leadership – and many senior Congressmen whose careers had been defined by party service, e.g. six past or present Congress Presidents and 14 Provincial Congress Committee Presidents. The most venerated and experienced leaders of India's dominant political party were exceedingly active in the Constituent Assembly, particularly Jawaharlal Nehru and Vallabhbhai Patel. By and large, members of the Constituent Assembly were men, and several women, who had risen up through the party ranks and who had been involved with the independence movement for decades. In other words, India's constitution-making process was dominated by the leading lights of its dominant political party, individuals who in turn had closely identified the advancement of their political interests with the success of the Congress Party. Evidencing its organizational prowess was the Congress Assembly Party, which the Congress Party had set up for the purposes of constitution-making. Before independence, even before the precise structural contours of the sovereign successor state were known, this Congress Assembly Party was at work debating and drafting constitutional provisions.

While the overwhelming dominance of a few leaders might well have spurred on the autocratic imposition of leadership decisions, Congress leaders instead went to great lengths to seek the representation and buy-in of different social groups in India, even groups that were not Congress constituents. When elections to the Constituent Assembly occurred in July 1946, the leaders of the Congress Party – generally those in the Congress Working Committee – took particular care to broaden minority representation in the Constituent Assembly beyond just Muslims and Sikhs, to include Parsis, Anglo-Indians, Indian Christians, members of Scheduled Castes and Tribes, and women. While Provincial Congress Committees were generally free to select their own representatives to the Assembly, Congress leaders did send circulars to the Provincial Congress Committees, either about the needed demographics of that province's

Assembly representatives, or in some cases, directing the PCCs to include prominent individuals. In 1939, Jawaharlal Nehru had written: "The Congress has within its fold many groups, widely differing in their viewpoints and ideologies. This is natural and evitable if Congress is to be the mirror of the nation."[10] At a time when Congress stood at the apex of its institutional legitimacy and when its leaders enjoyed a virtual monopoly within the constitution-making body, its leaders might readily have steamrolled opposition, as was done in other post-colonial democracies with a dominant political party. Congress instead sought to engage opposing political perspectives in the forging of an Indian constitution simply because it was how Congress had organized support and functioned before independence, when maintaining Congress' unity necessitated active efforts to co-opt political competitors.

The active choice of Congress leaders to broaden the Constituent Assembly's membership at a time when its immediate strategic position did not require it to do so reflected a party that was substantively democratic in nature. These democratic processes were forged over the pre-independence decades by an urban, educated middle class needing to co-opt opposition to sustain a prolonged, successful anti-colonial movement. Progressively, however, as the party institution itself developed and became more complex, decisions were increasingly defined by the party rather than short-term class interests, sometimes even when class interests pulled in the opposite direction.

The fact that Congress had institutionalized a commitment to a defining element of democracy – elections based on universal adult suffrage – explained its subsequent decision to formalize universal adult franchise within the Indian constitution. The 1928 (Motilal) Nehru Report was the first official document to suggest universal adult suffrage as Congress policy and its primary author admitted that adult suffrage was initially a facile way of dealing with the different claims of religious communities to political representation.[11] Universal suffrage, which Gandhi lobbied for at the Round Table Conferences between 1930 and 1932, was definitively mainstreamed as Congress policy after the 1932 Poona Pact. At the moment of independence however, most of the top leaders of Congress represented in the Constituent Assembly were drawn from upper caste and middle class backgrounds. These leaders might have sought to limit adult suffrage in some way, as there was no longer an immediate need

[10] Nehru (1941b: 139).
[11] Nehru Report of 1928: 92–93, NMML.

to mobilize subordinate social groups. Yet Congress elites had been able to mobilize political support through this commitment to adult franchise. Retrenching on its decades-long promise of universal franchise by instituting property or literacy qualifications would have certainly alienated some of its support base. Moreover, Congress' civil disobedience campaigns had effectively demonstrated the party's ability to control the nature, form, and extent of mobilization by activating the hierarchical patronage networks over which dominant peasants provided. Overall then, universal franchise did not appear to threaten Congress' political success at the same time that opposition to it would have cost the party political support.

Consequently, while the Congress-dominated Constituent Assembly did debate the form that universal suffrage would take, namely as to whether the individual or the village council (in the form of the traditional village ruling body, the *panchayat*) should form the basic electoral unit, there was no real debate about whether universal suffrage should form the basis for the electorate. Some prominent leaders of the Constituent Assembly, such as the Deputy Speaker, stated that he had "doubts as to whether universal suffrage would work in this country. Left to myself, I would have preferred that the village ought to have been made the unit [of suffrage]."[12] This kind of a system, where local village councils served as a sort of electoral college, would have been more institutionally conservative than universal suffrage, as it would have required the votes of individuals within an Indian village to be mediated by village elders who typically represented traditional upper castes. But Congress leaders rejected indirect elections and wrote universal adult suffrage into the constitution at a time when their narrow class interests did not compel them to do so – reflecting the workings of an institutional rather than a purely class logic.

Narrowly defined class interests alone cannot be said to explain Congress leaders' adoption of a liberal democratic order, since no more than several thousand, socially prominent Indians had directly participated in representative government. Introducing property or educational requirements for the franchise, however, would have come at a cost, both in terms of losing some of the support that such elites had effectively mobilized in the lead-up to independence and in terms of contradicting the egalitarian ideational foundations of Indian nationalism that had for decades served as the stated goal of the independence movement. At the

[12] M.A. Ayyangar, CAD (India), Vol. XI, 663.

same time, since core distributive conflicts had been successfully managed before independence, retrenching on the promise of universal adult franchise provided little tangible benefit. That universal franchise was ultimately implemented was thus reflective of the fact that the party as an institution rather than class interests directly shaped the decisions of Congress Party leaders. The *content* of Congress' institutionalized commitments before independence thus promoted the adoption of defining democratic institutions after independence.

A constitution governing a large, variegated electorate was also adopted in a relatively short time in India because the constitution-making process was largely governed by party procedures that were honed prior to independence but that continued to govern decision-making after independence. In their three years of constitutional deliberations between 1947 and 1949, the Congress-led Constituent Assembly leadership generally made decisions by first seeking consensus within itself and subsequently seeking to bring the rank and file into line through persuasion. Congress leaders reached decisions on controversial constitutional issues not just through a bare majority of votes but through consensus when possible or through votes of supermajorities. When Congress leaders disagreed, this disagreement was notably resolved not by undermining or eliminating party opposition, but through extensive debate, appeals to patriotism, and ultimately, party discipline. And finally, where Congress leaders agreed upon constitutional issues but were opposed by important sections of public opinion, as in the case of the creation of linguistic states, top Congress leaders were responsive to demands from below and eventually relented to public opinion. Regularized party procedures and a commitment to creating broad consensus – organizational and ideational features of the party which were created to pursue class interests in the pre-independence period – critically explained the speedy adoption of a stable and a democratic constitution within a few years of India's independence.

The robust intra-party organization of Congress was evidenced in an additional number of ways. Even though Congress' leader, Jawaharlal Nehru, had a special leadership position, having long ago been anointed by Gandhi as his successor, the Congress "high command" included men of considerable stature who could and did challenge Nehru on numerous issues, including Vallabhbhai Patel, Rajendra Prasad, K.M. Munshi, and A.K. Ayyar. Unlike Pakistan's Muslim League, the internal structure of India's independence party was somewhat democratic, meaning that most party leaders could be and were overruled by groups of other

Congress leaders. When party chiefs disagreed, such as they did over the extent and manner in which large landlords were to be compensated in the course of *zamindari* abolition, the ensuing debate was often heated and lengthy. But ultimately, these leaders agreed to compromise. Finally, though leadership was in fact crucial in making constitutional decisions, it bears emphasizing that this leadership was created via the party in the decades before independence, both because such individuals had risen up through party ranks and because many of these leaders had demonstrated nationalist commitment by substantial personal sacrifice, including loss of private property and incarceration.

The ability to debate matters within the Congress-created Assembly Party – an organization created by the Congress Party leadership to enable Congressmen to freely debate constitutional matters off-record before they were formally brought to the floor of Constituent Assembly and made part of the public record – was another example of the importance of party organization in managing conflict. By creating such organizations, the Congress Party functioned as the ultimate instrument of consensus and accommodation. To be sure, debate over constitutional matters frequently assumed frank and sometimes acrimonious form. But the leadership of the Constituent Assembly sought regularly to emphasize, throughout the framing of its constitution, the importance of persuasion. Congress leaders pursued two overarching goals in the creation of a constitution, "one [was] the urgent necessity in reaching our goal [of promulgating a constitution] and the other, that we should reach it in the proper time, *with as great a respect for unanimity as possible*" [emphasis added].[13]

If debate did not serve to produce consensus among the party rank and file, party leadership often intervened, with Nehru or Patel being regularly called on to address the Constituent Assembly on important matters. Patel was known to "hold court" with Assembly members in sunrise walks in Delhi's Lodi Gardens.[14] When disagreements over constitutional provisions occurred, either within the leadership or within party rank and file, notably democratic procedures – persuasion, accommodation, consensus, and ultimately, submission to party vote – were used to create compromise. Moreover, though Congress leaders wished a constitution would be speedily adopted, they also prioritized consensus over speed. As such, the first Prime Minister stated to the Assembly just prior

[13] Jawaharlal Nehru, January 22, 1947, CAD (India), Vol. II, 319.
[14] Austin (1972: 314–315).

to the adoption of the Aims and Objects Resolution, the first resolution passed by the House:

I should like the House to consider that we are on the eve of revolutionary changes, revolutionary in every sense of the word ... Therefore, let us not trouble ourselves too much about the petty details of what we do, those details will not survive for long, if they are achieved in conflict. *What we achieve in unanimity, what we achieve by cooperation is likely to survive. What we gain here and there by conflict and by overbearing manners and by threats will not survive for long.* [Emphasis added.][15]

Contentious issues – such as the expropriation of private property or the recognition of linguistic states – were deliberately left until the end of the Constituent Assembly's work at the behest of its key leaders, allowing for most of the constitution to assume shape before the most difficult issues were tackled. The Congress President (and not the Prime Minister as in Pakistan) presided over the Assembly, preserving the official dominion of the party (rather than the governing executive) over the constitution-making process, meaning that the Assembly was insulated to some extent from being used as a means to pursue specific Congress policy goals. And as a last resort, Congress did have an Assembly Whip, which occasionally worked to keep party members in line with the majority of the party. All this is evidence of the decision-making effectiveness of the Congress Party, an effectiveness which was initially forged during the pre-independence struggle when an urban, educated, middle-class elite created the party as a means of gaining political power.

The resolution of the most contentious constitution-making issues – federal power-sharing and the creation of linguistic states – illustrates how Congress' organizational discipline and shared ideational vision was responsible for the brokering of compromise and the ultimate creation of a constitution. On the question of federal power-sharing between provinces and center, Congress was able to speedily broker compromises on center–state relations with a minimum of disagreement, both because Congressmen had long adhered to a shared programmatic platform which necessitated a strong central government and because of the party's organizational discipline, in which party members abided by decisions with which they themselves did not agree.

Despite debate between those advocating the constitutional centralization of power – the "centralizers" – and those advocating greater

[15] J. Nehru, January 22, 1947, CAD (India), Vol. II, 323.

devolution of power – the "provincialists," Congressmen ultimately came to an agreement on the need for a strong central government because the implementation of Congress' programmatic goals necessitated a strong central government. Well prior to independence, Congress leaders had agreed on the need for a federal constitution which would give expression to the diversity of India's social and economic structures. In 1936, Nehru had stated that it was "likely that free India may be a Federal India, though in any event there must be a great deal of unitary control."[16] The more exact specifications of federalism within constitution, meaning the specific distribution of powers among constituent states and the federal center, were worked out shortly after independence, between the spring of 1947 and the fall of 1949 within the Union Powers Committee, chaired by Prime Minister Jawaharlal Nehru.

There was debate between provincial Congress leaders, who sought constitutional powers for the provinces, and the national Congress leaders, who were keen to allocate more power to the central government. Many of the individuals elected to the Assembly had already governed in provincial governments between 1937 and 1939, naturally leading them to clamor for provincial autonomy. Since top-level Congress leaders stood at the apex of that organization, they correspondingly favored greater centralization of powers for the federal government, as it would effectively arm them with greater powers. Compromise between these camps involved lengthy debate over what powers should be allocated to central versus provincial governments. Top-level Congress leaders eventually won over "provincialist" opposition, reflecting the former's 30-plus years of experience in leading a coordinated national movement.

The ideational goals of Indian nationalism – particularly goals of social and economic betterment – moved the federalism debate in the direction of a strong central government. When the Drafting Committee considered the specific powers accorded to the federal government, Congress centralizers won over the provincialists by appealing to socialist ideals of the independence movement.[17] India's foremost constitutional historian in fact states that "the most singular aspect" of India's Constituent Assembly debates over federalist provisions is the relative *absence* of a deep cleavage between centralizers and provincialists when contrasted starkly with the debates over the creation of the federalist provisions in the American constitution for example. This was because there was a

---

[16] J. Nehru, *Indian Annual Register*, 1936, Vol. II, 226.
[17] Objectives Resolution. CAD (India), Vol. I, 5.

general agreement that only a relatively empowered central state would be able implement the development agenda that had for decades been the stated goal of the Indian independence movement.

As detailed above, Congress leaders had for decades advocated social uplift and created organizations to advance these goals. Even relatively conservative Congress members such as Vallabhbhai Patel had famously led an anti-colonial agitation that sought to grant greater revenue rights to upwardly mobile peasant communities. Congress leaders had for decades agitated for social betterment and now felt that many of these goals could only be achieved through a strong central government. The creation of a centralized constitution, which legitimated national leadership at the expense of local and provincial leaders, was justified in party by "a solemn promise to the people of India that the legislature will do everything possible to renovate and rebuild society on new principles."[18] India's influential constitutional advisor wrote at the time that raising the Indian living standard would probably require a strong central government.[19] Appeal to the ideational content of Indian nationalism, content defined during the pre-independence period, thus helped to create consensus on the need for a strong federal government.

All this does not mean that provincialists did not protest against the federal government's centralization of powers, as seen in the debate over the proposed Article 226, which allowed the federal government to temporarily take over provincial governments with a two-thirds majority in the Council of States. But despite real debate and vocal opposition, debate proceeded along rational lines, with Congress provincial representatives eventually acquiescing to arguments made by the centralizers for the need for expanded powers and passing Article 225 into the Constitution with a one-year sunset clause.[20] The provincialists eventually assented to the centralists, even though the former possessed different immediate political interests on this issue, because as Congressmen, they all shared the goal of Congress success in constitution-making and a Congress identity based on clear programmatic commitments. These combined to explain the relatively facile adoption of a federal constitution specifying a reasonably strong central (albeit federal) government.

Beyond the party's programmatic goals, historical events accompanying Partition created further pressure for the creation of a strong central

---

[18] Panniker (1961: 63–64).
[19] Rau (1960: 313–315).
[20] Austin (1972: 200–203).

government because the dissolution of the state had underscored the fissiparous tendencies inherent within the Indian state. Provincial governments before independence had intensified the communal killings during Partition which killed hundreds of thousands of people. The horror of this communal bloodshed was used by the centralists to undermine provincial claims to power. It is thus perhaps no surprise that a joint session of the Union and Provincial Constitution Committees, meeting just after Partition, decided that a federal constitution entrusting strong residuary powers within the central government should be created. While resistance to a strong federal government did exist, the fact of Partition gave Congress leaders an additional excuse, beyond fulfilling the social and economic goals of the Congress platform, to create a strong central government.

Whereas compromises over the federal provisions of India's constitution were resolved with a relative minimum of contention, the single most difficult issue in India's constitution-making was the question of reorganizing administrative units around India's regional languages. As was true for Pakistan, the recognition of regional languages proved to not only be a highly emotive issue, but one which was associated with regional and ethnic domination, which determined provincial education policies, and which practically determined access to the resources and status associated with employment in the government civil services. Moreover, the Congress Party had long acknowledged the right of linguistic provinces to formal recognition. The legitimacy of linguistic provinces had been indirectly accepted by Congress as early as 1905 when Congress supported the annulment of the partition of Bengal, had been definitively embraced in 1920 when Congress reorganized itself by linguistic units, and had been reiterated on several prominent occasions before independence, including in Congress' election manifesto of 1945–6. Congress' long-stated policy thus clearly affirmed a right to linguistic self-determination.

After independence, however, when the unity of the Indian state was deeply in question, Congress leaders reneged on their oft-repeated commitment to linguistic self-determination because they feared India's centrifugal tendencies. Given the recent secession of two regions from India and several princely states that were asserting their right to independence, the central Indian state in the immediate post-independence environment was perceived as intensely fragile. It was for this reason that Congress' top leaders – Nehru, Patel, Prasad, and Rajagopalachari – all uniformly and consistently sought to reverse Congress' well-established   position on the creation of linguistic provinces. Any legislation which encouraged the recognition of difference, they felt, would give fillip to those separatist tendencies which had fed the fires of Pakistan. In 1948, the Constituent Assembly appointed a committee of jurists and civil servants to look into the linguistic reorganization of states. The Dar Commission, as it became known, unsurprisingly concluded that the linguistic re-formulation of provinces should be delayed because of the need for a "deeper [national] unity" and that the "formation of provinces on exclusively or even mainly linguistic considerations is not in the larger interests of the Indian nation."[21]

When the report failed to mollify the advocates of linguistic reorganization, Congress leaders used the familiar and institutionalized tactics of delay and co-optation to eventually seek accommodation with political forces from below. To mollify public sentiment, another committee – this time known as the JVP committee – was formed to further investigate the issue, which included Congress' two most powerful leaders as well as, notably, the foremost proponent of linguistic reorganization, Pattabhi Sitaramayya. The April 1949 JVP report, which was published as the Constituent Assembly's debates were drawing to a close, recognized that Congress had "given its seal of approval to the general principle of linguistic provinces" but that it was nonetheless "incumbent upon us therefore to view the problem of linguistic provinces in the context of today. That context demands, above everything, the consolidation of India and her freedom ... [and] demands further stern discouragement of communalism, provincialism, and all other separatist and disruptive tendencies." This report concluded that "We would prefer to postpone the formation of new provinces for a few years so that we might concentrate during this period on matters of vital importance and not allow ourselves to be distracted by this question." Nevertheless, the report left a window open for future accommodation: "However, *if public sentiment is insistent and overwhelming, we, as democrats, have to submit to it*" [emphasis added].[22] Though the debate over linguistic provinces, which was constantly referenced in the Constituent Assembly, was not settled in the process of constitution-making, the debate did lead the Assembly to include an article which allowed for the Parliament to alter provincial boundaries with the consent of the involved provinces.

[21] Report of the Linguistic Provinces Commission, December 1948, Paragraphs 141 and 152. Central Secretariat Library, New Delhi.
[22] JVP report (for the three members of the committee, Jawaharlal Nehru, Vallabhbhai Patel, and Pattabhi Sitaramayya), pp. 2, 4, 5, 15. Central Secretariat Library, 1949, New Delhi.

Though strongly opposed to the creation of linguistic provinces, the most powerful leaders of Congress sought to co-opt rather than repress their political opponents. Ultimately, rather than quashing the demands of their political opponents through the imposition of martial law, as was done in Pakistan, they ultimately reaffirmed the basic democratic principle of submitting to demands from below. In 1948, the leaders of India's independence movement perceived India to be an infant state which had already experienced secession and whose integral unity was open to question. In 1948, then, the demand for linguistic states appeared deeply threatening. By 1953, however, the national political situation appeared considerably different. The secession of key states had been averted, the princely states had been successfully absorbed into the Union of India, a constitution proclaiming a relatively strong central state been ratified, national elections had revealed Congress' dominance, and the colonial institutions of the military and bureaucracy had been effectively subordinated to Congress rule. Even by the early 1950s, then, the unity of the Indian state was no longer in question.

It was from this position of relative strength that Congress leaders, and Prime Minister Nehru in particular, acceded to sub-national demands for the creation of linguistic states. Nehru was now in possession of far greater political power than he was in 1948 and he could more easily afford to compromise. When a former Gandhi associate, Potti Sriramulu, died while fasting for the creation of a separate state of Telegu speakers, the ensuing political unrest led the Congress Prime Minister to accede to the demand for an Andhra state. The accommodation of other linguistic groups quickly followed suit through the appointment of a States' Reorganization Commission (SRC; notably composed of non-Congressmen) in 1954 to make general recommendations. The Congress-dominated government accepted the SRC recommendations in 1956 and organized a variety of new states along linguistic lines. By the mid 1950s, the Congress Party simply possessed more political power and thus felt more willing to compromise with democratic demands.

The role of the dominant political party as a vehicle for regime stability could be seen in multiple realms during India's constitution-making process. The Congress Party was able to effectively set up organizations, such as the Constituent Assembly Party, which co-opted opposition and sought consensus. While the constitution-making process in India was certainly characterized by disagreement, it did not lack a coherent party institution and multiple tiers of leadership that could effectively

broker compromises to overcome such disagreement. The existence of
the Congress Party enabled India to quickly adopt a stable constitution
enshrining constituent elements of democracy such as universal adult
franchise.

Despite the fact that Congress functioned independently of class interests in the post-independence period, however, it is crucial to remember
that the supremacy of India's dominant political party was initially built
on, and therefore fundamentally enabled by, the foundation of a coherent
distributive coalition. That the Congress Party still reflected the interests
of a particular alliance of classes is most clearly in evidence in the constitutional debate over the abolition of large landowning estates, or *zamind-
aris*. The most notable feature of the Constituent Assembly debates on
zamindari abolition is that there was unanimous support among Congress
leaders for the general proposition that the large *zamindari* landholdings
be abolished. The debate in the Constituent Assembly was in no way
about *whether zamindari* tenures should be abolished, but rather, over
whether there should be any compensation for their abolition, the definition of such compensation, and whether compensation should ultimately
be justiciable. That there was no debate over whether *zamindari* abolition should be pursued was unambiguous evidence that large landowners
did not form part of the core Congress support base.[23] The Congress-led
constitutional resolution over the abolition of *zamindari* tenures is clear
evidence that Congress was simultaneously a conservative and a revolutionary movement. The movement was revolutionary in the sense that it
did not represent the distributive interests of large landowners who sat
at the apex of India's rural social structure but was conservative in that
it did also not genuinely represent the interests of India's lower classes.
The Congress coalition most clearly represented upwardly mobile middle
classes, urban and rural alike.

---

[23] Dr. Ambedkar later wrote of the debate over property expropriation in the Constituent
Assembly, "The Congress Party, at the time that Article 31 was being framed was so
divided within itself that we did not know what to do, what to put and what not to
put. There were three sections in the Congress Party. One section was led by Sardar
Vallabhbhai Patel, who stood for full compensation ... Our Prime Minister was against
compensation ... Our friend Mr. Pant [Chief Minister of the United Provinces, which
later became Uttar Pradesh] wanted a safe delivery for his baby [the UP Zamindari
Abolition Bill] ... So he had his own proposition. There was thus a tripartite struggle and
we left the matter to them to decide in any way they liked." Parliamentary Debates, Rajya
Sabha, Official Report, Vol. IX, No. 19, March 19, 1955, Columns 2450–2452. Note that
there was no debate over *whether* zamindari abolition was to occur, but only over *how
much compensation* was to be paid.

To restate in summarized form, it was the Congress Party, and more specifically its class composition, its organizational coherence, and its shared ideological vision, which enabled India to quickly broker constitutional compromises along democratic lines. Summing up his thoughts on India's draft constitution, the Chairman of the Drafting Committee (notably himself *not* a Congressman) stated:

> The task of the Drafting Committee [of the Indian Constituent Assembly] would have been a very difficult one if this Constituent Assembly had been merely a motley crowd, a tessellated pavement without cement, a black stone here and a white stone there in which each member or each group was a law unto itself. There would have been nothing but chaos. This possibility of chaos was reduced to nil by the existence of the Congress Party inside the Assembly which brought into its proceedings a sense of order and discipline.[24]

Though the debates in the Constituent Assembly were hardly characterized by unanimity, Congress' procedural discipline, its commitment to a shared programmatic platform, and less visibly but no less crucially, its underlying class basis of support, all crucially facilitated democratic compromises on the same issues upon which Pakistan's constitution-making process foundered.

Musical chair politics in Pakistan

The core challenges facing Pakistan's First Constituent Assembly during its existence (1947–54) were how to apportion power between the central and provincial governments and between the two geographically separate wings of the country – power-sharing dilemmas that a weak governing party was not able to solve. These problems were created by the demographic contours of the new state: a popular majority – 55 percent of the population – resided in East Pakistan while a large minority lived in West Pakistan, primarily concentrated in the province of the Punjab.

A popular majority of the country (in Bengal) desired the creation of a constitution which reflected its proportionate share of power, but the landlords of the Punjab (and to a lesser extent, Sindh) were not inclined to relinquish power and submit to a parliament which they could not control. The leaders of Pakistan's governing political party, the Muslim League, were unable to discipline the provincial leaders in either province,

---

[24] Ambedkar speech on draft Constitution, November 25, 1949, CAD (India), Vol. XI, 972–981.

an immediate consequence of the way the League created and organized provincial support in the lead up to independence, namely by wholly reinforcing the social and economic power of the rural landed aristocracy in West Pakistan and by allying with a redistributive peasant movement in East Pakistan. Upon independence, when the Punjabi rural landed aristocracy no longer possessed clear interests in supporting the governing political party, it easily undermined both the centralizing imperatives of the central government and the democratizing imperatives of the Bengali majority. The inability of the governing political party in Pakistan to discipline or accommodate its constituent units led to the slow, steady aggrandizement of executive authority by the civilian bureaucracy with the support of the military.

The partition of colonial India exacerbated the already substantial class cleavages characterizing the Muslim-majority provinces which became Pakistan. The Muslim League had achieved Pakistan by creating a tenuous coalition between the large landed aristocracy in West Pakistan and the cultivating tenantry in East Pakistan. The accompanying differences in social structure between Pakistan's two geographical wings, already stark before independence, intensified as a result of independence because both these Muslim-majority provinces were split, with approximately one-half of each province joining Pakistan. Eastern Punjab, with a more equitable distribution of land, joined India. Consequently, landholding in West Pakistan had become *less* equitable: in Pakistani Punjab, 0.5 percent of the population now owned 20 percent of the cultivable land while in Sindh, 1 percent of the population owned 30 percent of the cultivable land. In West Pakistan as a whole, about 6,000 individuals possessed landholding in excess of five hundred acres, and it was these large landholders who by and large wielded political power in the provincial Muslim League and in the Pakistan Constituent Assembly.[25]

In contrast, East Pakistan's socio-economic structure had become *more* equitable. Approximately three-quarters of the land in East Pakistan was owned by large, absentee Hindu landlords who fled to India upon independence.[26] Ownership of this land was effectively transferred to the

---

[25] National Planning Board, The First Five Year Plan 1955–1960: 309. National Documentation Centre, Central Secretariat Library, Islamabad. Hereafter NDC.

[26] Firoz Khan Noon speech to Second Constituent Assembly, February 14, 1956. Pakistan Constituent Assembly Debates [hereafter CAD (Pakistan)] Vol. 1, 3056. The Memorandum of the Bengal Congress Committee to the Boundary Commission similarly states that 80 percent of the urban property belonged to *bhadralok* Hindus.

Muslim cultivating peasantry in control of the East Pakistan Muslim League by virtue of a 1950 land reform bill limiting land ownership to 33 acres.[27] The Pakistan Constituent Assembly delayed its consent to this legislation for several months, likely because neither the landlords nor the *mohajirs* in West Pakistan were interested in promoting such progressive legislation. Stark differences in distributive interests, which had been papered over before independence in the bid to protect Muslim interests at a national level, emerged with a vengeance after independence when the vague rallying cry of "Islam in danger" could no longer serve as a unifying national identity.

Class-based differences over national political goals, intensified by the demographic changes accompanying independence, were additionally compounded by the dominance of Punjabis in Pakistan's state institutions. Prior to independence, the Muslim League movement had virtually equated the achievement of a sovereign Muslim state with an improvement in the economic conditions of Bengali cultivators, a demand made possible by the overlap of the class and religion cleavage in undivided Bengal. Upon independence however, it seemed to Bengalis that Hindu landlords were simply being substituted by West Pakistani landlords, both politically and economically. Despite the early advent of English education in Bengal, few Bengali Muslims had risen to high levels in the civil services, with the result that West Pakistanis represented 57 of the 60 top-level civilian bureaucrats, some of whom now assumed the top government posts in East Pakistan.[28]

Such disparity was even more apparent among top military officers, among whom just four (of 308) were Bengali, a glaring disparity given that Bengalis formed a majority of the population. Moreover, West Pakistani government domination appeared to translate directly into preferential economic policies at the expense of East Pakistan, even though the jute exports of East Pakistan earned a substantial portion of Pakistan's foreign exchange credits. By one count, 86 percent of the central government expenditure on provinces, including provincial financial assistance, capital expenditures, grants, and foreign aid, went to West Pakistan while just 14 percent went to East Pakistan, despite the latter's majority.[29] This great disparity in government resource allocation led some Pakistani observers to note that the streets of Karachi, the-then

[27] *Dawn*, April 20, 1951.
[28] Either at the level of Secretary or Joint Secretary. *Dawn*, January 18, 1956.
[29] *Dawn*, January 9, 1956. Similar figures are cited in Lambert (1959: 52–53).

capital of Pakistan, were "paved with jute sales," jute being the cash crop of East Pakistan.[30]

To be sure, the East–West disparity in both social structures and government patronage was aggravated by its coincidence with linguistic, cultural, and racial cleavages. West Pakistanis were lighter-skinned, considered themselves *ashraf* Muslims, and spoke a variety of regional languages such as Punjabi, Pushtu, Sindi, and Baluchi. For these Muslims and for the Muslim League leaders from the United Provinces, only Urdu was considered a distinctly Muslim language and thereby served as a unifying symbol of the Pakistan movement. East Pakistanis spoke predominantly Bengali, however, and had very little exposure to Urdu. The question of which languages were recognized as national became emotional and evocative in its own right during the first decade of Pakistan's independence, but the emotional resonance of the language issue was built *in part* on the foundation of class because the national recognition of a language had clear repercussions on Bengalis' access to government patronage. If Bengali as well as Urdu were considered a national language, examinations for government civil service positions would become distinctly more accessible to Bengalis. Thus, while the conflict over a national language involved more than economic spoils, even these ethnic demands were partly based on economic considerations.

The inability of Pakistan's dominant political party to broker compromises between these class-based interests or to discipline provincial interests to a national interest was directly responsible for three successive failures to produce a Pakistani constitution. As the Congress did in India, the Muslim League dominated the Constituent Assembly in Pakistan and was thus the primary organizational driver of constitutional compromises. Of the 74 delegates of the Assembly, 59 of 61 Muslims belonged to the Muslim League.[31] Already by independence, Jinnah's failing health forced him to play an ever-smaller role in national politics. Upon his death in September 1948, executive leadership of the country passed (both as the Muslim League President and as Pakistan's Prime Minister) to Liaquat Ali Khan, a refugee from the United Provinces who, like Jinnah, had no political base of his own within Pakistan.

In March 1949, Prime Minister Khan produced an "Objectives Resolution," which stated the goals of the Pakistani constitution in a very general form. The Resolution stipulated that the territories of Pakistan

---

[30] Interview with Ejaz Haider. February 23, 2005.
[31] Choudhury (1954: 20).

should form autonomous units. Sufficiently ambiguous and broad as to provoke little opposition from the provincial politicians who wielded the real political and social power in Pakistan, this Objectives Resolution was adopted by the Constituent Assembly. By September 1950, however, the Constituent Assembly's Sub-committee on Representation produced the first substantive outline of legislative representation, which proposed that Pakistan's parliament would be bicameral, divided between a House of the People, elected by direct vote, and a House of Units, elected by the provincial legislatures of Punjab, Bengal, Sindh, North-West Frontier, and Baluchistan. The Report proposed that both houses possess equal powers in budgetary matters, motions of confidence, and removals of heads of state.

The first precise specification of the power allocation in a future constitution produced severe discord along two cleavages, both between the provincial leaders who wished to protect their autonomy and among the provinces for control over the center, conflict that a weak political party was unable to reconcile or subordinate.[32] The most strident opposition to this first constitutional draft came from the Bengalis, whose opposition to the Constitution centered on the proposed form of representation in the central legislature.[33] All Units were to be treated equally in the upper House of Units, where Bengalis formed just a fifth of the upper house. Though Bengalis would be assured a popular majority of the lower house through proportional representation, the upper House of Units was vested with powers equal to that of the lower House of the People. Effectively then, the voice of a majority of Pakistan's population in Bengal could be reduced to a legislative minority in a joint session of the two houses, to which Bengalis vociferously protested.

Though Bengalis were also opposed to the proposed adoption of Urdu as the sole national language, Bengalis were most aggravated by the prospect of becoming a legislative minority despite their popular majority.[34] The Working Committee of the Bengal Muslim League was unambiguous in its denunciation of the report. The Bengal-based *Pakistan Observer* called the report a conspiracy at the hands of a "power-drunk oligarchical ruling clique in Karachi" that aimed to turn Bengal "into a colony of

[32] Mozaffar (1981) shows that while *mohajirs* or refugees from the United Provinces held 29 percent of Pakistan's Cabinet positions in 1947, including all the important ones, by 1958 *mohajirs* had been marginalized to such an extent that they held just 8 percent of the important Cabinet positions.

[33] Khan (2005: 69).

[34] CAD (Pakistan), Vol. VII, 183, NDC. Also, Choudhury (1954: 72–73).

West Pakistan."[35] In the month following the publication of the report, the *Observer* published five editorials and 80 letters about the Interim Report, every one of which was critical of the proposed constitution.[36] Bengalis wanted both greater autonomy from the center and greater representation within any government structure. Like in India, the task of allocating constitutional powers to the federal center or to constituent states provoked heated discussion. But unlike in India, the dominant political party was not able to broker a resolution, which eventually led to a breakdown in the constitutional process.

West Pakistani provinces were also dissatisfied with the proposed constitution's strong centralization of power in the form of a head of state with extensive emergency powers. Top-level Muslim League leaders, who were predominantly refugees from the United Provinces, saw this as necessary because they were aware that provincial politicians held the real political power in Pakistan. That the League had little support in the provinces was already demonstrated in the workings of provincial politics in the few years between independence (1947) and the Interim Report (1950). Within a week of independence, the central government had dismissed the provincial government of the North-West Frontier Province because it was led by a party which had opposed the creation of Pakistan. The League Ministry which subsequently formed was so weak that it was unable to form a legislative majority for months and ultimately consolidated power only by arresting approximately 250 political opponents.[37] A similar struggle was also apparent in a second province, Sindh. The Sindh provincial government had stridently opposed the central government's attempts to re-constitute Karachi, located in Sindh, as an independent federal territory, since doing so would remove the federal capital from provincial jurisdiction. It was for this reason that Jinnah dismissed Sindh's Chief Minister Khuhro in 1948. Unable to garner its own political support, however, the government of Prime Minister Liaquat Ali Khan was forced in 1949 to strike a bargain with Khuhro, reinstating him as President of the Sindh Muslim League in return for his political support of the Muslim League in the federal government. These developments illustrated yet again how the central Muslim League leadership was dangerously reliant on the support of provincial leaders.

[35] *Pakistan Observer*, October 13, 1950.
[36] Rehman (1982: 43).
[37] Binder (1963: 131).

The weakness of central Muslim League leaders vis-à-vis provincial Muslim Leaguers is most clearly evidenced in their relations with
Punjabi landlords. Since independence, the Chief Minister of the Muslim
League Ministry in Punjab was a powerful landed aristocrat, the Nawab
of Mamdot.[38] In 1948, the Governor of Punjab, a retained British civil
servant, complained to Jinnah of the League's provincial Chief Minister,
who he claimed was "prepared at any time to sacrifice the administration
to the retention of power and patronage."[39] In particular, the Governor
accused the Chief Minister of distributing abandoned property to his own
political supporters and therefore advocated that Daultana, also a large
landlord, replace Mamdot as Chief Minister. Jinnah, who himself directed
the central government's refugee agency, attempted to engineer the Chief
Minister's resignation in the summer of 1948. The proposed successor to
the Punjabi Chief Minister (Mamdot) "had known Mamdot for a long
time and did not wish to oppose him."[40] Unable to reach his desired
outcome, Jinnah told the Punjab Governor that he no longer wished to
intervene.[41] Even the direct intervention of Pakistan's charismatic leader
at the apex of his powers had failed to compel one Punjabi landlord
to act against another, demonstrating how class interests trumped party
loyalty. Indeed, the central government admitted that it was too weak
to impose its will on Punjabi landlords. After Jinnah's death, the new
Governor-General Nazimuddin wrote to the Punjab Governor: "We
must recognize that [Chief Minister] Mamdot has got the support of a
very large majority of the Muslim League Assemblymen and it does not
pay to have a Ministry without support in the Province."[42] By 1949, the
Punjab Governor wrote to the Prime Minister: "Mamdot has, to everyone's knowledge, defeated the centre, even the Quaid [Jinnah] ... and the
feeling is growing that the centre is powerless."[43] Provincial party leaders
in Punjab had successfully opposed the League's central leadership, evi
dencing just how little ideational loyalty and organizational discipline
Pakistan's dominant political party possessed.

Already in the very early post-independence years, then, the inability
of its dominant political party to discipline its provincial politicians was

---

[38] Griffin (1993).
[39] Mudie to Jinnah, *Mudie-Jinnah Letters*, MSS Eur. F64/14–15, IOL.
[40] McGrath (1996: 49). Based on his 1992 interview with Daultana.
[41] May 18, 1948, Jinnah to Mudie. Mudie-Jinnah Letters, MSS Eur. F164/14–15, IOL.
[42] Mudie-Nazimuddin Letters, India Office Library, London, MSS Eur. F164/51, IOL.
[43] Mudie-Liaquat Ali Khan Letter, dated January 10, 1949. MSS Eur. F164/51, IOL.

the most important differentiating factor in setting Pakistan on a different democratization trajectory. Only by making deals with the provincial landed aristocracy, as had been done in Punjab and Sindh, or by intimidation and arrest, as had been done in NWFP, could Pakistan's dominant political party stay in power and win regional elections. An opposition politician, Suhrawardy, wrote: "These elections were rigged with a vengeance in the interest of the Muslim League ... The same League governments and party were in power and the same kind of people had been returned [by the elections]. Namely, those belonging to the feudal aristocracy, except in the NWFP where Khan Abdul Qayyum Khan had taken care to see that a large number of illiterates were elected so that no one in the legislature would ever be able to challenge his supremacy."[44] In effect, the Muslim League maintained support in West Pakistan only by reinforcing the power of the landed aristocracy while its support in East Pakistan disintegrated.

Pakistan's first attempt at constitution-making was stalled because of provincial objections to a strong central government. In the absence of a political party able to aggregate and prioritize interests, constitution-making broke down over two key issues, one of which was the struggle between weak national politicians and strong provincial politicians. Though the differences among Punjabi (West Pakistani) and Bengali (East Pakistani) politicians were also pronounced, these groups jointly opposed the creation of a strong central state. The Punjab-based *Pakistan Times* responded to the 1951 Basic Principles Committee Interim Report by denouncing its "conferring of dictatorial powers" on state officials, particularly the Head of State. Giving the Head of State the right to appoint provincial heads was a "severe curtailment of provincial autonomy." The "concentration of legislative and executive power at the apex of the constitutional pyramid was certain to expose the Centre to the temptation of interfering too much, with or without warrant, in the affairs of the Federal units."[45] The General Secretary of Bengal Provincial Muslim League felt that a constitution based on the Interim Report would "establish a pure and simple dictatorship" while the Bengal Muslim League Working Committee suggested amending the constitution to provide for "maximum autonomy to the province including control over communications, commerce, development and industries."[46] Based on these

[44] Suhrawardy (1987: 83).
[45] *Pakistan Times*, September 30, 1950.
[46] *Pakistan Observer*, October 31, 1950.

vociferous objections in September and October, the Prime Minister (also the leader of the Muslim League) was forced to withdraw the Interim Report on the constitution in November 1950, ostensibly to take suggestions from the public.

Subsequent attempts to create a constitution faltered on the second key issue – the apportionment of power between the country's eastern and western wings. From its very first meetings, provincial Muslim League leaders consistently and vociferously denounced central Muslim League leaders for not providing provinces with sufficient authority on governing matters.[47] Consequently, there was little constitutional resolution on the nature of state–center relations. By 1951, public pressure was beginning to build on the Constituent Assembly to produce a constitution. The Constituent Assembly had by now been at work for four years with little to show. The deadline for public suggestions had ended in January 1951, and by December, the Constituent Assembly had still not ratified a constitutional draft. The Punjab-based newspaper *Nawa-i-Pakistan* wrote an accusatory editorial in December 1951 condemning the "incompetence and singular inactivity" of the Assembly and demanding to know "for how many hours did the Constituent Assembly meet in more than four years of its existence and how long did its subcommittees sit to work on the task assigned to them?"[48] Two days after this editorial, *Dawn*, the semi-official government newspaper, announced that the Assembly's sub-committee reports would be finalized within months and during the summer of 1952, the constitution-making process did seem to be moving forward.[49]

In December 1952, the next constitutional draft was presented to the Constituent Assembly by the Prime Minister. The next constitutional draft was rejected by a Punjabi landed aristocracy that perceived little need to assent to a curtailment of its power. The December 1952 draft had accommodated the Bengali complaints about diluting the influence of a democratic majority, but by doing so, elicited the opposition of the Punjabi landlords who felt that their influence in the central government was being diminished. This constitutional draft also envisaged a bicameral legislature, but distributed power in the upper house, the House of Units, among ten regions. East Pakistan, which formed a demographic majority, was given 60 of 120 seats. The remaining 60 seats were distributed

---

[47] CAD (Pakistan), Vol. I, 85–127. See also Callard (1957: Chapter V).
[48] *Nawa-i-Pakistan* on December 5, 1951, as quoted in Rehman (1982: 19).
[49] Rehman (1982: 20) and McGrath (1996: 87).

among nine geographical units in West Pakistan. Power was similarly apportioned in the lower house, the House of People, which was vested with the lion's share of the legislative authority.

This constitutional proposal thereby effectively treated East Pakistan and West Pakistan as equal units. Given that East Pakistan had a popular majority, however, a constitution creating legislative equality between East and West Pakistan was perhaps the most that Punjabis could expect within a democratic framework. Yet the Punjabi press vehemently and nearly uniformly opposed this second draft of the constitution precisely because of legislative parity. Punjabis feared that the Bengalis, already a majority, would be able to legislatively dominate the Punjabis by creating alliances with smaller units in West Pakistan. Bengali domination was a threat because Bengal had a different social structure which led it to propose very different political policies.[50] This fear was also perhaps reasonable, since the constitutional proposal had been favorably received in one other small province, the NWFP.[51]

Like the first attempt then, the second attempt at constitution-making culminated in deadlock over the key issue of power-sharing between the provinces. The Punjab Muslim League withdrew its support for the constitutional Report, denouncing it on the grounds that East Pakistan unfairly formed one "unit" while West Pakistan was composed of "nine units."[52] But East Pakistan, with a popular majority of 55 percent, was entitled to at least half of the seats in a democratic legislature functioning on the principle of "one man, one vote." The Punjabi Muslim League, led by the landed aristocrat Daultana, now proposed that Pakistan should have a unitary rather than federal form of government, presumably because it offered the best chance of preventing a Bengali-dominated legislature from emerging. Punjab-based newspapers endorsed unitary government, while newspapers based in the smaller units of West Pakistan all strongly opposed a unitary form of government.[53] The central government, as generally represented by the newspaper *Dawn*, also disagreed with the Punjabi endorsement of a unitary government. Nevertheless, Punjabi opposition to the constitutional draft was so strong that Prime Minister Nazimuddin withdrew the report on January 21, 1953.

---

[50] For example, the East Pakistan Muslim League was strongly supportive of land reform, as it had been before independence.
[51] Choudhury (1954: 75).
[52] *Dawn*, Karachi, January 12, 1953.
[53] Rehman (1982: 51–52).

To distract the rest of the country from the constitutional negotiations, Punjabi landlord politicians in control of the League fomented a series of religious riots with the aim of undermining the central government. The Chief Minister of the Punjab, the head of the Punjab Muslim League, and a powerful landed aristocrat, Mian Mumtaz Daultana, was the central player in engineering an attack on the central government. Since the Muslim League had built its support up in the Punjab by basing its demand for Pakistan on religion, religious leaders generally felt entitled to lobby the state to adopt pro-Islamic policies after independence, even though most League leaders were opposed to the influence of religion on politics. Islamic *ulema* or religious leaders in the Punjab were particularly exercised over implicit state recognition of the Ahmadis, an Islamic sect which did not recognize Mohammed as the last prophet, and lobbied the government to declare the Ahmadis un-Islamic. The pressure of religious leaders, though not unimportant, could have been sidelined if League politicians at both national and provincial levels uniformly opposed their demands. However, the landed aristocracy's support for the *ulema*, when such support suited their specific political goals, elevated their demands to national prominence.

Said differently, religious demands only became a threat to the central government's authority when powerful Punjabi politicians joined forces with religious groups to undermine the central government's proposed constitution. In other words, it was the opposition of provincial landlords, and not the religious leaders in and of themselves, which destabilized the central government. On the very same day on which the Prime Minister withdrew his proposed constitution, a delegation of *ulema* threatened violence through "direct action" if Ahmadis were not declared a religious minority. Acceding to this request would effectively have amounted to providing religious leaders with veto authority over state policy-making, something most League leaders had consistently opposed.

The Chief Minister of Punjab, a powerful provincial landlord, thereupon issued a public statement not only supporting the demands of the anti-Ahmadis (particularly the Jamaat-i-Islami, led by Maulana Maududi) but charging that the central government had responsibility for resolving this conflict because he hoped to undermine the central government.[54] Prime Minister Nazimuddin responded by arresting the leaders of the anti-Ahmadi movement in March, causing severe outbreaks of violence in the Punjab, particularly Lahore. To quell these riots, the Prime

[54] Noon (1993: 234).

Minister ordered the military into Lahore, where it proclaimed martial law, and dismissed the Punjabi Chief Minister Daultana according to Section 92A of the Government of India Act. Within a few weeks of martial law ending in Lahore, the Governor-General, a civilian bureaucrat, autocratically dismissed the Prime Minister, effectively shelving his constitutional draft, "on the pretext of the worsening economic situation."[55] The struggle between provincial politicians had thus effectively led to the autocratic dismissal of both a provincial and a national administration by a civilian bureaucrat with the tacit support of the military. Had the Muslim League party functioned as a coherent governing force, the civil service would have had no justification for dismissal. Instead, constitutional deadlock provided the civilian bureaucracy with an opportunity to steadily aggrandize governing power.

The third and final attempt to forge a democratic constitution by a League-dominated Constituent Assembly followed a now-familiar pattern – deadlock over power-sharing along center–province and inter-provincial dimensions – and signaled the continuing inability of the Pakistan's dominant political party to create consensus within its ranks. In 1953, Prime Minister Mohammed Ali Bogra, newly appointed by the Governor-General, made the resolution of constitutional deadlock his foremost priority. This meant resolving issues over provincial power-sharing because "it is within the knowledge of everybody that on account of this difference of opinion between East Bengal [East Pakistan] and West Pakistan in the matter of the composition of the Houses [that] the work on constitution-making was stopped."[56] The Prime Minister and the League-dominated Constituent Assembly now attempted to resolve the deadlock by introducing the concept of parity between the eastern and western wings of Pakistan, providing for a bicameral legislature in which power was equally apportioned between the legislative houses and distributing seats in such a way as to provide for equal representation between the eastern and western zones of the country in a joint session of the parliament. Moreover, the proposal provided both the East and West with legislative checks, since any legislative measure could only be passed if 30 percent of the members from each zone voted for the measure.[57] At the same time as it attempted to broker compromises between East and West Pakistan, the Bogra proposal still clearly reflected the desire of

[55] Khan (1967: 49).
[56] Nurul Amin, CAD (Pakistan), Vol. XV, 183, October 14, 1953.
[57] Choudhury (1954: 76–78).

League politicians in the Assembly to create a strong central government, entrusting as it did the federal government with wide-ranging powers.

This proposal made steady progress and, by November 1953, provincial power-sharing had been approved by all the provincial representatives in the Assembly: "In these 130 paragraphs all the essential aspects of the constitution have been covered in regard to that part which deals with the Islamic character of the constitution *as also the most controversial part, namely, the federal structure*" [emphasis added].[58] Though the Bogra formula offered reasonable assurances to both wings of the country, its ratification was halted by West Pakistani feudal landlords who were not prepared to see their political power circumscribed at the hands of a democratic Bengali majority and by civilian bureaucrats who were not prepared to cede power to the elected Constituent Assembly.

This last attempt at constitutional compromise failed because both the civilian bureaucracy and the League leadership in the Constituent Assembly were threatened by the success of an opposition political movement. The new Prime Minister, installed by the Governor-General precisely because of his political weakness, began to develop political ambitions of his own. To stay in power, however, he needed to respond to political developments in Bengal, where growing disaffection with the Muslim League had translated into a massive exodus from that party. An alliance of Bengal-based political parties led by the Awami League had espoused a platform which reflected Bengali interests for the March 1954 elections, including provincial autonomy on all matters but foreign affairs, currency, and defense.

The results of the 1954 provincial elections in Bengal signaled a stunning defeat for the Muslim League, which, though it had won overwhelming support prior to independence, now possessed just ten of 239 seats. The new United Front coalition, led by an erstwhile member of the Muslim League, won an outright majority. The success of the United Front undermined the legitimacy of a Prime Minister leading a League-dominated Constituent Assembly, which now appeared not to represent a majority of the country. At this particular moment then, both unelected and elected arms of the central government shared an incentive to see the provincial government of Bengal dismissed. The Constituent Assembly nodded to the substance of Bengali demands by addressing some of the United Front's platform within the proposed constitution, such as the use of Bengali as a national language. But unlike in India,

---

[58] A.K. Brohi. CAD (Pakistan), Vol. xv, 748.

provincial challenges could not be addressed within the dominant political party which consequently dismissed a democratically elected regional government on the pretense of labor unrest and "disruptive forces and enemy agents."[59]

What happened in Bengal in 1954 represented a microcosm of post-independence political developments in Pakistan: an influential member of the Muslim League defected from Pakistan's dominant political party and formed an opposition party which defeated the Muslim League in provincial elections. As a result of this success, he was summarily dismissed from government by one civilian bureaucrat with the support of the Constituent Assembly and replaced by another civilian bureaucrat, thereby reinforcing the autocratic writ of the bureaucracy. Between 1955 and the military coup in 1958, Huq returned to the central government however, serving as a Cabinet member and as Governor of Bengal.

In short, an influential League leader had quit the party because it did not reflect his interests as a Bengali. Once his independent success posed a threat to the bureaucracy-controlled central government however, this leader was removed and subsequently co-opted into a bureaucratically controlled government. Had the League been able to forge compromises that kept its key supporters within the party ranks, it could have prevented the civilian bureaucracy from aggrandizing power – as the Congress did in India.

Thus, the weakness of Pakistan's dominant political party, and in particular its inability to forge consensus among different class-based interests, enabled and even encouraged civilian bureaucrats to gradually enlarge their power within the state. By early 1954, it was a mere matter of time before the Muslim League was completely sidelined by the civilian bureaucracy. In October 1954, an alliance of civilian bureaucrats and Punjabi landlords coalesced to prevent the ratification of the League's constitution. Though the League-dominated Constituent Assembly had already agreed to the provincial power-sharing formula, the new governing Punjabi Chief Minister Firoz Khan Noon (a large landlord) and Governor-General Ghulam Mohammad both withdrew their support of the constitution.[60]

The League-dominated Constituent Assembly attempted to assert its power over the Governor-General by constitutionally stripping him of

---

[59] "Pakistan Ousts East Zone Chief, Charges Treason," *New York Times*, May 31, 1954.
[60] McGrath (1996: 122).

the ability to dismiss provincial governments and binding him to the advice of his ministers. In return, the Governor-General dismissed the Constituent Assembly and banned public meetings for two months, marking a decisive win for the power-aggrandizing bureaucracy in the struggle between elected and unelected institutions.[61] The Bengalis in the Constituent Assembly, who had been elected a few months previously in provincial elections, now supported its dissolution because they were political opponents of the United Front. This "bureaucratic coup," and the inability of League politicians to challenge it, meant that governing power now rested firmly in the hands of civilian bureaucrats.

With the dismissal of the First Constituent Assembly in 1954, the leadership of Pakistan's dominant political party ceased to possess any meaningful influence on Pakistani politics, though the bureaucratic oligarchy running the central government maintained the fiction of constitutional rule until 1958. Possessing 25 of 80 seats, the Muslim League was still the largest party in the Second Constituent Assembly, but it was no longer in a position to command a majority.[62] The breakdown of the Muslim League as a party led to a proliferation of governments, with many of the same several dozen leaders cycling through key Cabinet positions until the military coup of 1958. In 1955, a Second Constituent Assembly, indirectly elected by provincial ministries, met and ratified a constitution which merged the provinces of West Pakistan into one unit and provided for parity with East Pakistan, but this was a constitution which the bureaucracy-dominated central government had created and presented to the fragmented Second Constituent Assembly for rubber-stamp approval.

Unsurprisingly given its provenance, this constitution also provided for a strong central government and enlarged the powers of the Governor-General, who hereby became President. The newly ratified constitution, technically parliamentary in character, was in actual fact a highly centralized system in which a strong President had the power to dissolve provincial and national governments, appoint a Prime Minister, control budgets, and veto national and provincial laws. In other words, parliamentary government would be allowed to function so long as it did

---

[61] S.S. Pirzada stated that it was unambiguously the motion to strip the Governor-General of his powers which led the Constituent Assembly to be dismissed in 1954. When the Governor-General dismissed the Prime Minister, General Ayub Khan was apparently standing behind a curtain in the room. Interview with S.S. Pirzada, Jinnah's Personal Secretary, March 10, 2005.

[62] Choudhury (1954: 92–93).

not impinge upon Presidential prerogative. The Presidency, in turn, was firmly controlled by the civilian bureaucracy.

Between 1954 and 1958, four Prime Ministers cycled through power, the clearest manifestation yet of musical chair politics. In August 1955, Prime Minister Bogra, a Bengali politician, was replaced by Chaudri Mohammed Ali, a civilian bureaucrat, who presided over a United Front–Muslim League coalition government. With representatives in both executive positions of President and Prime Minister, the civilian bureaucracy set about consolidating central power. Because it sought to maintain the fiction of representative government, however, the bureaucracy also needed the support of provincial politicians who directly controlled their own patronage networks. When one set of powerful Punjabi landlords in the Muslim League demanded the resignation of the leader of another set of Punjabi landlords who had left the Muslim League to form the Republican Party, the deadlock ultimately led to the Prime Minister's resignation.[63] With Ali's resignation, the party leading Pakistan's independence movement officially ceased to control the central government. The second Ministry, led by the Bengali politician Suhrawardy between September 1956 and October 1957, formed a coalition between the landed aristocrat-dominated Republican Party and the peasant-dominated Awami League which lasted just over a year and which broke down over the question of whether the One Unit scheme of provincial representation should be abolished or not – the same issue that had plagued constitutional negotiations since 1950.[64] The third Ministry of I.I. Chundrigar lasted just two months and collapsed in December 1957 after the Punjabi landed aristocrats in the Republican Party withdrew their support.

Beginning in December 1957, the final civilian Ministry, led by a powerful Punjabi landed aristocrat and the head of the Republican Party Firoz Khan Noon, formed a coalition government of six different parties. The prospect of national elections, which may have legitimated provincial politicians, led President Iskander Mirza, a civilian bureaucrat, together with the Army Chief of Staff, Ayub Khan, to abrogate the constitution, abolish political parties, and declare martial law on October 8, 1958. Within the same month, the military formally took over, announcing a military regime that was to last for 11 years and that inaugurated a regular pattern of military coups in Pakistan. The full suspension of civilian government, initially at the hands of civilian bureaucracy and shortly

---

[63] Jalal (1990: 227–235), Khan (2005: 120–121).
[64] Khan (2005: 121–122).

thereafter by the military leadership, ended the fiction of democratic government and granted the military the *de jure* power to run Pakistan's government.

The rise and fall of four administrations in as many years before Pakistan's first military coup signaled the absence of a coordinating and disciplining political party. Had the Muslim League been an ideologically coherent party, it could have prevented its support bases from deserting the organization the moment the party did not serve their needs. Opposition parties such as the Awami League and the Republican Party would not have formed, or at least would have been a good deal weaker. Had the League been composed of a consensually united elite, the Muslim League could have provided the space for the resolution of intra-party differences by resort to regularized rules or shared progammatic commitments. Fundamentally however, such a party did not exist and this difference most clearly explained the divergent regime trajectories of India and Pakistan.

In sum, constitution-making in Pakistan's first decade stalled because Pakistan's dominant political party was unable to draw on shared distributive goals, on party discipline, or on a compelling ideational commitment to facilitate power-sharing compromises. The Muslim League's inability to resolve provincial conflicts was, in turn, a direct result of the way it had mobilized support in the lead up to independence. Instead of cultivating grassroots support within party structures, the Muslim League had built support for the creation of Pakistan by wholly reinforcing the social and economic power of the rural landed aristocracy and religious leaders in one part of the country and by allying with a peasant movement in the other part of the country. Though this class-based cleavage coincided with linguistic and ethnic cleavages, post-independence constitutional deadlock was notably over class based issues.

Because of the conflicting distributive interests of its core supporters, Pakistan's dominant political party could not reliably mobilize its own supporters around a specific policy platform, much less define procedures for distributing and transferring power. After independence, when the rural landed aristocracy no longer had any incentive to submit to the discipline of the dominant political party, it quickly exited the party and held the League-dominated Constituent Assembly hostage to its demands. In the context of repeated constitutional deadlock, a direct manifestation of party weakness, Pakistan's civilian bureaucracy and military slowly aggrandized power and eventually dismissed the Constituent Assembly, thereby ending Pakistan's infant democratic experiment.

III. FORGING AN ACCOUNTABLE CHIEF EXECUTIVE

The role of its dominant political party in explaining the democratic divergence between India and Pakistan is also exemplified in whether and how these countries selected an elected chief executive, the hallmark of a *democratic* regime. Even by minimalist definitions, democracy is defined as an "institutional arrangement for arriving at political decisions in which individuals acquire the power to decide by means of a competitive struggle for the people's vote."[65] The most powerful position for which this competitive struggle matters is that of the chief executive, either the Prime Minister or the President in most systems of governance.

An elected Prime Minister in India

Upon independence, both Pakistan and India were governed by the 1947 Independence of India Act, which left executive power in the hands of a Governor-General until a new constitution was promulgated by each country's Constituent Assembly. In India, the Governor-General/ President remained a titular figurehead. Congress leaders almost universally agreed to the Westminster form of government because these leaders had attained power through a party that essentially modeled parliamentary government. As a result, Congress leaders had little to lose by adopting a representative form government. Having mobilized against an autocratic colonial regime for decades, nationalist leaders were experientially primed to understand the pitfalls of an autocratic executive and therefore quickly sought to subordinate unelected positions of power to elected leadership. Thus, the elected position of Prime Minister quickly assumed ascendancy over the position of Governor-General/President in India because its independence party forged consensus and resolved conflict among key elites.

Before India was formally independent, the Congress-dominated Constituent Assembly was generally of the opinion that India would adopt the Westminster system of government, whereby the chief executive would be an elected position, typically the leader of the largest party elected in Parliament. In this arrangement, the President would be a figurehead with largely ceremonial powers who was to be elected by an electoral college consisting of the national and provincial legislatures. In speaking to the Constituent Assembly, the future Prime Minister Nehru

---

[65] Schumpeter (1942: 269).

said: "we want to emphasize the ministerial character of the Government, that power really resided in the Ministry and in the Legislature *and not in the President as such*" [emphasis added].[66] This relationship – where an elected Parliament and elected provincial legislatures were given the power to appoint the President – was the exact opposite of what developed in Pakistan, where the position of unelected Governor-General/President quickly assumed governing primacy. Indeed, these different decisions were constitutive of divergent regime outcomes in India and Pakistan.

India was able to reach consensus about the role of the Indian President largely because, in order to lead a controlled anti-colonial agitation before independence, Congress leaders had established and honed a streamlined system of centralized party control. At a time when the broader anti-colonial struggle provided a unifying framework, Congress leaders had given some thought to the position of the Congress President in a future sovereign state. Congress' Nehru Report of 1928 stipulated that the future executive branch of an independent India would be formally headed by a Governor-General and that everyday operating power would be in the hands of a Council of Ministers. In 1939, Congress was forced to clarify the role of presidential powers after the election of Subhas Chandra Bose to Congress President. At the time, Bose maintained that this position should be as powerful as an American President, in other words, accorded supreme executive governing authority. Older Congressmen disagreed and argued that the Congress President should function like a constitutional monarch while the Congress Working Committee, a body that effectively functioned as the counterpart to a future Parliament, should decide matters of policy. When Bose appealed to the AICC delegates to empower their President, the Congress Working Committee resigned, which induced Bose to also tender his resignation. The AICC subsequently elected a new President. Bose, who then got elected as the President of the Bengal Provincial Congress Committee, organized Bengali opposition, was dismissed from his office for not toeing the party line, and barred from holding executive office for three years. This effectively illustrates how Congress leaders had already chosen to concentrate power in the Congress Working Committee, the forerunner to the national Cabinet.

---

[66] Jawaharlal Nehru, "Speech on the Principles of the Union Constitution," July 21, 1947. CAD (India), Vol. IV, 713

Before independence, the Congress Party was indeed modelling a democracy by holding its President fully accountable. As Vallabhbhai Patel remarked, "I wholly dissent from the view that the President has any powers of initiating policy save by consent of the Working Committee. More than once the Working Committee has asserted itself in the teeth of opposition of Presidents."[67] That provincial ministries were also controlled by the Working Committee on major issues of policy was also clearly demonstrated in the prompt resignation of these ministries by an order from the Congress Working Committee that participation in colonial governance was no longer consistent with the independence struggle in 1939.

When members of the Indian Constituent Assembly considered the position of India's governing executive after independence, they envisaged that governance on most matters of policy would be undertaken by a strong, centralized, but democratically accountable Parliamentary executive. As with the drafters of the American constitution, Congress leaders strove to create governance structures which limited both the potential anarchy of factionalism and the potential tyranny of government. Congress leaders thus deliberately sought to limit the power given to the unelected head of state. Though the President was given power to protect minorities and decide certain electoral procedures, B.N. Rau, the Constituent Assembly's appointed constitutional advisor, opined that the position of the President should be that of a figurehead or "as far as possible, be the same [as] between the King and his ministers in England,"[68] a point which was made repeatedly throughout the Constituent Assembly debates. The Chairman of the Drafting Committee wrote of the Governors, who mirrored the function of the President at provincial levels: "I do not accept that even under election there would be any kind of rivalry between the Prime Minister and Governor, for the simple reason that the Prime Minister would be elected on the basis of policy while the Governor could not be elected on the basis of policy because *he could have no policy, not having any power*" [emphasis added].[69]

Having fought an autocratic colonial state over a period of decades, members of the Congress-dominated Constituent Assembly were keenly aware of the dangers of an autocratic executive and therefore expressly vested the President with limited powers. When discussing the powers of

---

[67] Indian Annual Register, 1939, Vol. I, 314–316.
[68] Rau (1960: 71).
[69] May 31, 1949, CAD (India), Vol. VIII, 468. Emphasis added.

the President, Assembly members again and again wished to minutely specify the executive powers of the President, which many advocated should be severely limited.[70] The fear of executive centralization of power in fact led the Drafting Committee in 1948 to recommend the inclusion of an Instrument of Instructions that would specifically instruct the President to choose the Prime Minister on the basis that he or she would be most likely to command a majority in Parliament. Just a month before the Constitution's ratification, the Chairman asked "If [in] any particular case the President does not act upon the advice of his ministers, will that be tantamount to a violation of the Constitution and will he be liable to impeachment?" To which the Chairman replied: "There is not the slightest doubt about it."[71] The Congress-dominated Constituent Assembly was nearly unanimous in the desire to limit the executive writ of the President, the only opposition being on the part of those individuals who wanted to *more* clearly limit the President's power.[72] That the dangers of an autocratic executive were very much on the minds of Congressmen is echoed in the parting words of the Chairman of the Assembly's Drafting Committee, who warned in his final speech to the Constituent Assembly that:

If we wish to maintain democracy not merely in form, but also in fact, what must we do? The first thing in my judgment we must do is to hold fast to constitutional methods of achieving our social and economic objectives ... The second thing we must do is to observe the caution which John Stuart Mill has given to all who are interested in the maintenance of democracy, namely *not to lay their liberties at the feet of even a great man, or to trust him with powers which enable him to subvert their institutions.* [Emphasis added.][73]

Despite these injunctions, India's first President did test the limits of presidential power. In September 1951, just after the Hindu Code Bill invalidating Hindu personal law was introduced into Parliament, President Rajendra Prasad (a devout Hindu) wrote to Prime Minister Nehru "expressing the desire to act solely on his own judgment" when assenting to Parliamentary bills. President Prasad was effectively exploring the possibility of attempting to use his position to oppose a bill being passed by the Parliament, tantamount to a direct challenge of legislative

[70] Austin (1972: 137).
[71] CAD (India), Vol. X, 269–314.
[72] CAD (India), Vol. X, 269–314.
[73] Ambedkar speech on draft Constitution, November 25, 1949, CAD (India), Vol. XI, 972–981.

authority by an unelected executive head of state.[74] The Prime Minister immediately communicated the President's inquiries to the Attorney General, among others, who wrote back in great detail that "by Article 74(1) the President is required to act in all matters with the aid and advice of his Council of Ministers." Another respondent to Prasad's inquiry stated that "the President's note raises points of such constitutional importance that, if conceded (they) will upset the whole constitutional structure envisaged at the time when the Constitution was passed (and will) make the President a kind of dictator." He followed with an unequivocal interpretation that the President "could not withhold his assent to Parliamentary bills because he had no appellate authority over the Cabinet."[75] Prasad assented to these arguments and no longer pursued the expansion of Presidential authority, respecting the rules enshrined in the newly adopted constitution.

Thus, within the first decade of independence, the Indian President was not just in name but also in practice restricted to acting as a mere figurehead while Congress ministers executed policy. All this did not mean that there was unanimity on constitutional issues. As the 11 volumes of India's Constituent Assembly Debates attest, on any number of issues quite the opposite was true. Nonetheless, the procedural discipline of the Congress Party crucially facilitated compromises on these conflicts. It was possible to reach agreement on the form and function of the various organs of the state – agreements formalized within a constitution – because India's governing political party had either already created consensus or had created a binding process of decision-making among its elites.

Aggrandizing Governor-Generals in Pakistan

The absence of institutionalized support for the dominant political party in Pakistan meant that party leaders needed to rely on autocratic rule to govern, thereby quickly setting Pakistan on a divergent democratic path from India. In Pakistan, key Muslim League leaders sought to entrench an unelected head of state in Pakistan's early post-independence years because, absent a reliable coalition of supporters, party leaders could only rule by autocratic decree. That Pakistan had been achieved at all had been largely due to the efforts of the dominant party's charismatic leader, M.A. Jinnah. In colonial India, it was Jinnah's leadership rather

---

[74] Austin (1972: 140–141).
[75] Austin (1972: 141–142).

than the existence of a developed party organization that had governed the Muslim League. Much the same was true of an independent Pakistan, i.e. the state functioned largely via charismatic rather than institutionalized leadership.

Moreover, that charismatic leader quite tentatively endorsed democratic means of decision-making. British administrators working out the transfer of power in the pre-independence years had feared that Jinnah intended to assume dictatorial powers for himself. When Jinnah stated he wished to become Pakistan's Governor-General during the constitutional negotiations over the colonial handover of power, he was reminded by the departing colonial Viceroy that the position of the Governor-General was to be a figurehead, whereupon Jinnah reputedly retorted: "In my position it is I who will give the advice and others who will act on it."[76] Even before independence, Jinnah was wary of instituting parliamentary government in Pakistan.[77] Above and beyond Jinnah's own personal beliefs regarding the desirability of democracy, however, the fact of a weak political party in Pakistan meant that Jinnah was not bound to function within the parameters of procedures that circumscribed his powers.

The absence of any organizational check on Jinnah's leadership, evident before independence, was only exacerbated after independence when Jinnah chose to assume the position of an unelected rather than elected executive. By choosing to govern from the *unelected* position of Governor-General rather than the elected position of Prime Minister, the leader of Pakistan's dominant party inaugurated a pattern of an unaccountable chief executive in Pakistan. The first major act of Pakistan's Constituent Assembly was to confer upon Jinnah (in his personal capacity rather than as the head of the Muslim League, a position from which he had resigned) the position of Governor-General. Astonishingly, during the Cabinet meeting on December 30, 1947, it was unanimously decided that Jinnah should formally preside over the Cabinet and that "*where the opinion of a majority of the Cabinet conflicted with Jinnah's opinion, that Jinnah's opinion should be 'final and binding'*" [emphasis added].[78]

The importance of this decision for locking in distinct institutional patterns should not be underestimated. Particularly because this was an early period where the conventions for this new state were being formulated, the elevation of an unelected position to one possessing supreme

---

[76] See Viceroy's Personal Report No. 11, July 4, 1947. *TP*, Vol. XII, 127.
[77] Interview with S.S. Pirzada, Jinnah's Personal Secretary, March 10, 2005.
[78] Pakistan Cabinet Meeting Minutes, December 30, 1947. File 21/CF/48, NDC.

governing authority was an extraordinary circumvention of the democratic process. That the unelected Governor-General rather than the
elected Constituent Assembly or Prime Minister was the more active
governing figure in Pakistan's early history is evidenced by that fact that
between 1947 and 1956, the Governor-General issued 376 ordinances
whereas the Constituent Assembly passed only 160 laws.[79]

It is not difficult to understand why Jinnah and subsequent League leaders sought appropriation of extra-constitutional powers to non-elected
positions – it was a direct response to the League's weak political control
over the areas that became Pakistan. Since most Muslim League leaders
had been based in what was now India, they were now *mohajirs* who
possessed little to no political support in the newly created Pakistan.[80]
The League's vague appeals to an Islamic identity, while sufficient to rally
some electoral support for Pakistan in colonial India, did little to unify
those provinces once this ostensibly Islamic state had been achieved.
Provincial Assemblies were dominated by traditionally powerful feudal
families with little allegiance to the independence party, which is why
such provincial leaders strongly opposed any discretionary power for the
Governor-General.[81]

For their part, League leaders understood too well that they were
in a weak position to discipline provincial leaders who had been lured
into a League coalition by promises of maintaining power, rather than
by any shared programmatic platform. It was for this reason that the
League-dominated Constituent Assembly attempted to persuade the
departing colonial Viceroy to provide the Governor-General with the
authority to dismiss provincial Ministries and instead govern directly
through the unelected provincial Governors, something the Viceroy
refused to do.[82]

The pattern of an unelected chief executive seeking to pre-empt
challenges to his authority – a pattern which continues to characterize
Pakistan to this day – plagued Pakistan's political system immediately
upon Jinnah's death in September 1948, as one weak leader after another
sought to aggrandize executive power. Had the League developed a
robust party organization which provided for the orderly succession of
power among a cadre of experienced party leaders, as the Congress did

[79] Newberg (2002: 37).
[80] Mozaffar (1981).
[81] Newberg (2002: 37).
[82] Louis Mountbatten to Earl of Listowel, Viceroy's Report No. 17, L/PO/6/123, IOL.

in India, the League may have been more able to govern effectively. As it was, however, weak political leaders who succeeded to a position of executive leadership used autocratic means to prevent challenges to their own political power.

Upon Jinnah's death, governing political power shifted to Prime Minister Liaquat Ali Khan, a UP League politician who appointed an ineffectual Bengali politician and landlord, Khwaja Nazimuddin, to the position of Governor-General. Liaquat Ali Khan was perhaps the only individual, aside from Jinnah, who was identified as a national rather than provincial League leader. Appointing a Bengali Governor-General was Liaquat Ali Khan's way of seeking local political support at the expense of the most pressing threat to League power, which came from Punjabi and Sindhi landlords. Because he possessed no political constituency in Pakistan and because the League had never elaborated, much less rallied, support for a clear set of programmatic policies, the new Prime Minister had no way of asserting control over provincial politics.[83]

With the assassination of Liaquat Ali Khan in 1951, no League leaders of a national stature existed, as the League had not developed a cadre of members who rose up through the party's organizational infrastructure. In the absence of a League leader who could effectively govern at a national level without being seen as representative of regional or sectional interests, individuals vied for access to political power by mobilizing their own institutional or geographical bases of support. A civilian bureaucrat who had served as Finance Minister under Jinnah and Liaquat Khan, Ghulam Mohammad, continued the developing pattern of governing from the unelected and constitutionally titular position of Governor-General. Mohammed apparently engineered his accession to the position of Governor-General, while the former Governor-General, Nazimuddin, now became Prime Minister. This agreement was completed from behind closed doors, without any consideration for the Constituent Assembly, the institution which was formally vested with the powers of nominating a Prime Minister and determining the line of succession. The pattern of unelected chief executives circumventing elected institutions thus continued to strengthen.

Between 1951 and 1953, national politics in Pakistan generally represented a tug of war between the Governor-General Mohammed and the Prime Minister Nazimuddin, with both men attempting to mobilize

---

[83] A newspaper noted of the Punjab's League Ministry, "There could be no difference on policy, simply because there is no policy." *Civil Military Gazette*, May 23, 1948.

their respective constituencies (the bureaucracy and the Punjabis for Mohammed and the religious establishment and the Bengalis for Nazimuddin) to establish political ascendancy over one another. After the Nazimuddin-led Constituent Assembly produced a constitutional report in 1952 which would have effectively increased the power of Bengalis, Punjabi politicians encouraged the politicization of a religious movement seeking to marginalize the *Ahmadis* in order to destabilize the Nazimuddin government. A prominent Punjabi politician himself writes: "This situation [of anti-Ahmadi agitations] was brought about by people who wanted to get into power at the Centre. They thought that by creating unrest, the men at the helm of affairs in the centre would have to go. The old tried method of attacking a religious minority sect called Ahmadis was used to inflame the minds of otherwise peaceful people."[84] In other words, the politicization of religious identities was not motivated by religious sentiment, but by a desire to aggrandize the political power of the Governor-General and his sometime Punjabi supporters at the expense of Bengalis and civilian bureaucrats.

This tug of war culminated in the Governor-General affecting an extra-constitutional *coup d'état* in 1953 by dismissing a Prime Minister who had the confidence of his Cabinet and his Constituent Assembly (which until it promulgated a new constitution, functioned as a parliament). In the spring of 1953, the *ulema* leading the anti-Ahmadi agitation in the Punjab were arrested, leading to rioting and violence in Punjab's biggest city, Lahore. The central government, effectively being challenged by provincial politicians collaborating with the *ulema*, called in the military to institute martial law. The Punjabi Chief Minister Daultana, also the leader of the Punjabi Muslim League, and a powerful large landlord, was dismissed by Prime Minister Nazimuddin, ostensibly under a section of the 1947 Act.[85] Within a few weeks of the dismissal, Governor-General Ghulam Mohammad also dismissed Prime Minister Nazimuddin, citing the inefficiency of his administration in coping with food shortages and problems of law and order. The Governor-General, with the support of an army which disliked Nazimuddin's proposed cut in defense expenditures, was effectively seeking to enlarge his personal power. While the Prime Minister had cited Section 92(a) of the 1935 Government of India Act to dismiss a provincial governor, the Governor-General possessed no

[84] Noon (1993: 246).
[85] McGrath (1996: 94).

authority to dismiss what was formulated as a fully sovereign Constituent Assembly.[86] As such, the dismissal of the Constituent Assembly amounted to an extra-constitutional coup by a civilian bureaucrat who had, through his Defense Minister Iskander Mirza, close ties to the military. One of Pakistan's leading newspapers opined that:

> The Governor-General's communiqué explaining his action had force at one point, and much that he said in it could not but have met with ready response in the public mind. But the spirit of the Constitution is even more important than the letter, and the use of such powers by the Head of State is not to be lightly regarded if democratic institutions are to be firmly established in Pakistan.[87]

The Prime Minister was correct in asserting that his dismissal at the hands of the Governor-General was "illegal," "unconstitutional," and "against the basic principles of democracy."[88] Though the Governor-General reinstated much of the Prime Minister's Cabinet, it is notable that the three most powerful and influential members of the Muslim League were permanently dismissed.[89] Nazimuddin was still President of the Muslim League, but the key provincial ministers would not serve in the Muslim League working committee unless the new Prime Minister, appointed by the Governor-General, was also appointed to the working committee. By 1953, the Muslim League began to adopt anyone in the position of Prime Minister (who was in turn effectively appointed by the Governor-General) as its President, evidencing how the party followed rather than led political decision-making.[90] Pakistan's major political party had effectively become the handmaiden of the Governor-General.

The unelected Governor-General continued to consolidate autocratic powers at the expense of the elected head of state. The Cabinet, which ostensibly advised the Prime Minister, was appointed entirely by the Governor-General. The next Prime Minister, Mohammed Ali Bogra, a member of the Bengali landed aristocracy, was chosen by the Governor-General because he had the advantage of being Bengali (thereby placating the province's desire for access to national political power) while simultaneously possessing little political capital of his own and therefore posing no risk to the Governor-General. As many mainstream Bengalis continued to feel themselves sidelined in national

[86] Interview with S.S. Pirzada, Jinnah's Personal Secretary, March 10, 2005.
[87] *Dawn*, April 21, 1953.
[88] *Pakistan Times*, April 19, 1953.
[89] McGrath (1996: 97).
[90] Syed (1989: 51).

politics, a proliferation of opposition parties formed in Bengal. A coalition of these splinter opposition parties – the United Front – overwhelmingly defeated the Muslim League in the March 1954 regional elections. The success of this new political coalition in Bengal not only challenged the Governor-General's powers, but those of the existing Constituent Assembly (which United Front leaders now argued was unrepresentative of Bengal), and the Muslim League leaders. Consequently, these actors all supported the central government in its dismissal of the newly elected provincial leadership in April 1954.

With the Bengali threat sidelined, musical chair politics continued. The Bengali-dominated Constituent Assembly, which recognized the increasingly autocratic tendencies of the Governor-General as a threat to its own aspirations to serve as a Parliament, produced a final draft of the Constitution in September which categorically stripped the Governor-General (who would in the new Constitution be President) of his rights to dismiss Prime Ministers and provincial leaders. Notably, a divided Constituent Assembly was able to come to agreement with key religious leaders on a constitution, evidencing that religious leaders did not possess a veto on key governing decisions. The Governor-General, who understood the threat to his personal power, and who was backed by the civilian bureaucrats who felt themselves more competent to govern than a parliament, dismissed the Prime Minister and the Constituent Assembly on December 24, 1954. According to both newspaper reports and reports of the Army Commander and Chief and other officers present at the dismissal, the Governor-General with his civilian counterparts and not the army was orchestrating these events at the time.[91] By the end of 1954, with the tacit assistance of the military, an autocratic head of state fully sidelined all elected institutions, instituted press censorship, and called the military into a governing coalition. Subsequent court challenges to the constitutionality of the Governor-General's actions were effectively dismissed by handpicking pliant judges.[92]

This second bureaucratic coup in 1954 made it unlikely that Pakistan could, in the near future, adopt any kind of stable political system that relied on political parties to forge consensus, a trademark of any stable regime, democratic and authoritarian alike. The Muslim League, whose weakness initially enabled and encouraged the Governor General to

[91] Interview with S.S. Pirzada, Jinnah's Personal Secretary, March 10, 2005.
[92] Newberg (2002: Chapter 2).

assert autocratic executive privileges, was also further weakened by the center's autocratic tendencies. The new "Constituent Convention" which the Governor-General decreed would come into being in May 1955 was elected from existing provincial assemblies, where the Muslim League had already lost political representation since independence. With three major parties and half a dozen minor parties, the new Constituent Assembly witnessed ever greater instability in governing coalitions, with coalitional groups changing nearly every month. The proliferation of parties, and the consistent instability of successive governments, augured increasing regime instability in Pakistan.

Between 1955 and 1958, government instability at national and provincial levels grew so acute that it was just a matter of time before a bureaucrat or military officer assumed full dictatorial powers, especially because the military had by now finalized security alliances with the American government. When Governor-General Ghulam Mohammad relinquished his post due to bad health in 1955, the position of chief executive was handed over to an individual who represented both the military and the civil service, Iskander Mirza. Mirza was a Sandhurst-trained military cadet who had chosen to serve in the civilian bureaucracy under colonial rule, who was appointed Defense Secretary upon Pakistan's independence, and who now served as Minister of the Interior. Executive power was now in the hands of a civilian bureaucrat who had close ties with the head of the military. Together with the Commander-in-Chief of the Pakistan Army, General Ayub Khan, President Mirza rallied the support of military and civilian bureaucracy behind an evermore centralized and autocratic national government. The 1956 constitution of Pakistan retained the ability of the Governor-General, now President, to not only dismiss but to appoint his Prime Ministers.

The increasing centralization of power within the Presidency was accompanied by a further decline in party organization. Four Prime Ministers were appointed and resigned between 1956 and 1958, over a variety of issues such as disagreements over institutional parity between the western and eastern wings or the loss of party support in provinces. Government instability at the national level mirrored, and was often caused by, similar instability at the provincial levels. In Punjab, feudal landlords freely circulated between the newly created Republican Party and the increasingly moribund Muslim League. In Bengal, ministries changed with increasing frequency, some lasting a few days. In September 1958, a paperweight thrown in the Bengali Provincial Assembly killed the

Deputy Speaker, this being cited as a reason for constitutional abrogation in early October 1958.[93]

The military coup which followed was therefore the natural culmination of the successive instability in Pakistan's governments. As political violence proliferated throughout the provinces during 1957 and 1958, riots were commonplace enough that the police were often unable to provide for law and order and called in the army. In 1958, the appearance of a variety of new threats, including the threatened secession of a Balochi ruler, led the head of state to fully end any pretence of ruling by constitutional mandate. Together, President Mirza and the Army Commander-in-Chief Ayub Khan outlawed political parties, dismissed the national and provincial legislatures, suspended civil rights, and instituted martial law on October 7, 1958.

It was the military, however, and not the civilian bureaucracy, which held ultimate power by commanding the army personnel now running the state. When President Mirza tried to place General Ayub Khan in the position of Prime Minister (a position which, given its history, signaled political subordination to the President) later that month and allegedly attempted to rally other Generals against the Commander-in-Chief, the army chief instead assumed complete control over state affairs, citing the need to rid the country of its inefficient and corrupt politicians.[94]

The military coup which formally ended Pakistan's tentative democratic experiment occurred not because the military or even the bureaucracy was initially intent on quashing democratic processes, but because Pakistan lacked an organizationally robust party which could broker consensus among its elites and provide a stable much less democratic basis for governing. Pakistan's dominant political party, with no political base of its own, could not rule without recourse to autocratic power, thereby further marginalizing the capacity of the party to govern effectively. In the absence of a party which served as a predictable route to power, individuals allied themselves with whatever political partners promised such access, thereby promoting a regularly shifting constellation of political coalitions based not on a shared governing platform but only on a shared desire to access political power.

This was "big shuffle" politics, where chief executives rotated among a small coterie of ministers, army generals, party leaders, and top bureaucrats in order to prevent new centers of power from coalescing. Politics

---

[93] Newberg (2002: 123).
[94] Khan (1967: 73) and Khan (1983: 8–9).

at its highest level resembled a fast-paced game of musical chairs.[95] And indeed, the first decade of Pakistan's independent history witnessed the rise and fall of eight separate administrations, the shortest one lasting a mere two months. In this climate of political instability, intervention by the military, the most coherent state institution as well as the institution possessing the de facto monopoly of violence, was an inevitable outcome.

IV. CONCLUSION

In 1947, both India and Pakistan were created as sovereign states through the efforts of their respective independence parties. These parties were based on different multi-class coalitions, had evolved specific nationalisms, and had created differing levels of party organization. Both of these newly independent states experienced provincial opposition to the centralizing imperatives of the governing political party. But in India, a relatively centralized political party quickly created a centralized state structure because this party was supported by a stable and coherent class coalition that institutionalized power-sharing procedures before independence.

In Pakistan, such a party was not created in the pursuit of class interests before independence and, consequently, class politics formed an insurmountable challenge to the creation of a stable, much less democratic regime. While a strong political party in India enabled the creation of a democratic constitution within a few years of independence, Pakistan's weak political party governed by seeking to arrogate autocratic powers to itself. Unable to draw on stable bases of support or to marshal consensus around the creation of power-sharing structures, each successive governing administration in Pakistan became less stable. This instability invited bureaucratic and eventually military intervention.

At first glance, it might appear that substantively different variables explain the post-independence regime trajectories of India and Pakistan. While the installation of uniform and substantively democratic procedures in India is explained by an institutional dynamic, the breakdown of Pakistan's infant democratic experiment is explained by a class dynamic. Yet these different dynamics were created by a similar analytical process. An institutional dynamic was only able to provide for regime

---

[95] Migdal (2001: 73).

stability in the event that a prior compromise on distributive interests had been worked out.

Class interests were demonstrably embedded within its party institution, which is why, for example, the formal abolition of large landlord tenures hardly appears to have been a struggle in India. By contrast, the coalition of support for Pakistan's independence movement, because it represented an incoherent distributive coalition, could not and did not strike the kind of distributive compromises which enabled the development of a robust party institution prior to independence. The dominant political party appears to be the primary explanation for India's and not Pakistan's democratic outcome simply because in Pakistan, a strong political party did not come into being.

6

The institutionalization of alliances in India, Pakistan, and beyond

The dominance of historically defined social classes and the strength of their pre-independence political parties were primarily responsible for the divergent democratic trajectories in India and Pakistan. I began this study by laying out the book's core causal claims. The theoretical framework developed in the book was inductively arrived at by an examination of these two empirical cases. But the core analytics of this argument, which centralizes the institutionalization of alliances before transitional moments, may have wider applicability to the regime trajectories of other, post-colonial developing countries.

This concluding chapter thus begins by synthesizing the initial causal claims with the empirical materials presented throughout the book. The second section discusses the contribution of this argument to broader debates over post-colonial democratization. And a third and final section discusses how the theory developed here may possess analytic purchase on another post-colonial regime trajectory.

I. THE PUZZLE ... AND THE CLASS COALITION AND POLITICAL PARTY ANSWER

The central puzzle motivating this study has been why, despite broadly similar institutional inheritances and colonial legacies, did India's and Pakistan's democratic trajectories quickly diverge upon independence? Most theories of democratization would have predicted that these new democracies were similarly unlikely to endure. Yet, by the end of their inaugural decade, India's and Pakistan's regime trajectories had dramatically diverged.

To explain this puzzle, I demonstrated in Chapter 2 that distinct social classes created the independence movements of each country as a means of advancing historically conditioned interests and that these movements were substantively pro-democratic in the case of India and anti-democratic in the case of Pakistan. Specifically, I showed how the establishment and growth of the British colonial state during the nineteenth century spurred on the emergence of an urban, educated middle class that superseded traditional status groupings. A shared participation in urban professional life, a shared English education, and a shared alienation from the colonial power structure as well as from traditional Indian society encouraged the forging of bonds among this new class. This class sought upward mobility and, in the particular circumstance of a well-developed state and an under-developed economy, pursued upward mobility by seeking access to state power. As the size of the urban, educated middle class steadily outgrew available employment opportunities, this class petitioned the colonial government for a more representative political regime – initially in a haphazard, decentralized fashion. In 1885, the urban, educated middle class created a national organization called the Indian National Congress to more effectively lobby for more representative political institutions. As such, it was a *pro-democratic* movement.

The second chapter also shows that Pakistan's independence movement was founded by a geographically concentrated, colonially entrenched and religiously distinct landed aristocracy that sought to protect its class interests by seeking to prevent democratic reform. In 1906, this threatened group of landed aristocrats founded the Muslim League to lobby against the introduction of representative political institutions and, to the extent that such institutions would be created, for extra-proportional and separate representation for Muslims on the basis of their historical contribution to colonial rule. Protecting religious identity was not the substantive impetus for political organization, however. Rather, religion was a readily available vehicle for political organization, providing a cultural touchstone for a group whose power was threatened by the advance of representative political institutions. A geographically concentrated religious minority thus translated a distinct social identity into a political identity for the discrete purpose of protecting distributive interests. Since this political organization generally opposed representative political institutions and specifically lobbied for extra-proportional representation that contradicted a defining element of democracy, this was an *anti-democratic* movement. Overall, the second chapter established that class interests, understood in a historically specific context, critically conditioned the organizational goals of the respective independence movements. In turn, the goals of these movements exerted a crucial influence on the likelihood of a representative regime being established.

In Chapters 3 and 4, I substantiated that these class interests motivated the formation of strong and weak political parties. In the third chapter, I documented how each political party, in the decades before independence, instrumentally espoused different kinds of nationalist ideologies in order to mobilize support for their class goals. By the end of World War I, accumulating political and economic grievances and repeated government failures to grant meaningful political reform unified an urban, educated middle class around the need for mass mobilization. In 1920, the educated, urban middle class adopted Gandhian nationalism as a means of more successfully promoting a demand for political reform. Congress popularized an Indian nationalism that was not just defined negatively, or in opposition to the colonial regime, but also espoused programmatic principles that helped to create a public sphere in which traditional status distinctions were rejected, at least in principle. A sophisticated intellectual, economic, and social critique of British rule and the careful manipulation of symbolic issues, by juxtaposing the interests of all indigenous classes against those of the colonial state, defined a programmatic Indian nationalism. Congress leaders absolutely espoused this ideology out of self-interest, in order to create a more unified national movement that could effectively countervail colonial claims of Congress representing a "microscopic minority." But by institutionalizing this party-defined egalitarian nationalism, broad segments of Indian society grew ideationally committed to Congress as a party. As such, by independence, Congress had become a political and ideational end in itself, rather than simply a means to an end.

In contrast, the third chapter showed that Pakistan's ruling political party articulated a nationalist ideology which remained largely instrumental throughout its pre-independence struggle and which consequently never came to motivate party supporters on its own terms. Given the dominant class interest represented in the Muslim League and the available choice of alliance partners in Muslim-majority provinces, the League was unable to espouse a nationalist ideology other than one shallowly based on a shared religious identity. Pakistani nationalism was primarily defined negatively, in opposition to rule by the Hindu-dominated Congress, rather than in terms of principles or programs around which its support bases became committed. Thus, the third chapter evidenced the variation in the fact and in the substance of an ideational commitment to the independence party in each country.

In the fourth chapter, I demonstrated the variation in the second and third defining dimensions of a strong political party, namely distributive coherence and intra-party organization, in the respective independence parties of India and Pakistan. Beginning in 1920, the educated, urban middle class leading the Indian National Congress forged alliances with myriad classes, but primarily with the rural middle class. Throughout the 1930s and 1940s, though to varying degrees across space and time, Congress gained support among the rural middle class by promising more favorable tax and land distribution policies. The rural middle class, or the dominant peasantry, presided over hierarchical and clientelistic networks. Though Congress rhetorically purported to represent the rural poor, Congress' platform, based as it was on a non-violent ideology that impeded revolutionary mobilization, substantively protected the interests of dominant peasants who could deliver the votes of subordinate social groups. Congress also gained the support of commercial middle classes, who stood to gain by Congress' policies as well as, eventually, the support of indigenous capitalists, a growing social and economic force. Upon independence, then, Congress primarily represented the interests of the rural and urban middle class. This was a coherent distributive coalition because it shared stable interests in limited redistribution away from the colonial regime and the large, landed aristocracy.

The fourth chapter also showed that the core coalition of support for Pakistan's independence movement shared very little in the way of distributive interests. The threat of continued political reform in colonial British India created an opportunity for a moribund Muslim League to resurrect itself by capitalizing on colonial government's desire to delay political reform. Led by a minority of Muslims from a Hindu-majority province, the Muslim League could not claim to be the national voice of Muslims if it proved unable to gain a political following in the two populous Muslim-majority provinces. The precarious position of the Muslim League was thrown into stark relief during the 1937 provincial elections, in which it polled extremely poorly in both critical Muslim-majority provinces while Congress contrastingly won outright electoral majorities in most provinces. Just a decade before independence, the Pakistan independence movement teetered on the brink of political extinction.

To perpetuate its organizational relevance, the Muslim League struck coalitions of convenience with organized political groups in the two key Muslim-majority provinces, groups whose distributive interests stood in almost diametric opposition to each other. Specifically, the League created alliances with the Unionist Party, representing the landed aristocracy of the Punjab, and the Krishak Praja Party, representing the small peasantry of the Bengal. These political organizations looked favorably upon an alliance with the Muslim League because they began to understand that colonial guarantees of non-interference in provincial affairs would mean little if British India became politically sovereign under Congress hegemony. During the late 1920s and 1930s, as the vagaries of political competition had led to heightening of religious identities as vehicles for advancing class-based interests, these erstwhile cross-communal political organizations began to cleave along religious lines in order to protect sectional social and political privileges. While a coalition between a Muslim landed aristocracy and a Muslim peasant movement made short-term strategic sense from a national perspective, these groups formed a fundamentally unstable coalition because they lacked shared distributive goals.

The fourth chapter also details the variation in the third defining dimension of political party strength, namely intra-party organization. India's independence party developed an increasingly differentiated and complex but still centralized party organization before independence. In 1920, ubiquitous local, regional, and national Congress offices were created at district and municipal levels, which served to mobilize and organize popular support throughout colonial India. Non-discriminatory guidelines for Congress membership and office-holding were created, and regular efforts were made to discipline members who did not adhere to Congress ideology. Congress created multiple levels of leadership, and the upper echelons of Congress leadership were drawn from the lower levels of Congress membership in an internally consistent way, thereby giving limited political expression to the lower class social base of the emerging nationalist movement. Top Congress leaders were charismatic indeed, but even its top leaders could be and were challenged by coalitions of other leaders. Moreover, second and third tiers of leadership were created.

In contrast, the Muslim League created little in the way of a developed party infrastructure in the decades before independence. Particularly in those areas which came to constitute Pakistan, the League either organized few grassroots party offices, or did so only in the year or two preceding independence. The all-India League leadership was not drawn from among its lower ranks in a representative fashion, but simply at the behest of its single charismatic leader. The League also created no second or third tier of party leadership whose career success would be defined by advancement within the party organization. Indeed, there was no incentive to do so because the Muslim landed aristocracy dominating the League possessed little interest in establishing institutions that shared power with the subordinate social classes that constituted a popular majority.

The fifth chapter showed how the variation in the dominant class interests and political party strength established in the previous chapters accounted for post-independence democratic divergence in India and Pakistan. After August 1947, when India and Pakistan were carved out of British India, both countries struggled with the inevitable challenges of state-building, including absorbing a massive refugee influx, integrating erstwhile semi-sovereign princely states, fending off external security threats, and establishing the writ of the newly independent state. While the colonial inheritances of each state were not identical, neither were such inheritances massively inequitable. Instead, the markedly different strengths of their dominant political parties, in each case reflecting an underlying distributive logic, explained the divergent democratic trajectories of India and Pakistan.

In both states, Constituent Assemblies dominated by their respective independence parties were tasked with formulating the power-sharing agreements that would come to define India's and Pakistan's respective regime outcomes. In India, the most contentious constitutional issues after independence – federal power-sharing and the creation of linguistic states – were rapidly resolved through the dominant party's organizational discipline and democratic decision-making procedures. In this way, the party brokered regime-building compromises, notably even when such compromises were not in the short-term interests of some party members, underscoring how the political party itself played an independent role in negotiating regime stability.

Moreover, the ideational content of India's Congress nationalism supported the installation of a defining element of democracy in India, universal adult franchise. Once independence had been achieved, Congress leaders could well have reneged on the promise of universal suffrage by introducing educational requirements for the franchise. But the composition of party support, in particular its organized support among subordinate social classes, militated against such a choice. Reneging on

Congress' institutionalized promise of universal adult franchise would have certainly alienated some portion of its support base. Since the party's mass mobilization drives had effectively demonstrated the party's ability to contain redistributive demands, there appeared to be little cost to instituting universal adult franchise. Overall, the *presence* of ideational agreement and developed organizational infrastructure explained why India was able to speedily forge regime-building compromises as exemplified in the constitution while the institutionalized *content* of India's nationalism explained Congress' decision to govern itself democratically, even when dominant class interests were not strictly promoted by this choice.

At the same time that the chapter showed how an institutional dynamic was responsible for India's creation of a stable, democratic regime, it highlighted that the apparent supremacy of an institutional dynamic over politics in independent India still reflected an underlying class logic, as evidenced by debate over *zamindari* abolition. That the formal abolition of large landlord tenure hardly appears to have been a struggle in the post-independence period is a clear testament to the fact that a distinct class coalition undergirded India's independence party.

While a strong and organizationally democratic political party enabled the creation of a stable and democratic constitution in India, the weakness of Pakistan's dominant political party led to intensifying political instability and eventual military intervention within the same period. In the absence of an institutionalized party that served as a predictable route to power, powerful social groups simply exited the party when doing so advanced short-term political goals. The result was a dizzying circulation of political entrepreneurs who created short-term coalitions for the sole purpose of accessing and maintaining political power. When changing circumstances altered political calculations and political support evaporated, these coalitions of convenience quickly fell from power. As the political instability intensified, colonial bureaucrats and then military officers aggrandized autocratic powers to govern, eventually culminating in the military coup of 1958.

Taken together, these chapters emphasize that the different democratic trajectories of India and Pakistan are explained by a similar analytics. The installation of a constitutionally consistent and procedurally democratic regime in India after independence is explained by a party dynamic, but this party institution was only able to emerge because a prior compromise on distributive interests had been struck and consolidated before independence. Meanwhile, the breakdown of Pakistan's infant democratic experiment is explained by a class dynamic because the deep distributive conflicts within its independence coalition meant that an institutional dynamic was never able to emerge. In other words, India's political party was able to develop into a strong institution because it represented a coherent distributive coalition while Pakistan's political party remained weak because it did not.

Because the Congress Party represented a coalition with stable distributive interests, it was able to organize and institutionalize a national interest and to develop its own causal relevance to political decision-making, even overcoming strict class interests on occasion. By contrast, the core coalition supporting Pakistan's independence party, representing both an entrenched landed aristocracy and a peasant movement, did not evolve the kind of distributive compromises which enabled the subsequent development of a programmatic party platform or a robust organizational infrastructure.

II. REVISITING BROADER QUESTIONS

What is new or surprising about the foregoing analysis? This book contributes to the study of comparative democratization by underscoring how the prevalent theoretical emphasis on the structural requisites of democracy needs to be softened. More than anything, the explanation of democratic developments in India and Pakistan highlights that one important way in which distributive conflicts between social groups causally affect regime outcomes is through group incentives to construct political parties before the transition to independence. The case of India shows that, if well institutionalized, political parties are able to influence group understandings of whether democratization is desirable in a manner that can countervail low levels of economic development.

The long shadow of colonial rule

The comparative historical analysis of India and Pakistan highlights the centrality of political parties as an important influence on post-colonial democratization while emphasizing that the creation of such political institutions hinges on the prior conciliation of the powerful social groups. An exclusive theoretical focus on the economic origins of democracy therefore, as measured by per capita GDP, Gini coefficients, or income quintiles, as has been central to recent explanations of democratization, is inadequate to explain the regime trajectories of these countries.

This is not to say that a greater scarcity of resources, all else being equal, does not raise the costs of accepting redistributive regimes for certain social groups, thereby narrowing the scope for stable political compromises. But as the establishment of stable power-sharing institutions in the post-colonial, low-income setting of India has shown, structural legacies are hardly destiny and can indeed be counterbalanced by pre-independence patterns of mobilization and organization.

Distributive conflicts – conflicts over such things as tax burdens and access to jobs – were indeed foremost in the minds of those social classes organizing and institutionalizing political movements in India and Pakistan. Yet the dramatically different regime outcomes in these countries highlight that distributive conflicts played out in a particular historical context in which social groups understood their interests relative to a distribution of power that was not defined exclusively in relation to other social groups, but also in relation to a colonially defined distribution of power. Key social groups chose alliance partners, built organizations, and espoused ideologies in response to that distribution of power, effectively building markedly different kinds of political parties.

In particular, this study found that when powerful social groups felt their socio-economic mobility was impeded by the workings of colonial regime, such groups were more likely to mobilize mass support and organize robust political institutions to challenge a powerful colonial state. When, instead, powerful social groups felt that colonial patronage protected their interests, there was much less incentive to organize. In the context of a relatively developed state apparatus and a relatively under-developed market economy characteristic of post-colonial polities, then, how social groups pursued upward mobility and how they chose to mobilize popular bases of support was not defined by economic interests alone but also by whether and how their class interests were protected by the colonial regime. This suggests that colonial patterns of patronage critically influenced the post-independence regime trajectories of colonial countries by affecting group incentives to mobilize and institutionalize political parties.

The linchpin role of political parties

The argument developed herein emphasizes that the strength and nature of their dominant political parties upon independence largely explains India's and Pakistan's democratic trajectories. These countries' dominant political parties were both created by powerful social groups pursuing material interests in a particular historical context. But only one group ultimately created a political party representing a coherent distributive coalition, espoused a programmatic nationalism, and organized robust party infrastructure, all of which directly explains regime stability and type upon independence. A central contention of my research is therefore that the relationship between distributive conflict on the one hand and regime stability on the other hand is mediated through the construction of robust political institutions, typically political parties, which can themselves alter how distributive conflicts matter for regime outcomes.

This assertion builds on two established literatures concerned with regime outcomes. First, an analytical emphasis on the relative distribution of power among class groups is historically well grounded in the study of comparative democratization, with myriad scholars causally linking varying constellations of class coalitions and concomitant patterns of social mobilization to regime outcomes.[1] But such literature has tended to privilege the changing distribution of power between social classes and the alignments of social classes prior to regime-founding moments. For example, Rueschemeyer *et al.* (1992: 287) conclude that political parties can independently influence the prospects for democratization, though their empirical treatment of cases in Europe and Latin America devotes little analytic space to how political parties emerge from and in turn condition class interests. By highlighting how material interests led to political organization, my argument embraces and builds on this research tradition.

But at the same time, my research also underscores how this literature has generally neglected to devote space to the precise mechanisms which translate the interests of coalitions into regime outcomes, mechanisms which are often political parties. Party formation may initially be motivated by narrow political or material interests. But once created, parties can do much more than serve as a locus for aggregating determined preferences. Party institutions can themselves condition the strategic interests of powerful social groups. In India and Pakistan, the strength of dominant political parties, though constructed by each country's multi-class coalitions for discrete political ends, independently and most proximately explained the divergent post-independence regime trajectories.

---

[1] Moore (1966), Rueschemeyer *et al.* (1992), Paige (1997), Yashar (1997) and Collier (1999), among others.

The argument developed above therefore suggests that while understanding the changing distribution of power between social classes and the coalitions they forged is crucial to understanding post-colonial regime outcomes, relating the strength and coalitions of social classes to regime outcomes also necessitates understanding the degree to which regime-founding coalitions are institutionalized. During the post-colonial, regime-founding years in India and Pakistan, it was above all the presence of a robust political party which provided for the creation of stable constitutional rules for sharing and transferring power, the hallmark of regime stability. To the extent that regime stability is defined as the consensual routinization of political rules, the dominant political party at independence, and not the class actors which the party initially represented, was responsible for directly creating such rules. This suggests that the strength of the dominant political party at independence can be as causally relevant as the nature of supporting class coalitions in influencing post-colonial regime stability and type, especially because the functioning of an effective party can alter the underlying interests that originally supported the creation of the party.

The legacy of coherent distributive coalitions

The argument developed above contributes to another body of scholarly literature concerned with explaining regime stability through the functioning of political parties, as exemplified by Huntington (1968), but resounding through the institutionalist literature such as North (1990) and still reflected in recent work on regime outcomes such as Magaloni (2006) and Brownlee (2007). These scholars all share a theoretical focus on the causal relevance of political parties by highlighting the different ways in which ruling political parties are able to provide for regime stability.

The argument developed in the case of India and Pakistan draws attention to the pivotal importance of political parties in explaining regime stability. But I also show that viewing political parties as the primary explanation for regime stability neglects to move further back along the causal chain of explanation and to problematize the circumstances under which political parties first gained and institutionalized the support of key elites. Huntington (1968) famously stated that regime stability is at any time a function of both the extent of mobilization as well as the extent of institutionalization. The most important mechanism through which social mobilization was institutionalized, he also suggested, was political parties. But he said little about the circumstances that were conducive to creating institutionalized political parties that could channel mobilization into regime stability. Similarly, North (1990) showed how a variety of economic and political institutions impact economic outcomes by structuring incentives, facilitating information flows, and reducing strategic uncertainty, but this work also emphasized *that* institutions matter rather than explaining *how* and *why* such institutions were initially forged.

Yet the comparative historical analysis of regime origins in India and Pakistan demonstrated that, *at their inception*, political parties were no more than an array of social groups or factions coming together to pursue short-term gains and that their group incentives to coordinate power-sharing hinged critically on the nature of their class interests. These alliances eventually forged rules for sharing power and espoused ideologies that facilitated extended windows of cooperation. If and when these rules became regularized and national ideologies came to matter on their own terms, then political parties were able to function as brokers of regime stability, independently of the narrow interests of those social groups. But whether or not parties emerged as robust institutions first hinged on whether the allied social groups were able to achieve compromises on key issues of redistribution. More generally, this suggests that an institutional dynamic is only able to emerge and provide for regime stability when its dominant political party represents a stable compromise on key issues of distribution.

The fleeting window for institutionalization

The argument developed to explain the regime outcomes of India and Pakistan emphasized that political parties in those post-colonial states came into being to serve the needs of powerful and organized social groups who allied in a shared pursuit of upward mobility. When these social classes struck distributive compromises, espoused programmatic platforms, and evolved a complex party organization – in short, when they created robust political parties *before independence*, these parties were able to broker post-independence regime stability.

In India and Pakistan, as elsewhere, the granting of colonial independence did not fundamentally alter social or political structures, but it did often alter power-sharing incentives. The granting of colonial independence effectively transferred the reins of state power to groups who, once in control of state patronage, faced little incentive to relinquish or share this power. Where, as in India, power-sharing compromises had been struck and institutionalized before independence, power-sharing often continued in the same way after independence, effectively brokering regime stability. Where, as in Pakistan, power-sharing compromises on key issues of redistribution had not yet been worked out, the group inheriting the reins of state power had little incentive to share power with the powerful rural elite. Because the powerful rural elite was not invested in the party, this elite quickly exited and marginalized the party once it no longer served short-term political ends. Consequently, the powerful landed aristocracy was able to quickly destabilize regimes that did not serve their short-term distributive interests, resulting in the intensifying instability of successive governments that ultimately fed military intervention.

The evidence presented in the cases of India and Pakistan thus emphasized that parties are significantly more likely to function as agents of regime stability after independence if multi-class support is not just created but institutionalized before the transition to independence. The timing of party institutionalization mattered crucially because the incentives to create such institutions often shifted markedly through the granting of independence. Before independence, powerful social groups possessed incentives to forge and institutionalize distributive compromises in their shared pursuit of accessing the state. If this coalition did not institutionalize coalitional compromises before independence, then there was markedly less incentive to do so after independence because the granting of independence created new winners and losers whose power-sharing incentives changed. Those winners inheriting the reins of state power after independence faced little incentive to share power with those who did not. But if the winners did not institutionalize mechanisms of power-sharing, particularly with rural allies in what were overwhelmingly agricultural economies, these regimes were unlikely to persist.

In making this argument, this book joins an emerging vein of research which underscores the critical window of transition for understanding post-colonial regime trajectories. Though the concept of "critical junctures" and the path-dependent re-production of an initial structural pattern was conceived by Collier and Collier (1991) and Mahoney (2001), more recent literature such as Smith (2005) and Riedl (2008) has centralized the moments of colonial independence and post-independence democratic transitions in their explanations of post-independence regime character, showing that the transition to independence locks in place distinct patterns of power-sharing, often within political parties. Where political parties had mobilized, organized, and institutionalized widespread political support before these transitions, regime stability was more likely to emerge under party auspices. Where, however, the dominant political party neither struck distributive compromises nor institutionalized power-sharing mechanisms before independence, post-independence regime instability was likely to ensue.

III. EXTENSIONS BEYOND SOUTH ASIA

This book has substantiated the claim that the nature of dominant class interests and the strength of dominant political parties before independence critically influenced the nature and stability of the post-independence regime trajectories in two countries in South Asia. To what extent is this argument simply unique to these two countries? The central task of this last section is to briefly assess the possibility of using this theoretical framework to explain post-colonial regime trajectories in other parts of the world.

To examine whether an analytic focus on social group interests and political party strength may account for post-independence regime trajectories in other cases, I would seek evidence that stable democracies in the post-colonial decade were forged by powerful social groups (possibly but not necessarily class actors) that, in the pre-independence decades, pursued their strategic interests by creating coalitions among middle-class groups that broadly agreed upon distributive issues and that institutionalized these agreements within a strong political party. After independence, my theory would predict that this strong political party would formalize power-sharing compromises within state institutions, effectively providing for regime stability while the historically understood nature of class interests would influence the adoption of democratic norms.

While any future research agenda should more systematically and definitively test the applicability of the argument, this section will cursorily examine whether a post-colonial regime outcome in another region can be largely explained by reference to the nature of distributive alliances formed and institutionalized in the pre-independence period. It is particularly apt to examine other low-income countries which gained independence from colonial rule since these cases are similar in some important structural dimensions. These countries were typically governed by an imperial power until after World War II, when financial and legitimacy concerns forced gradual decolonization. During their colonial periods, the European imperial powers had often created large bureaucracies to staff these colonial states and made key governing decisions from within the parameters of the imperial state, providing limited opportunities for indigenous elites to practice plebiscitarian politics. Moreover, these colonies were often characterized by overwhelmingly agricultural economies and little industrialization, which meant that access to state employment and patronage afforded, relative to the market, an attractive means of upward mobility for any indigenous, urban, professional groups which may have emerged under colonial rule. Colonial independence often transferred power to these urban, professionalized elites, which had sometimes created rural alliances before independence. For my argument to travel beyond the cases of India and Pakistan, the salient distributive cleavages need not always be based exclusively on class interests. Lipset and Rokkan (1967) argued that the interests of a variety of social group identities, which can but need not necessarily be classes, could be politicized and subsequently frozen into place as the basis for future political organization, while others in this tradition have shown that, once created, initial electoral alignments often endure because there are institutional incentives for reproducing such alignments.[2] Following in this tradition, I theoretically centralize the existence and organization of key social cleavages at the moment of independence in explaining regime outcomes.

I will briefly examine one another case, Malaysia, where the regime outcome in the post-independence decade was a stable, if imperfect and ethnically divided, democracy. A cursory examination of Malaysian history provides support for the argument that the institutionalization of an alliance between powerful social groups with historically conditioned interests in democracy was the most important cause of Malaysia's democratic stability in the post-independence decade.[3] While the primary social cleavage in colonial Malaysia was ethnic rather than religious, the alliance created among powerful ethnic groups and the ensuing party institutionalization during the colonial period most directly caused the establishment of a stable democratic regime upon independence.

[2] Bartolini and Mair (1990).
[3] I wish to thank Erik Kuhonta for his careful reading of this section. The description of Malaysian history throughout the next several paragraphs draws heavily on Means (1970), von Vorys (1975), and Kuhonta (2011: Chapter 3).

Broadly speaking, Malaysia witnessed a prolonged period of British colonial rule that had politicized three social groups: an urban commercial middle class, an urban, educated professional class staffing the colonial civil service, and aristocratic rural elites whose weakening relative power was buttressed by the colonial state. The latter two social groups – the bureaucratic elite and the rural landed aristocrats – shared an ethnic Malay identification which the colonial regime had perpetuated while the economically dominant commercial class who formed nearly half of the population of peninsular Malaysia was predominantly Chinese. Unlike in British India, where the commercial and professional middle class came together to pursue their shared interest in upward mobility, the commercial and professional middle class in British Malaya was divided by an ethnic cleavage that reflected important economic differences. Overlapping political and ethnic cleavages initially led the urban, educated, professional middle class to align with the traditional landed aristocracy in order to protect the privileges traditionally accorded them – rights to rule for the Malayan sultans and privileged access to government schools and employment for a select urban, educated Malay elite.

Ethnic and religious identities had always formed possible political cleavages in colonial Malaysia, but only the combination of historical circumstances and imminent colonial reform with its potentially significant redistributive consequences actually spurred on ethnically based political organization.[4] The Japanese occupation during World War II, which persecuted the Chinese minority, impelled political organization in the form of a communist insurgency among segments of Chinese community. During this time, Chinese insurgents also heightened ethnic cleavages by, for example, advocating for elimination of some of the traditional sultans. But though the salience of ethnicity was heightened by the Japanese occupation, it was only when the British colonial regime began negotiations for the gradual devolution of power in 1945 that mass political mobilization and organization ensued. The proposed Malayan Union put forth by the colonial government simultaneously suggested reducing the political powers of the Malay sultans and enabling the non-Malay immigrant community to easily obtain citizenship rights, thereby threatening the privileged access to state employment of the Malay bureaucratic elite. In short, when proposed democratic reform threatened the entrenched position of the educated middle class in government, this group mobilized

---

[4] Means (1970: 53).

and formed a political organization called the United Malays National Organization (UMNO). A traditional and weakening ruling class whose political power was underwritten by the colonial state and an emerging professional class entrenched within the colonial state feared distributive losses if colonial independence granted non-Malay communities full rights to citizenship. As such, UMNO was a substantively conservative movement aimed at maintaining the extra-proportional political representation of the Malay community. Here, as in the cases of India and Pakistan, the distributive interests of social groups, interests that were critically impacted by the position of each group within the colonial system of control, assumed ethnic form and spurred on political organization, initially a reactionary interest in preventing fully representative political institutions.

By the time of political independence, however, the professional and commercial middle class, though divided by ethnicity, would form and institutionalize a pro-democratic alliance. While the class interests of both the commercial and the professional middle classes would be served by a democracy which would ensure their relative economic and political dominance, the enfranchisement of the commercial Chinese class would also threaten the heretofore ethnically monopolized source of upward mobility for the Malay professional class. UMNO, i.e. the ethnically Malay bureaucratic elite and traditional rural aristocracy, mobilized mass support across the country on the basis of a Malay national identity by highlighting distinctive cultural symbols. When this movement succeeded in getting the British to scuttle the Malayan Union plan and instead create the Federation of Malaya, UMNO became the premier political voice of the Malay community.[5] As in British India, political organization among one powerful social group impelled political organization among other powerful social groups. The Malayan Communist Party (MCP), which was created by Chinese Malayans opposing Japanese occupation between 1941 and 1945, protested against the Federation. By 1948, this protest had mutated into a full-scale insurrection and motivated the British to declare a state of emergency.

After 12 years of bloody conflict under this emergency, the colonial government, the bureaucratic Malay elite, and the moderate Chinese business elite all shared an interest in preventing communists from growing politically dominant and created a strong political party to do so. At the end of World War II, the colonial government promoted the creation

[5] Von Vorys (1975: 80).

of a cross-ethnic Malay and Chinese alliance by simultaneously reducing sources of inter-ethnic tension and by supporting inter-ethnic cooperation. For Malays, they did this by solidifying UMNO's political position as the premier political organization of Malays and by greatly expanding the positions for indigenous government bureaucrats.[6] For the Chinese commercial class, British colonialists encouraged the creation of the Malayan Chinese Association (MCA), led by Chinese capitalists to undermine the communist movement. The MCA served as a charity focused on social uplift for the Malayan Chinese community as well as a political organization. The colonial government legitimated UMNO and MCA leaders as the political representatives of their ethnic constituencies and championed their cooperation, eventually formalizing their coalition in a permanent body called the Alliance. The Alliance was a single, cross-ethnic party that advocated programmatic albeit still ethnically based policies.[7] Now representing the politically and economically dominant social groups, the Malay government bureaucrats entrenched within the state and the Chinese business community dominant in the economy, this middle-class coalition effectively mobilized to win a series of local pre-independence elections. This was the state of political affairs when Malaysia became independent.

Upon independence in 1957, the Alliance brokered the state-building compromises that formalized Malaysian democracy, evidencing how historically conditioned class interests drove the adoption of regime type through a strong party able to broker power-sharing disputes. At the same time, the ethnic divides that had been formalized before independence continued to be a salient political cleavage. In particular the nativist form of nationalism espoused by and institutionalized in Malaysia would eventually undermine the quality of that democracy. This brief review of Malaysia's pre-independence patterns of colonial political mobilization thus substantiates the argument that the nature of the distributive interests represented in coalition and the institutionalization of this coalition within a strong political party before independence critically explains both the type and stability of its post-independence regime outcome.

This chapter has concluded by summarizing the argument of the book with reference to empirical materials presented throughout the previous chapters. It then highlighted the ways in which the argument advances

---

[6] Von Vorys (1975: 91).

[7] Von Vorys (1975: 96) and Means (1970: 124).

current debates on democratization by showing that two distinct bodies of literature, both of which have examined regime outcomes, can be analytically linked. Finally, an overview of one other case has suggested that the pre-independence party institutionalization of varying distributive coalitions does not uniquely account for the post-independence regime trajectories of India and Pakistan alone and may well travel beyond the cases studied here.

References

SECONDARY SOURCES

Acemoglu, D. and J. Robinson. *Economic Origins of Dictatorship and Democracy* (Cambridge University Press, 2006).

Acemoglu, D., S. Johnson, J. Robinson, and P. Yared. "Income and Democracy." *American Economic Review*, Vol. 98, Issue 3 (2008), 808–842.

Adams, N.L. and D.M. Adams. "An Examination of Some Forces Affecting English Educational Policies in India: 1780–1850." *History of Education Quarterly*, Vol. 11, No. 2 (summer, 1971), 157–173.

Ahmed, K. *A Social History of Bengal* (Dacca: Raushan Ara Ahmed, 1970).

Aiyappan, A. *Social Revolution in a Kerala Village: A Study in Culture Change* (New York: Asia Publishing House, 1965).

Ali, I. *The Punjab Under Imperialism, 1885–1947* (Karachi: Oxford University Press, 2003).

Ali, S. "Collective and Elective Ethnicity: Caste among Urban Muslims in India." *Sociological Forum*, Vol. 17, No. 4 (December, 2002), 593–620.

Anderson, B. *Imagined Communities* (London: Verso Press, 1983).

Appadurai, A. *The Social Life of Things: Commodities in Cultural Perspective* (Cambridge University Press, 1986).

Argov, D. *Moderates and Extremists in the Indian National Movement, 1883–1920* (London: Asia Publishing House, 1967).

Arnold, D. *The Congress in Tamilnad: Nationalist Politics in South India, 1919–1937* (New Delhi: Manohar, 1977).

Austin, G. *The Indian Constitution: Cornerstone of a Nation* (Bombay: Oxford University Press, 1972).

Balachandran, G. *John Bullion's Empire* (Surrey: Curzon Press, 1996).

Bamford, P.C. *History of the Non-Co-operation and Khilafat Movements* (Delhi: Deep Publications, 1925).

Bartolini, S. and P. Mair. *Identity, Competition, and Electoral Availability* (Cambridge University Press, 1990).

Bellin, E. *Stalled Democracy: Capital, Labor, and the Paradox of State-Sponsored Development* (Ithaca: Cornell University Press, 2004).

Bermeo, N. "Myths of Moderation: Confrontation and Conflict during Democratic Transitions." *Comparative Politics*, Vol. 29, No. 3 (April, 1997), 305–322.

Binder, L. *Religion and Politics in Pakistan* (Berkeley: University of California Press, 1963).

Blaug, R. and J. Schwarzmantel. *Democracy* (New York: Columbia University Press, 2001).

Boix, C. *Democracy and Redistribution* (Cambridge University Press, 2003).

Boix, C. and S. Stokes. "Endogenous Democratization." *World Politics*, Vol. 55, No. 4 (July, 2003), 517–549.

Bose, S. *Agrarian Bengal: Economy, Social Structure and Politics, 1919–1947*, 1st edn (Cambridge University Press, 2007).

Brown, J.M. *Gandhi's Rise to Power* (Cambridge University Press, 1972).

Brown, J.M. and M. Prozesky. *Gandhi and South Africa: Principles and Politics* (Pietermartizburg: University of Natal Press, 1996).

Brownlee, J. *Authoritarianism in an Age of Democratization* (New York: Cambridge University Press, 2007).

Callard, Keith. *Pakistan: A Political Study* (London: George Allen & Unwin, 1957).

Chadda, M. *Building Democracy in South Asia* (Boulder: Lynne Rienner, 2000).

Chandra, B. *The Rise and Growth of Economic Nationalism in India: Economic Policies of Indian National Leadership, 1880–1905* (New Delhi: People's Publishing House, 1966).

Chandra, B., M. Mukherjee, A. Mukherjee, K.N. Panniker, and S. Mahajan. *India's Struggle for Independence, 1857–1947* (New Delhi: Viking, 1989).

Chandra, K. *Why Ethnic Parties Succeed: Patronage and Ethnic Headcounts in India* (New York: Cambridge University Press, 2004).

Chatterji, J. "The Fashioning of a Frontier: The Radcliffe Line and Bengal's Border Landscape, 1947–52." *Modern Asian Studies*, Vol. 33, No. 1 (February, 1999), 185–242.

Choudhury, G.W. *Constitutional Development in Pakistan* (Dacca: Green Book House, 1954), 19–20.

Cohen, S.P. *The Idea of Pakistan* (Washington, DC: Brookings University Press, 2004).

Collier, R.B. *Paths Toward Democracy: The Working Class and Elites in Western Europe and South America* (New York: Cambridge University Press, 1999).

Collier, R.B. and D. Collier. *Shaping the Political Arena: Critical Junctures, the Labor Movement, and Regime Dynamics in Latin America* (Princeton University Press, 1991).

Dahl, R. *Polyarchy* (New Haven: Yale University Press, 1971).

Das, D. *India from Curzon to Nehru & After* (London: Collins, 1969).

Desch, M.C. *Civilian Control of the Military: The Changing Security Environment* (Baltimore: Johns Hopkins University Press, 2001).

Diamond, L. and R. Gunther. *Political Parties and Democracy* (Baltimore: Johns Hopkins University Press, 2001).

Epstein, D.L., R. Bates, J. Goldstone, I. Kristensen, and S. O'Halloran. "Democratic Transitions." *American Journal of Political Science*, Vol. 50, No. 3 (July, 2006), 551–569.

Fine, G.A. and K. Sandstrom. "Ideology in Action: A Pragmatic Approach to a Contested Concept." *Sociological Theory*, Vol. 11, No. 1 (March, 1993), 21–38.

Fish, M.S. "Islam and Authoritarianism." *World Politics*, Vol. 55, No. 1. (October, 2002), 4–37.

Freitag, S.B. "Sacred Symbol as Mobilizing Ideology: The North Indian Search for a 'Hindu' Community." *Comparative Studies in Society and History*, Vol. 22, No. 4 (October, 1980), 597–625.

Geddes, B. "Authoritarian Breakdown: An Empirical Test of a Game Theoretic Argument." Paper presented at the Annual Meeting of the American Political Science Association, Atlanta, GA. 1999. Available at: www.uvm.edu/~cbeer/geddes/ab.pdf.

Gellner, E. *Thought and Change* (University of Chicago Press, 1965).

George, A. and A. Bennett. *Case Studies and Theory Development in the Social Sciences* (Cambridge, MA: Massachusetts Institute of Technology Press, 2005).

Gerring, John. *Case Study Research: Principles and Practice* (Cambridge University Press, 2007).

Gilmartin, D. "Religious Leadership and the Pakistan Movement in the Punjab." *Modern Asian Studies*, Vol. 13, No. 3 (1979), 485–517.

Gourevitch, P. "The Second Image Reversed: The International Sources of Domestic Politics." *International Organization*, Vol. 32, No. 4 (autumn, 1978), 881–912.

Griffin, L.H. *The Punjab Chiefs* (Delhi: Sang-e-Meel, 1993).

Guha, R. (ed.). *Sub-altern Studies* (Delhi: Oxford University Press, 1994).

Haggard, S. and R.R. Kaufman. *The Political Economy of Democratic Transitions* (Princeton University Press, 1995).

Hall, P. "Aligning Ontology and Methodology." *Comparative Historical Analysis in the Social Sciences* (Cambridge University Press, 2003), 373–404.

Hardiman, D. *Peasant Nationalists of Gujarat: Kheda District, 1917–1934* (New Delhi: Oxford University Press, 1981).

Hasan, M. (ed.). *India's Partition: Process, Strategy, and Mobilization* (New Delhi: Oxford University Press, 1993).

Hassan, R. "Religion, Society, and the State in Pakistan: Pirs and Politics." *Asian Survey*, Vol. 27, No. 5 (May, 1987), 552–565.

Hiemsath, C. *Indian Nationalism and Hindu Social Reform* (Princeton University Press, 1964).

Higley, J. and M.G. Burton. *Elite Foundations of Liberal Democracy* (Lanham: Rowman & Littlefield, 2006).

Hill, J.L. "Congress and Representative Institutions in the United Provinces" (Duke University, unpublished PhD thesis, 1967).

Horowitz, D. *Ethnic Groups in Conflict* (Berkeley: University of California Press, 1985).

Huntington, S. *Political Order in Changing Societies* (New Haven: Yale University Press, 1968).

Huntington, S. *The Soldier and the State: The Theory and Politics of Civil-Military Relations* (Cambridge, MA: Belknap Press, 1957).

Huntington, S. *The Third Wave* (Norman: University of Oklahoma Press, 1993).

Hutton, J.H. *Caste in India: Its Nature, Function and Origins* (Oxford University Press, 1951).

Jaffrelot, C. *Pakistan: Nationalism Without a Nation?* (London: Zed Books, 2002).

Jalal, A. *Democracy and Authoritarianism in South Asia: A Comparative and Historical Perspective* (Cambridge University Press, 1995).

Jalal, A. *The Sole Spokesman: Jinnah, the Muslim League, and the Demand for Pakistan* (New York: Cambridge University Press, 1985).

Jalal, A. *The State of Martial Rule: Origins of Pakistan's Political Economy of Defence* (Cambridge University Press, 1990).

Jeffrey, A. "Temple-Entry Movement in Travancore, 1860–1940." *Social Scientist*, Vol. 4, No. 8 (March, 1976), 3–27.

Jeffrey, R. "Matriliny, Marxism, and the Birth of the Communist Party in Kerala, 1930–1940." *The Journal of Asian Studies*, Vol. 38, No. 1 (November, 1978), 77–98.

Jeffrey, R. "The Punjab Boundary Force and the Problem of Order, August 1947." *Modern Asian Studies*, Vol. 8, No. 4 (1974), 491–520.

Jeffrey, R. "A Sanctified Label – 'Congress' in Travancore Politics, 1938–1948," in D.A. Low (ed.), *Congress and the Raj: Facets of the Indian Struggle 1917–47* (Oxford University Press, 2006), 435–472.

Karl, T. *The Paradox of Plenty: Oil Booms and Petro-States* (Berkeley: University of California Press, 1997).

Khan, H. *Constitutional and Political History of Pakistan* (Karachi: Oxford University Press, 2005).

Khan, M.A. *Generals in Politics: Pakistan: 1958–1982* (New Delhi: Vikas Publishing House, 1983).

Kitschelt, H. *The Transformation of European Social Democracy* (Cambridge University Press, 1994).

Kohli, A. *Democracy and Discontent: India's Growing Crisis of Governability* (Cambridge University Press, 1990).

Kohli, A. (ed.). *The Success of India's Democracy* (Cambridge University Press, 2001).

Kothari, R. *Politics in India* (Boston: Little Brown, 1970).

Krishna, G. "The Development of the Indian National Congress as a Mass Organization, 1918–1923." *The Journal of Asian Studies*, Vol. 25, No. 3 (May, 1966), 413–430.

Kuhonta, E. *The Institutional Imperative: The Politics of Equitable Development in Southeast Asia* (Stanford University Press, 2011).

Kumar, R. "Class, Community or Nation? Gandhi's Quest for a Popular Consensus in India." *Modern Asian Studies*, Vol. 3, No. 4 (1969), 357–376.

Lambert, R.D. "Factors in Bengali Regionalism in Pakistan." *Far Eastern Survey*, Vol. 28, No. 4 (April, 1959), 49–58.

Levitsky, S. "Institutionalization and Peronism: The Concept, the Case and the Case for Unpacking the Concept." *Party Politics*, Vol. 4, No. 1 (1998), 77–92.

Levitsky, S. and L. Way. "Linkage versus Leverage: Rethinking the International Dimension of Regime Change." *Comparative Politics*, Vol. 38, No. 4 (July, 2006), 379–400.

Lipset, S.M. "Some Social Requisites of Democracy: Economic Development and Political Legitimacy." *American Political Science Review*, Vol. 54 (1959), 69–105.

Lipset, S.M. and S. Rokkan. *Cleavage Structures, Party Systems, and Voter Alignments: An Introduction* (New York: Free Press, 1967).

Londregan, John B. and Keith T. Poole. "Poverty, the Coup Trap, and the Seizure of Executive Power." *World Politics*, Vol. 42, No. 2 (1990), 151–183.

Low, D.A. (ed.). *Congress and the Raj: Facets of the Indian Struggle 1917–47* (Oxford University Press, 2006).

Luebbert, G. *Liberalism, Fascism, or Social Democracy: Social Classes and the Political Origins of Regimes in Interwar Europe* (New York: Oxford University Press, 1991).

Maddison, A. *Class Structure and Economic Growth: India and Pakistan Since the Moghuls* (London: Allen & Unwin, 1971).

Magaloni, B. *Voting For Autocracy: Hegemonic Party Survival and its Demise in Mexico* (New York: Cambridge University Press, 2006).

Mahoney, J. "After KKV: The New Methodology of Qualitative Research." *World Politics* 62, No. 1 (January, 2010), 120–147.

Mahoney, J. *The Legacies of Liberalism: Path Dependence and Political Regimes in Central America* (Baltimore: Johns Hopkins University Press, 2001).

Mainwaring, S. and T. Scully (eds.). *Building Democratic Institutions: Party Systems in Latin America* (Stanford University Press, 1995).

Markovits, C. *Indian Business and Nationalist Politics, 1931–1939* (Cambridge University Press, 1985).

Martin, B. *New India: British Official Policy and the Emergence of the Indian National Congress* (Berkeley: University of California Press, 1969).

McDonald, G. "Unity on Trial: Congress in Bihar," in D.A. Low (ed.), *Congress and the Raj: Facets of the Indian Struggle 1917–47* (Oxford University Press, 2006), 289–314.

McGrath, A. *The Destruction of Pakistan's Democracy* (Karachi: Oxford University Press, 1996).

McLane, J.R. *Indian Nationalism and the Early Congress* (Princeton University Press, 1977).

Means, G.P. *Malaysian Politics* (New York University Press, 1970).

Metcalf, T.R. *Ideologies of the Raj* (Cambridge University Press, 1994).

Migdal, J. *State in Society: Studying How States and Societies Transform and Constitute One Another* (Cambridge University Press, 2001).

Mines, M. "Muslim Social Stratification in India: The Basis for Variation." *Southwestern Journal of Anthropology*, Vol. 28, No. 4 (winter, 1972), 333–349.

Misra, B.B. *Indian Middle Classes: Their Growth in Modern Times* (New York: Oxford University Press, 1961).

Misra, B.B. *The Indian Political Parties: An Historical Analysis of Political Behaviour up to 1947* (Delhi: Oxford University Press, 1976).

Moore, B. *The Social Origins of Dictatorship and Democracy: Lord and Peasant in the Making of the Modern World* (Boston: Beacon Press, 1966).

Mozaffar, S. "The Politics of Elite Transformation in Pakistan: A Study of Recruitment to the Central Cabinet, 1947–1977" (unpublished dissertation, Miami University, 1981).

Mukherjee, A. and M. Mukherjee. "Imperialism and Growth of Indian Capitalism in Twentieth Century." *Economic and Political Weekly*, Vol. 23, No. 11 (March, 1988), 531–546.

Newberg, P. *Judging the State: Courts and Constitutional Politics in Pakistan* (Cambridge University Press, 2002).

North, D. *Institutions, Institutional Change, and Economic Performance* (New York, Cambridge University Press, 1990).

O'Donnell, G. "Delegative Democracy." *Journal of Democracy*, Vol. 5, No. 1 (January, 1994), 55–69.

O'Donnell, G. and P.C. Schmitter. *Transitions from Authoritarian Rule: Tentative Conclusions from Uncertain Democracies* (Baltimore: Johns Hopkins University Press, 1986).

Oldenberg, P. *India, Pakistan, and Democracy: Solving the Puzzle of Divergent Paths* (New York: Routledge, 2010).

Page, D. *Prelude to Partition: The Indian Muslims and the Imperial System of Control* (New Delhi: Oxford University Press, 1999).

Paige, J.M. *Coffee and Power: Revolution and the Rise of Democracy in Central America* (Cambridge, MA: Harvard University Press, 1997).

Panniker, K.M. *Hindu Society at Crossroads* (New Delhi: Asia Publishing House, 1961).

Posen, B. *The Sources of Military Doctrine: France, Britain and Germany Between the World Wars* (Ithaca: Cornell University Press, 1984).

Potter, D. *India's Political Administrators, From ICS to IAS* (Oxford University Press, 1986).

Pouchepadass, J. *Champaran and Gandhi* (New York: Oxford University Press, 1998).

Przeworski, A. and N. Limongi. "Modernization: Theories and Facts." *World Politics*, Vol. 49, No. 2 (January, 1997), 155–183.

Przeworski, A., M. Alvarez, J.A. Cheibub, and F. Limongi. *Democracy and Development: Political Institutions and Well-Being in the World, 1950–1990* (Cambridge University Press, 2000).

Rahman, M. *From Consultation to Confrontation: A Study of the Muslim League in British Indian Politics, 1906–1920* (London: Luzac, 1970).

Rashid, H. *The Foreshadowing of Bangladesh: Bengal Muslim League and Muslim Politics, 1936–1947* (Dhaka: Asiatic Society of Bangladesh, 1987).

Rawls, J. *A Theory of Justice* (Cambridge, MA: Harvard University Press, 1971).

Reeves, P.D. "The Politics of Order: 'Anti-non-Cooperation' in the United Provinces, 1921." *The Journal of Asian Studies*, Vol. 25, No. 2 (February, 1966), 261–274.

Rehman, I. *Public Opinion and Political Development in Pakistan* (Karachi: Oxford University Press, 1982).

Revri, C. *The Indian Trade Union Movement* (Delhi: Orient Longman, 1972).

Riedl, R.B. "Institutions in New Democracies: Variations in African Political Party Systems" (PhD dissertation, Princeton University, 2008).

Robinson, F. *Separatism among Indian Muslims: The Politics of the United Provinces' Muslims, 1860–1923* (Delhi: Oxford University Press, 1993).

Rosen, S.P. *Societies and Military Power: India and its Armies* (Ithaca: Cornell University Press, 1996).

Ross, M. "Does Oil Hinder Democracy?" *World Politics*, Vol. 53, No. 3 (April, 2001), 325–361.

Rudolph, L. and S. Rudolph. *Explaining Indian Democracy: A Fifty Year Perspective, 1956–2006* (New Delhi: Oxford University Press, 2008).

Rudolph, L. and S. Rudolph. *The Modernity of Tradition: Political Development in India* (University of Chicago Press, 1967).

Rudolph, L. and S. Rudolph. *Postmodern Gandhi and Other Essays: Gandhi in the World and at Home* (University of Chicago Press, 2006).

Rueschemeyer, D., E. Stephens, and J. Stephens. *Capitalism, Development, and Democracy* (Cambridge: Polity Press, 1992).

Sachs, J.D. and A.M. Warner. "Sources of Slow Growth in African Economies." *Journal of African Economies*, Vol. 6, No. 3 (1997), 335–376.

Sarkar, S. *Modern India* (Delhi: Macmillan, 1983).

Sartori, G. *The Theory of Democracy Revisited* (Chatham: Chatham House, 1987).

Sayeed, K.B. *Pakistan: The Formative Phase* (Karachi: Pakistan Publishing House, 1968).

Schumpeter, J. *Capitalism, Socialism, and Democracy* (New York: Harper, 1942).

Schurmann, F. *Ideology and Organization in Communist China* (Berkeley: University of California Press, 1970).

Seal, A. "Imperialism and Nationalism in India." *Modern Asian Studies*, Vol. 7, No. 3 (1973), 321–347.

Selznick, P. *The Organizational Weapon: A Study of Bolshevik Strategy and Tactics* (New York: McGraw-Hill, 1952).

Selznick, P. *Leadership in Administration* (Berkeley: University of California Press, 1957).

Sen, S. *Muslim Politics in Bengal, 1937–1947* (New Delhi: Impex India, 1976).

Shah, G. "Traditional Society and Political Mobilisation: The Experience of Bardoli Satyagraha, 1920–1928." *Contributions to Indian Sociology*, No. 8 (1974), 89–107.

Shefter, M. *Political Parties and the State: The American Historical Experience* (Princeton University Press, 1994).

Skocpol, T. *States and Social Revolutions* (New York: Cambridge University Press, 1979).

Slater, D. *Ordering Power* (New York: Cambridge University Press, 2010).

Smith, B. "Life of the Party: The Origins of Regime Breakdown Under Single Party Rule." *World Politics*, Vol. 57, No. 3 (April, 2005), 421–451.

Stepan, Alfred C. and Graeme B. Robertson. "An 'Arab' More than a 'Muslim' Democracy Gap." *Journal of Democracy*, Vol. 14, No. 3 (2003), 30–44.

Stern, R.W. *Democracy and Dictatorship in South Asia* (Westport: Greenwood Publishing Group, 2001).

Syed, A.H. "Factional Conflict in the Punjab Muslim League, 1947–1955." *Polity*, Vol. 22, No. 1 (autumn, 1989), 49–73.

Talbot, I. *India and Pakistan* (London: Arnold, 2000).

Talbot, I. *Provincial Politics and the Pakistan Movement* (New York: Oxford University Press, 1988).

Tilly, C. *Coercion, Capital and European States, 990–1992* (Oxford: Blackwell, 1992).

Trivedi, L.N. "Visually Mapping the 'Nation': Swadeshi Politics in Nationalist India, 1920–1930." *The Journal of Asian Studies*, Vol. 62, No. 1 (February, 2003), 11–41.

Varshney, A. "Why Democracy Survives." *Journal of Democracy*, Vol. 9, No. 3 (1998), 36–50.

Varshney, A. *Ethnic Conflict and Civil Society: Hindus and Muslims in India* (New Haven: Yale University Press, 2003).

von Vorys, K. *Democracy Without Consensus: Communalism and Political Stability Malaysia* (Princeton University Press, 1975).

Wayne, S.J. *The Road to the White House* (Boston: Thomas Wadsworth, 2008).

Weber, M. *The Theory of Social and Economic Organization*, edited by Talcott Parsons (New York: Free Press, 1991[1947]).

Weiner, A.B. and J. Schneider. *Cloth and Human Experience* (Washington, DC: Smithsonian Institute Press, 1989).

Weiner, M. *Party Building in a New Nation* (University of Chicago Press, 1967).

Wells, I.B. *Jinnah: Ambassador of Hindu-Muslim Unity* (London: Seagull Books, 2006).

Wilkinson, S. *Votes and Violence: Electoral Competition and Ethnic Riots in India* (Cambridge University Press, 2006).

Wolpert, S.A. *Jinnah of Pakistan* (New York: Oxford University Press, 1984).

Yashar, D. *Demanding Democracy: Reform and Reaction in Costa Rica and Guatemala, 1870s–1950s* (Stanford University Press, 1997).

Yong, T.T. *The Garrison State* (Sage: New Delhi, 2005).

PUBLISHED PRIMARY SOURCES

Ahmed, A.M. *Fifty Years in Politics, As I Saw It* (Dacca: Naoroj, 1968).

Ambedkar, B. *Writings and Speeches of Dr. Ambedkar* (Bombay: Government of Maharashtra, 1979).

Aziz, K.K. (ed.). *Muslim Under Congress Rule 1937–1939: A Documentary Record* (Islamabad: National Commission for Historical Research, 1978).

Coupland, R. *India: A Re-Statement* (London: Oxford University Press, 1945).

Coupland, R. *The Indian Problem: A Report on the Constitutional Problem in India* (New York: Oxford University Press, 1944).

Gandhi, M.K. *Collected Works of Mahatma Gandhi* (Delhi: Government of India, 1958).

Gandhi, M.K. *Gandhi: An Autobiography: The Story of My Experiments With Truth*, edited by Mahadev H. Desai, original work published in 1948 (Delhi: Beacon Press, 1993).

Gokhale, G.K. *Speeches and Writings of Gopal Krishna Gokhale* (London: Asia Publishing House, 1967).

Hashim, A. *In Retrospection* (Dacca: Subarna Publishers, 1974).

Jinnah, M.A. *Some Recent Speeches and Writings of Mr. Jinnah*, edited by Jamal al-Din Ahmad (Lahore: S.M. Ashraf, 1947).

Khaliquzzaman, C. *Pathway to Pakistan* (Lahore: Longmans, Pakistan Branch, 1961).

Khan, A. *Friends not Masters* (London: Oxford University Press, 1967).

Khan, Sir S.A. *The Present State of Indian Politics: Speeches and Letters* (Allahabad: Pioneer Press, 1888).

Mansergh, N. (ed.). *The Transfer of Power, 1942–1947* (London: HMSO, 1982).

Menon, V.P. *The Story of the Integration of Indian States* (Delhi: Longmans, 1956).

Nehru, J. *An Autobiography: With Musings on Recent Events in India* (London: John Lane [1945]).

Nehru, J. *Towards Freedom: The Autobiography of Jawaharlal Nehru* (Boston: Beacon Press, 1941).

Nehru, J. *The Unity of India* (London: Drummond, 1941b).

Noon, F.K. *Dominion Status or Autonomous Provinces?* (unpublished pamphlet from NMML, Lahore, 1928).

Noon, F.K. *From Memory* (Islamabad: National Book Foundation, 1993).

Patel, S.V. *Collected Works of Sardar Vallabhbhai Patel*, edited by Pra Nath Chopra and Prabha Chopra (Delhi: Konark Publishers, 1990).

Pirzada, S.S. *Foundations of Pakistan: All-India Muslim League Documents, 1906–1947* (Karachi: National Publishing House, 1969).

Prasad, R. *Autobiography* (Bombay: Asia Publishing House, 1957).

Prasad, R. *Satyagraha in Champaran*, 2nd edn (Delhi: Navajivan Publishing House, 1949).

Ranade, G. and R. Ranade. *The Miscellaneous Writings of the Late Hon'ble Mr. Justice M. G. Ranade* (Bombay: Manoranjan Press, 1915).

Rau, B.N. *India's Constitution in the Making* (Bombay: Allied Publishers, 1960).

Suhrawardy, H.S. *Memoirs* (Dhaka: University Press, 1987).

Wavell, A.P. *The Viceroy's Journal*, edited by P. Moon (London: Oxford University Press, 1973).

Zaidi, A.M. (ed.). *Jinnah-Ispahani Correspondence, 1936–1948* (Karachi: Forward Publications Trust, 1976).

Zaidi, A.M. (ed.). *Proceedings of the Indian National Congress*, Various Volumes (Delhi: Indian Institute of Applied Political Research, 1990).

ARCHIVAL PRIMARY SOURCES

Central Secretariat Library, New Delhi, India (CSL)

Report of the Linguistic Provinces Commission (Dar Report), December 1948

Report of the Linguistic Provinces Committee (also known as JVP report, for the three members of the committee, Jawaharlal Nehru, Vallabhbhai Patel, and Pattabhi Sitaramayya), 1949
Parliamentary Debates

INDIA OFFICE LIBRARY (IOL)

British Intelligence Reports
Casey's Personal Diary
Committee Reports (various)
Cross Papers
Fortnightly Reports
Hailey Papers
Harcourt Butler Papers
Irwin Papers
Linlithgow Papers
Morley Papers
Mountbatten Papers
Mudie-Jinnah Letters
Parliamentary Papers
Reports of the Public Service Commission
Ripon Papers

NATIONAL ARCHIVES OF INDIA (NAI)

Government of India, Agricultural Labour Enquiry of 1951
Government of India, Home Political Records
Indian Annual Register
Reports of National Planning Committees

NATIONAL ARCHIVES OF PAKISTAN (NAP)

Shamsul Hasan Collection of Muslim League Papers

NATIONAL DOCUMENTATION CENTRE, CENTRAL SECRETARIAT LIBRARY, ISLAMABAD (NDC)

Cabinet Meetings, 1947–1958
Constituent Assembly Debates (CAD)
National Planning Board, Five Year Plans
The Report of the Court of Inquiry constituted under Punjab Act 11 of 1954 to Enquire into the Punjab Disturbances of 1953

NEHRU MUSEUM AND MEMORIAL LIBRARY (NMML)

All India Congress Committee Papers (AICC)
Constituent Assembly Debates (CAD)
Government of India, Census of 1901, 1921, 1931, 1941
Indian Annual Register
Indian Statutory Commission
Macaulay Minute on Education of 1835
Nehru Report of 1928
Purshottam Das Tandon Papers (PT)
Report of the Indian Education Commission of 1882–83
Report of the States' Reorganization Commission, Government of India, 1955

Index

minority rights, 8, 97
Mirza, Iskander, 188, 199, 201, 202
mohajirs, 33, 175, 196
Mohammad, Ghulam, 186, 197
Moore, Barrington, 15, 16, 18
Muhammadan Anglo-Oriental
    Defence Association of Upper
    India, 61
Munshi, Kanaiyalal Mankelal, 164
Muslim
    demographics, 57
Muslim League
    Bengal and, 137–150
    class alliances within, 129–150
    goals of, 63–64
    ideology of, 64, 86–98
    incoherent distributive coalition in,
        151
    membership of, 62–63, 64–65
    North-West Frontier Province and,
        178–179
    organization of, 64, 124–125,
        142–144, 146
    Punjab and, 124–129, 179–180
    Sindh and, 178
    United Provinces and, 124–129
    United Provinces dominance of, 63
Muslims
    Bengal and, 137–138
    United Provinces and, 57–59,
        124–129

Naoroji, Dadabhai, 49
National Agriculturalist Party, 124
National Planning Committee, 112
nationalism
    Congress and Indian, 73–86
    constitution-making and Indian,
        167–168
    definition of, 68
    Muslim League and, 86–98
    Pakistan and, 86–98
Nawab of Mamdot, 134, 179
Nazimuddin, Khawaja, 143, 147, 179,
    182, 183, 197, 198, 199
Nehru Report of 1928, 162, 191,
    234

Nehru, Jawaharlal, 1, 55, 71, 114,
    161, 162, 164, 167, 169, 232
Nehru, Motilal, 71, 79
Non-Cooperation movement, 82, 83,
    85
Noon, Firoz Khan, 88, 186, 188
North-West Frontier, 88, 125, 178
North, Douglass, 215, 216

Objectives Resolution, 176

Pakistan
    demand for, 93–95, 134–136,
        145–146, 147–149, 157
Pal, Bipin Chandra, 49
panchayat, 163
pan-Islamism, 91
partition of colonial India, 154–160
Patel, Vallabhbhai, 104, 114,
    117, 161, 164, 168, 169,
    192, 232
pirs, 130–131, 136
political parties
    causal independence of, 122
    class interests in, 18
    core coalitions in, 14–15
    defining strength of, 12–15
    linchpin role of, 213–215
    organization of, 13–14
    programmatic ideology of, 12–13
Poole, Keith, 29
Poona Pact of 1932, 162
Potter, David, 27, 229
Prasad, Rajendra, 80, 164, 169, 193
process tracing, 36, 37, 38
Przeworksi, Adam, 19
public sphere, 49, 73, 74, 76, 77, 78,
    82, 99, 207
Punjab
    military and, 29
    Muslim League and, 124–129
    Pakistan demand and, 134–136

Quit India movement, 82, 84

Rai, Lala Lajput, 49
Raja of Mahmudabad, 63, 143

CPSIA information can be obtained
at www.ICGtesting.com
Printed in the USA
LVHW02s0516210818
587530LV00010B/189/P

9 781316 635247